I0831372

Islandica

A Series in Icelandic and Norse Studies

Cornell University Library

PATRICK J. STEVENS, MANAGING EDITOR

VOLUME LV

The Partisan Muse in the Early Icelandic Sagas

(1200-1250)

THEODORE M. ANDERSSON

The Partisan Muse in the Early Icelandic Sagas (1200-1250)

Theodore M. Andersson

ISLANDICA LV

CORNELL UNIVERSITY LIBRARY
ITHACA, NEW YORK
2012

First published 2012 by Cornell University Library

Printed in the United States of America
Design and composition: Jack Donner, BookType

A complete version of this book is available through open access at http://cip.cornell.edu/Islandica

ISBN: 978-0-935995-14-5

Cloth printing 10 9 8 7 6 5 4 3 2 1

Contents

Preface

The present volume assembles several papers from the last ten to fifteen years in slightly corrected and updated form and combined in such a way as to argue a general thesis. Chapters 1–5 substantially reproduce previously published papers (listed before the Bibliography); chapters 6–7 are new, though based on earlier work. To some extent the last five chapters make an attempt to work out the chronology of the early sagas. A number of these have traditionally been dated in the middle or toward the end of the thirteenth century, but I argue that some are appreciably earlier. Part of the project is therefore to establish what the repertory of early sagas is likely to have been. The larger project is an experiment in literary history at the time when the first sagas came into being. Readers will inevitably find the detailed exposition of the texts under study somewhat trying, but it is necessary for the purpose of establishing the textual interplay and the historical framework.

The general argument is that these sagas, without being explicitly ideological, nonetheless interact with one another on political and literary matters. Relations between Iceland and Norway were particularly troubled in the period 1215–1220, and this seems to have been the time frame in which saga writing first blossomed, with the appearance of the most distinguished kings' sagas and the first notable sagas about Saga Age Iceland. It seems inevitable that the political tensions must have carried over into the nascent writing of the period; the Icelanders were surely concerned with the status of their own polity and its connections abroad, most especially its relationship to the mother country.

After some introductory consideration of the antecedent oral traditions, the Icelandic perceptions of self and others become the subject of chapters 3–5. They outline how a prefatory cultivation of royal panegyric yielded to a more searching and critical account of the Norwegian kings. In due course this critical posture affected the composition of native sagas, in which international antipathies are replaced by regional rivalries within Iceland. Chapter 6 explores a few relevant cases in the area of Eyjafjörður. But the literature was not long constrained by local antagonisms, and chapter 7 illustrates how saga writing soon freed itself from political concerns and embraced more personal and social issues. Taken together, the chapters try to illuminate how the earliest sagas evolved into the narratives that modern readers still find so remarkable.

My first acknowledgment goes to the Centre for Medieval Studies at the University of Bergen in Norway for three most agreeable spring seasons in 2006, 2007, and 2008. I am much beholden to Sverre Bagge and Else Mundal for their very warm welcome at the Centre and to all the colleagues in residence for much stimulation. They kept my interest in Norse-Icelandic matters alive for a decade after I retired from Indiana University. I am also greatly indebted to the staff of the Stanford University Library, especially to Mary-Louise Munill for her instantaneous provision of interlibrary loan books and to Eric Heath and his colleagues, who suffered and solved the most arcane questions. Finally, I owe a special debt of gratitude to Patrick J. Stevens and the staff of the Division of Rare and Manuscript Collections, Cornell University Library, for a month of generous hospitality and a cornucopia of Icelandic journals and books from the riches of the Fiske Collection.

T.M.A.
Menlo Park, CA
December, 2011

Abbreviations

ÅNOH Aarbøger for nordisk oldkyndighed og historie
ANF Arkiv för nordisk filologi
BA Bibliotheca Arnamagnaeana
ÍF Íslenzk fornrit. Hið íslenzka fornritafélag

Vol. 1 (pts.1 and 2): Íslendingabók; Landnámabók. Ed. Jakob Benediktsson (1968).
Vol. 2: Egils saga Skalla-Grímssonar. Ed. Sigurður Nordal (1933).
Vol. 3: Borgfirðinga sǫgur. Ed. Sigurður Nordal and Guðni Jónsson (1938).
Vol. 4: Eyrbyggja saga. Ed. Einar Ól. Sveinsson and Matthías Þórðarson (1935).
Vol. 5: Laxdœla saga. Ed. Einar Ól. Sveinsson (1934).
Vol. 6: Vestfirðinga sǫgur. Ed. Björn K. Þórólfsson and Guðni Jónsson (1943).
Vol. 7: Grettis saga Ásmundarsonar. Ed. Guðni Jónsson (1936).
Vol. 8: Vatnsdœla saga. Ed. Einar Ól. Sveinsson (1939).
Vol. 9: Eyfirðinga sǫgur. Ed. Jónas Kristjánsson (1956).
Vol. 10: Ljósvetninga saga. Ed. Björn Sigfússon (1940).
Vol. 11: Austfirðinga sǫgur. Ed. Einar Ól Sveinsson (1950).
Vol. 12: Brennu-Njáls saga. Ed. Einar Ól. Sveinsson (1954).
Vol. 14: Kjalnesinga saga. Ed. Jóhannes Halldórsson (1959).
Vols. 23–24: Morkinskinna. Ed. Ármann Jakobsson and Þórður Ingi Guðjónsson (2011).
Vol. 25: Færeyinga saga; Óláfs saga Tryggvasonar eptir Odd munk Snorrason. Ed. Ólafur Halldórsson (2006).

	Vol. 29: Ágrip af Nóregskonunga sǫgum; Fagrskinna—Nóregs konunga tal. Ed. Bjarni Einarsson (1985).
	Vol. 30: Sverris saga. Ed. Þorleifur Hauksson (2007).
	Vol. 34: Orkneyinga saga. Ed. Finnbogi Guðmundsson (1965).
	Vol. 35: Danakonunga sǫgur. Ed. Bjarni Guðnason (1982).
	Vols. 36–38: Heimskringla. Ed. Bjarni Aðalbjarnarson (1941–51).
JEGP	Journal of English and Germanic Philology
MHN	Monumenta Historica Norvegiae. Latinske kildeskrifter til Norges historie i middelalderen
NVAOS	Skrifter utgitt av Det Norske Videnskaps-Akademi i Oslo
OOLH	Finnur Jónsson, Den oldnorske og oldislandske litteraturs historie
SI	Scripta Islandica
Sjötíu ritgerðir	Sjötíu ritgerðir helgaðar Jakobi Benediktssyni 20. júlí 1977
SS	Scandinavian Studies
SUGNL	Samfund til udgivelse af gammel nordisk litteratur

CHAPTER 1

The Oral Prelude to Saga Writing

One of the consuming topics of twentieth-century medievalism was oral literature. The discussion was initiated by Milman Parry's Homeric studies in the 1920s, but it did not embrace medieval studies until the middle of the century when, in Europe, Ramón Menéndez Pidal issued his compendious critique of Joseph Bédier's inventionism, equivalent to Homeric unitarianism. In America Francis Peabody Magoun Jr. methodically applied Parry's formulaic analysis to *Beowulf*.[1] The opposition between Bédier and Menéndez Pidal never became truly thematic in Europe, but the formulaic and type-scene analysis of Old English texts became a cottage industry in the United States and was soon extended to other branches of medieval narrative literature. As early as 1966 Larry D. Benson published a disabling critique of the leap from formula to orality in Old English, but by this time the enterprise had acquired a momentum of its own and continued unabated.[2] It was propelled by a postwar expansion in the American universities, the concomitant phenomenon of "publish or perish," and (as at least one European scholar intimated) a peculiarly American taste for mechanics and quantification.[3] Here there is no need to review the massive applications of the Parry-Lord method to medieval literature because John Foley has provided an ongoing and frequently updated assessment of this work.[4]

Almost exactly contemporaneous with but quite separate from the growth of oral-formulaic studies, there emerged a renewed interest in the orality of the Icelandic sagas. These developments were parallel rather than interconnected for reasons that are readily understandable. Aside from the built-in insularity of all the subfields covered by the oral inquiry, perhaps most particularly the peripheral status of Old Icelandic studies, the sagas stand apart because they are in prose. Thus, whereas oral-formulaic studies, notably in Greek and Old English, focused increasingly on the formulism of the individual verse or verse segment, that avenue was closed to Icelandic prose studies.[5] Robert Kellogg tried to capitalize on the Parry-Lord method with an oral-formulaic analysis of Eddic poetry, but his initiative has not taken root.[6] More fruitful for saga studies was Lord's type-scene analysis, but the experiments in this style have been sporadic.[7]

Beginning in 1959—that is, at the time of Menéndez Pidal's neotraditionalist critique of Bédier—I reviewed the problem of orality in the sagas.[8] The situation in saga studies was in fact quite similar to the opposition between inventionism and traditionalism in *chanson de geste* studies, but the sequence of events was inverted. Whereas Bédier's inventionism came first for the *chanson de geste* and was challenged only fifty years later by the traditionalist Menéndez Pidal, in saga studies it was Heusler's traditionalism (what he called *Freiprosa*) that prevailed first and then gradually came under attack by a group of inventionist scholars in Iceland.[9] My own views, initially without knowledge of Menéndez Pidal's work, were traditionalist. I argued against the Icelandic view that the sagas were thirteenth-century fictions based on scattered and disorganized traditions and forged into narratives at the writing desk by individual "novelists." Based on references to oral transmission, genealogical discrepancies that could only have resulted from faulty oral transmission, and narrative variants too distant from one another to be explained by scribal interventions, I judged that the sagas must be derivative from full oral traditions.

A few years later I went further and argued that the native sagas exhibit structural and rhetorical principles in common that could only be understood in terms of highly developed oral practices.[10] If it can be shown that the sagas are structured in the same or similar ways and if the dramatic techniques remain constant throughout the corpus, such norms are unlikely to have been devised at a single blow at the beginning of the thirteenth century. It seemed to me more likely that form and rhetoric were inherited from an anterior oral tradition that gave shape to the narrative style of the sagas before they were actually written down.

The general and justified criticism of my book was that it oversimplified the structure of the sagas and overstated the common features. Structural abstraction was a symptom of the times and a reflex of the literary morphologies that were current in the 1960s—not so much Vladimir Propp's *Morphology of the Folktale,* which became popular in the United States at that time and clearly isolated a narrative morphology very different from the sagas, as the appearance of general morphologies of the novel.[11] Structure was one of the bywords of the decade. The reception of my book therefore tended to emphasize the structural component more than the rhetorical strategies, but as I now look back, I find myself more satisfied with the rhetorical observations, as will emerge below.

The gist of my study was the suggestion that there was such a thing as a complete oral saga before the written saga came into existence. Furthermore, I proposed that the form of the oral saga was conditioned by the confrontational patterns of Norse heroic poetry, which had put their stamp on the Icelandic saga traditions. The effect of the argument was to underline the native features of the sagas and to place them in a long-standing literary continuity rather than to emphasize their status as a thirteenth-century innovation. My argument also had the effect of portraying the sagas as more or less simultaneous surfacings of oral tradition, rather than as independent works in a literary evolution extending over a century or so. Such an argument capitalizes on the difficulty of dating the sagas and relating them to one another in an evolutionary chain. We do not know which is the oldest saga, but whichever we choose as a point of departure, it cannot serve very well to explain later developments in saga writing. It does not seem possible to establish a literary continuity in which one saga inspires the next and so on down the line. Each saga is idiosyncratic and appears to be a new beginning. It is thus possible to argue that they spring from independent oral roots rather than from systematic literary schooling.

At roughly the same time as my book appeared, I tried to underpin the notion of an oral saga by exploring the frequent references to oral tradition, such formulas as "people say," "some people say," "most people say," "it is told," "it is reported," and so forth.[12] I collected 231 references of this type and sorted through them to ascertain whether they could tell us anything about the nature of the oral transmissions. My conclusion was that 174 (ca. 75 percent) of the references were either stylistic mannerisms or likely to be spurious, but that the remaining fifty-seven (ca. 25 percent) constituted genuine evidence of orally transmitted narrative. This residue is located in nineteen different sagas and *þættir* and therefore suggests general recourse to oral tradition by saga writers. I went on to scrutinize the content of the fifty-seven authentic references and observed that thirty of them pertained to conflicts or to the settlement of conflicts. Given the fact that conflicts are the very stuff of the sagas, it therefore seemed reasonable to suppose that such references imply the widespread availability of oral traditions relative to the conflict situations that appear in the written sagas.

Because of the popularity of oral-formulaic analysis in the 1960s, my work on the sagas was no doubt understood to be a promotion of oral literature,[13] but such was not the case. In the 1970s I voiced opposition to the idea that *Beowulf* and the *Nibelungenlied* are in any sense recordings of oral tradition.[14] I considered both to be literary creations based only remotely on oral material. *Beowulf* appeared to me to be a Virgilian exercise in literary epic. In the case of the *Nibelungenlied* I argued that the immediate sources were written poems and that the poet's technique and point of view could be identified through the application of traditional literary analysis; that is to say, one can compare the end product with sources that are fairly easy to reconstruct in outline. I therefore considered the prose transmissions of Iceland to be an entirely different problem from the poetic traditions of England and Germany, and I was by no means an advocate of oral theory in general.

As I moved away from oral theory as it applied to literature in England and on the Continent, other students of Old Icelandic literature became more receptive to it. Lars Lönnroth in particular, having come to teach at the University of California, Berkeley, in the summer of 1965, became a spokesman for the oral-formulaic studies that were dominant in the United States but had gained little attention in Europe.[15] In the same year as the publication of Lönnroth's book on *Njáls saga*, the Icelandic scholar Óskar Halldórsson shifted the position of the "Icelandic School" significantly in a small but revolutionary book on *Hrafnkels saga*.[16] Sigurður Nordal's study of the same saga from 1940—well publicized in R. George Thomas's translation of

1958—still stood as the chief pillar of inventionism as applied to the sagas.[17] Nordal had argued that *Hrafnkels saga* should be understood as a fiction contrived by an author intent not on conveying traditional narrative but on achieving literary effect. Óskar Halldórsson argued that it was in all probability not a fiction but a version of tradition that had passed through the normal distortions that give the appearance of fiction. Since the publication of his book, Icelandic scholars have been more open to the idea that the sagas are based extensively on oral tradition.

The fruit of this evolving reassessment was harvested in the studies of Gísli Sigurðsson.[18] They mark a return to the study of narrative doublets in the sagas; that is, instances in which the same story is told in differing forms in different sagas. The problem for scholars had always been to determine whether these doublets are similar enough to allow for the assumption that one is a literary borrowing from the other, or whether they are so different that they must derive from independent and ultimately oral sources. Gísli Sigurðsson appears to have resolved the controversy in favor of the view that there were fully evolved stories that could be set down independently by different authors without reference to written versions.

In the United States Carol J. Clover rethought the problem of oral antecedents in an innovative essay published in 1986.[19] Located at a university richly endowed with resources on languages, literatures, and cultures throughout the world, she availed herself of those resources to gather material on the transmission of prose narrative in non-European cultures. She observed that these transmissions have two salient features. In the first place, "prose" is a term that does not adequately describe even the prose parts of these traditions. Aside from the fact that the traditions are almost universally prosimetrical, the prose sections normally employ a poetically heightened, rhythmic prose that is the very antithesis of what we find in the Icelandic sagas. The second striking feature of these narratives is that they are significantly shorter than the Icelandic sagas. Where they appear to be longer—as in the case of the Japanese *Tale of Heike* or the Turkish *Dede Korkut*—there is evidence that they have passed through a process of literary amalgamation in the written transmission.

On the basis of these observations Clover concluded that there is no evidence for the existence of a "long prose form" in the oral traditions of the world. The traditions that have been available for study turn out to be neither pure prose nor long. The effect of Clover's argument is to isolate the situation in Iceland: if Iceland did in fact have a long prose saga at the oral stage, that phenomenon would be unique in our wider experience. At the same time, however, there is abundant evidence that there were oral traditions of some kind in Iceland. If they were not a long form, they must therefore have been a short form, and the appearance of written sagas running to two or three hundred pages must represent a literary elaboration of episodic traditions. To explain the evolution from microform to macroform, Clover had recourse to the thinking of the Africanists Daniel Biebuyck and Isidore Okpewho, who had noted that African performers know more than they actually recite, and know in addition how their performed episodes fit into a larger narrative context. Clover referred to this larger context as the "immanent whole."[20] Icelandic storytellers presumably also knew an "immanent whole," but by analogy the international evidence suggests that they too told only parts of it at a sitting. Some attempt at rendering the "immanent whole" was a strictly literary venture and emerged for the first time in the written sagas as we have them.

Though allowing for the existence of the "immanent whole" in some real but unrealized form, Clover specifically opposed my own supposition that there were full-length oral stories precursory to the written sagas, because that supposition does not square with the international analogies. The alternative idea, that the written saga could represent an amalgamation of shorter narratives, had been current since the nineteenth century as an offshoot of the rhapsodic theory of the Homerists. The *þáttr* theory, as it was known, was the notion that individual subtales had been linked to produce longer narratives. The theory had been most fully articulated by the Swedish poet A. U. Bååth in 1888, but had subsequently been dismantled by Andreas Heusler in 1913 on the grounds that well-defined short narratives cannot simply be placed end-to-end in order to create a long saga.[21] Clover countered Heusler's objections by arguing that the short narratives were not fixed, unalterable tales but flexible episodes known to be parts of an "immanent whole" and therefore reconcilable with a longer narrative.

Clover offers a flexible solution reminiscent of the flexibility introduced into the Homeric discussion by Milman Parry. We are no longer obliged to imagine that a Greek rhapsode committed all of the *Iliad* or *Odyssey* to memory or that an Icelandic storyteller knew or performed the whole of *Egils saga* or *Njáls saga* as we know them. Rather, the Icelandic storyteller knew a number of incidents pertaining to Egill or Gunnarr or Njáll and could have told one or several incidents at one or several sittings. The oral flexibility hardened into a "long prose form" only at the written stage.

Clover's theory might also serve to explain both the narrative style of the sagas, which was preconditioned at the oral stage, and the diversity of macrostructures in the written sagas, which can take the form of biographies (e.g., the skald sagas), regional chronicles (e.g., *Vatnsdœla saga*), conflict stories (e.g., *Reykdœla saga*), or tales of exploration (e.g., the Vinland sagas or *Yngvars saga víðfǫrla*). These forms could also be combined, as in *Bjarnar saga Hítdœlakappa* (skald saga and conflict saga) or *Egils saga* (biography, skald saga, and conflict saga). What Clover's theory does not explain quite so well is how and why the first literary realizations of the "immanent saga" were so successful. If the first saga writers had no models in the prior tradition, how did they achieve such satisfactory wholes as *Egils saga*, *Gísla saga*, or *Laxdœla saga* on their first attempt?

Clover did, however, shift the debate significantly by widening the context, finding a middle ground between traditionalism and inventionism, and defining the oral materials more subtly. Unlike Heusler, Liestøl, and me she did not simply project the written sagas more or less as we have them back into oral forerunners but tried instead to discriminate between the oral and written stages and to suggest something about the transition from one to the other. She also leads us to think more flexibly about the denominations of oral narrative.

In a subsequent book Hermann Pálsson took a similar tack, though without reference to Clover's paper.[22] To some extent his study is antithetical to Clover's, but it also carries forward her project of identifying the oral components differently. It is antithetical to the extent that, rather than internationalizing the evidence, it focused in close detail on the Icelandic evidence. On the other hand, the argument is reconcilable with Clover's initiative by virtue of seeking to define the oral materials in a more nuanced way. It dissents from the idea that the sagas are based on oral stories peculiar to a particular locale and compares the traditions instead to "family heirlooms." They were not regionally confined because there was a far-flung marriage network in Iceland that would have ensured the circulation of oral information from one region to another.

The most readily ascertainable form of information was genealogical, but genealogy needs to be understood in two senses. On the one hand it comprised family relationships, such as those in the great compilations of *Landnámabók*. But it should also be taken to include *mannfræði* or personality lore; that is, details about the appearance, character, and actions of particular individuals. Hermann Pálsson explores how these personality sketches cropped up everywhere, presumably in oral and lost written accounts as well as in what has survived. He points out that *Njáls saga* is estimated to have "twenty-five carefully and skillfully executed character portraits" (p. 63) and suggests that the bulk of oral traditions served to portray persons from the Saga Age, although certain other narrative models, such as the love triangle (based on Brynhild and Sigurd) and the travel adventure, were also in circulation (p. 75).

At the end of his book he suggests that some sagas (*Grettis saga, Gísla saga, Njáls saga*) seem to subscribe to a five-part pattern, but he does not suggest that this form was adumbrated in oral tradition. Indeed, his position seems to be Cloverian in the sense that he assumes the written sagas to have been pieced together from memories and traditions about historical personalities. It is perhaps also Cloverian in the sense that it does not account well for the overall economy and drama of the saga as a whole. A sketch of Gísli's personality does not lead compellingly to the symmetrical intensity of *Gísla saga* as a narrative. It is the extraordinary plotting of the sagas that remains to be explained, and that is the task of the following pages.

Short-Term Traditions

We may begin with two sagas that have not, to my knowledge, been included in discussions of oral tradition in Iceland, *Sturlu saga* and *Guðmundar saga dýra*. Both deal with events in the second half of the twelfth century, and it is supposed that both were written in the early thirteenth century. The protagonist of the first, Sturla Þórðarson, the progenitor of the Sturlung family that came to dominate the political and cultural scene in the thirteenth century, died in 1183. The protagonist of the second, Guðmundr dýri Þorvaldsson, was a successful chieftain in the North and died in 1212. In Sturla's case the saga was probably written within fifty to sixty years of the events described, and in Guðmundr's case the saga seems to have been written very soon after his death.[23] The time that elapsed between the historical occurrences and the composition of the sagas was therefore relatively short, and the events described would still have been within living memory.

If we ask why these sagas have not been included in the ongoing discussions of oral tradition, at least two reasons suggest themselves. The first is that they are difficult to read. They are an almost impenetrable clutter of names and events. Such matters may well have been comprehensible to a contemporary audience that remembered or had heard about the events recounted, but these events are a jumble for modern readers who have no background. Nor is the accumulation of detail alleviated by any of the pointed dialogue, scenic focus, or sustained drama that is characteristic of the tales from Saga Age Iceland. Without taking careful notes, the modern reader finds it difficult to retain any sense of the narrative or how it is put together.

A second reason for the omission of these sagas from earlier discussions is what might be referred to as the straitjacket of genre. Ever since the days of Peter Erasmus Müller, the sagas have been divided up into discrete genres and have been studied genre by genre rather than as a global phenomenon.[24] Furthermore, the various genres have been ordered in a definite hierarchy, with by far the greatest attention devoted to the sagas about early Iceland, only a small and quite specialized literature devoted to the kings' sagas, and very little literary attention paid to the texts assembled in *Sturlunga saga*. The walling-off of genres runs quite counter to the practice of modern literary history, which is more likely to organize chronologically. Thus it would be quite normal to encounter a study of the narratives of a given national literature in the period 1800–1850, but no study exists of the Icelandic narratives in the key period 1200–1250. The genre boundaries are persistently observed. The alternative proposition advanced here is that a study of contemporaneous or nearly contemporaneous sagas traditionally assigned to different genres may give a different slant on the transmission of older narrative traditions.

Sturlu saga

The first three chapters of *Sturlu saga* confront the reader with a truly intimidating array of eighty-two names, aside from genealogical information. Indeed, these chapters amount to not much more than a listing of names, with no clear indication of which names will be important for the subsequent narrative. Only in chapter 4 does something approaching a story begin. The woman companion of a certain farmhand named Aðalríkr comes under suspicion of having stolen linen from Aðalríkr's employer, Skeggi Gamlason. The matter is not settled, and Aðalríkr eventually kills Skeggi. Skeggi is the *þingmaðr* (constituent or supporter) of Sturla and his father, Þórðr, so that it falls to Sturla to prosecute Aðalríkr, who has in the meantime taken refuge with Oddi Þorgilsson. The effect of the incident is thus to put Sturla Þórðarson and Oddi Þorgilsson in opposite camps and potentially at loggerheads.

Chapter 5 tells us that Aðalríkr is eventually able to get abroad with the aid of Oddi and Oddi's brother-in-law. Sturla learns after the fact that Oddi is at the bottom of this escape. In a second, unrelated incident there is an attempt to prosecute Sturla's cousin Gils Þormóðarson in a paternity case, but Sturla is able to break up the court proceeding and avert outlawry with a money payment. The chapter concludes with a summary statement: "Þessi voru af Sturlu upphöf fyrst, er hann átti málum at skipta við menn" [these were the first cases in which Sturla contended legally against others].[25] This is an important comment because it can be read to say a good deal about the nature of the story that is being told. It suggests a biographical focus on Sturla, and it suggests that an important aspect of a man's biography consists of his legal dealings or, more broadly perhaps, his contentious dealings of any kind with other people. Finally, it suggests that these dealings were remembered and therefore perhaps told serially. The dealings did not necessarily focus on two particular individuals in conflict but could instead involve the protagonist and a series of opponents.

Chapter 6 shifts the focus to the family of Oddi Þorgilsson. That is a meaningful shift because an underlying opposition between Oddi and Sturla has already been established. The refocusing on Oddi's group suggests that we have not heard the end of the troubles between Oddi, or his family, and Sturla. We learn, in fact, that the projected antagonist will not be Oddi himself, because he dies the next winter and his death is soon followed by the deaths of his sister Álfdís and their father, Þorgils, the following spring (1151). Oddi's brother, Einarr Þorgilsson, now becomes the leader of the clan, although it is noted that he is not learned in the law and has a lisp. The narrative at this point becomes much simplified and more surveyable; the reader has been led to focus on Einarr Þorgilsson at Staðarhóll and Sturla at Hvammr, their farms located respectively on the northern and southern sides of the peninsula extending into Breiðafjörður. The stage is now set for a regular conflict between the two parties, and that conflict is in fact the substance of the next thirty chapters down to the time when Sturla dies (1183), soon to be followed by Einarr (1185). A compressed synopsis of the action might look like this:

1. In a complicated sequence of events, Einarr Þorgilsson protects the ne'er-do-well Þórir inn fjǫlkunngi (the sorcerer) against the people at Hváll (not far from Staðarhóll), one of whom Þórir has wounded. Einarr offers his protection because Þórir has been resident with Einarr's foster father Þorgeirr Sveinsson.
2. Two of Þórir's equally scurrilous companions show up at Kambr in Króksfjörður (a little to the north) and attack Jón Þórarinsson, who was introduced in passing in chapter 3, because of injuries alleged but not explained. Jón kills one of his assailants, but people feel that the district governance was not what it once was under Þorgils Oddason and they begin to move away.
3. Yngvildr, who has been introduced in chapter 1 as the daughter of Þorgils Oddason and is therefore in the clan of the Staðhyltingar, is widowed, then becomes involved with Sturla's brother-in-law Þorvarðr Þorgeirsson. She gives birth to a child, but the matter is concealed and the birth is attributed to another woman. Sturla is suspected of being complicit in the cover-up. Sturla and Einarr Þorgilsson bring suit against each other and both are condemned to lesser outlawry.
4. On the way to a thingmeeting Einarr raids and plunders at Hvammr.

5. A dispute over shearing rights leads to a quarrel between Sturla's stepson Einarr Ingibjargarson and Einarr Þorgilsson.
6. The elderly priest Þorgrímr has his young wife abducted by a member of Einarr Þorgilsson's household. That leads to more tension between Einarr and Sturla when Þorgrímr appeals to Sturla for help. Sturla initiates a plan that results in the severe wounding of the abductor.
7. Sturla's stepson Einarr Ingibjargarson initiates a flirtation with the wife of Einarr Þorgilsson's þingmaðr Sigurðr kerlingarnef. Sigurðr appeals to Einarr Þorgilsson and thus provokes another confrontation between Sturla and Einarr, in which Sturla maintains the upper hand.
8. Viðarr Þorgeirsson, the son of Einarr Þorgilsson's foster father, is killed by a certain Kjartan Halldórsson in a quarrel over a woman. Sturla elects to shelter Kjartan and thus places himself once more in opposition to Einarr Þorgilsson.
9. Twenty-nine new characters are introduced. A household member of Einarr Þorgilsson's þingmaðr Erlendr Hallason beats a member of Sturla's household and in turn is killed by Sturla and his son Sveinn. A settlement is reached.
10. Einarr Þorgilsson lays claim to the inheritance of Ǫzurr auðgi in Búðardalr and disputes the claims of others, notably Oddr Jósepsson, who then appeals to Sturla.
11. Einarr Þorgilsson seizes everything he can lay his hands on in Búðardalr and constructs a fort around Staðarhóll. Sturla and Einarr Ingibjargarson collect whatever is left, leaving Einarr and Oddr Jósepsson behind in Búðardalr in command of the forces they have levied.
12. Einarr Ingibjargarson makes raids on Staðarhóll that culminate in a regular battle. The outcome favors the Búðdœlir, and Einarr Ingibjargarson is severely wounded.
13. The two camps consolidate, with each side supported by a bishop. A settlement is reached by arbiters, but Sturla thinks it is to his disadvantage and refuses to pay, at the same time taking the precaution to fortify Hvammr. An unwary Einarr Ingibjargarson is nearly caught by the Staðhyltingar.
14. Einarr Ingibjargarson takes service with King Magnús Erlingsson and falls at Íluvellir (1180). A new settlement is reached between

the parties at Staðarhóll and Hvammr, but Sturla continues to demur. The Staðhyltingar conduct a raid at Skarfstaðir south of Hvammr and then return north.

15. Ingjaldr at Skarfstaðir (the son of Sturla's foster father Hallr) learns what has happened and apprises Sturla, who sets out in pursuit of the Staðhyltingar. A great battle is fought on Sælingsdalsheiðr.
16. Both sides return home, leaving most people with the impression that this is the decisive moment at which the tide turns in Sturla's favor.
17. Sturla feuds with Þorleifr beiskaldi and Einarr Þorgilsson over a killing by one of Sturla's þingmenn. The settlement of the case obliges Sturla to pay a small fine.
18. A day laborer stops by at Hvammr and Hítardalr (where Þorleifr lives) and is treated to scathing remarks by Sturla and Þorleifr at each other's expense.
19. The story starts anew with a complicated action in which twenty-two additional characters figure. In this action Einarr Þorgilsson and Sturla find themselves on the opposite sides of a quarrel between Þorsteinn drettingr and Þórhallr Svartsson. Sturla's son Sveinn conspires with Þorsteinn against Þórhallr.
20. Yet another new narrative thread leads to an inheritance dispute in which Þórhallr is killed by two of Sveinn Sturluson's henchmen.
21. A seduction case causes a certain Álfr Ǫrnólfsson to switch his thing affiliation from Einarr Þorgilsson to Sturla.
22. Yet another inheritance dispute pits Einarr Þorgilsson against Sturla.
23. A whole new cast of characters, numbering twenty-eight, gives rise to two abductions, both of which are settled by Jón Loptsson.
24. Still another fresh narrative start, with forty-nine new characters, sets the stage for a further inheritance dispute, which is once again settled by Jón Loptsson.
25. The continuation of the dispute puts Sturla at loggerheads with Páll Sǫlvason at Reykjaholt.
26. Páll's wife Þorbjǫrg attacks Sturla with a knife, and he uses his moral advantage to get the dispute settled on his own terms.
27. Sturla makes an exorbitant demand for compensation that astonishes everyone and causes Páll to demur.

28. Páll appeals to Jón Loptsson, who is sympathetic to his case and deaf to Sturla's representations.
29. Sturla must finally defer to Jón Loptsson, who offers to foster his son Snorri at Oddi, but reduces the compensation he is owed from two hundred hundreds to thirty hundreds.
30. Páll rewards Jón richly.
31. Þorbjǫrg dies, and Sturla sees no reason for further hostilities. He himself dies in 1183, and Einarr Þorgilsson dies two years later.

A reader confronted with this summary is likely to find it quite opaque. The only gist of the story that will emerge is that there is an ongoing conflict between Sturla Þórðarson and Einarr Þorgilsson, each supported by a shifting group of family and friends. But even this minimal sense of structure is purchased at the cost of radical simplification. A number of the chapters show a complexity suggestive of a whole saga, and it requires heavy-handed omissions to reduce them to a couple of summary sentences. The action in the central chapters is not articulated in such a way as to make it coherent or memorable. As often as not, a new chapter gives the appearance of starting all over again, rather than attaching to the previous chapter in a continuous flow.

Furthermore, the narrative details of the conflict may strike the reader as both disconnected and repetitive, without any hierarchy in terms of relative importance or dramatic profile. The issues are familiar enough to saga readers, but they are not constructed in what we are accustomed to think of as saga style. The quarrels are provoked by woundings and slayings (1, 2, 9, 17), by sexual disputes of various kinds including paternity and parentage questions, abductions, and seductions (3, 6, 7, 8, 19, 21, 23), by inheritance disputes (10, 11, 20, 22, 24), by raids (4, 12, 14), and once (atypically) by a dispute over shearing rights (5). Sexual and inheritance disputes are the most common, the former at least being familiar from, for example, *Eyrbyggja saga, Gísla saga, Hallfreðar saga, Hávarðar saga Ísfirðings, Kormáks saga, Ljósvetninga saga, Njáls saga, Reykdœla saga, Vatnsdœla saga,* and *Víga-Glúms saga.* It is curious, however, that the inheritance disputes, which are well illustrated in *Sturlunga saga,* are so poorly represented in the classical sagas, with exceptions in *Egils saga, Laxdœla saga,* and *Vápnfirðinga saga.*[26]

The classical sagas tend to organize such quarrels and provocations in a mounting crescendo. The action of *Bjarnar saga Hítdœlakappa* passes through increasingly drastic stages—from insult to slander to assassination plots and finally to direct assaults—but this crescendo effect is missing in *Sturlu saga*, although the late introduction of Jón Loptsson might be considered an intensification. For the most part the provocations seem freely interspersed, in an order that the writer probably thought of as chronological. The materials are arranged serially rather than dramatically. Only the battles of the Staðhyltingar against the Búðdœlir (12) and on Sælingsdalsheiðr (15) approach the scenic articulation characteristic of the classical sagas. In the first of these actions, the details are limited to information on the wounds and casualties inflicted during the encounter, but in the action on Sælingsdalsheiðr there is a considerably greater deployment of detail. Ingjaldr informs Sturla of the raid, and Sturla wordlessly takes down his weapons and then responds to his wife's query with pointed understatement. She in turn incites his followers. The pursuit is set in relief with information on the route taken by each group and the dialogue in each camp, as well as the words that pass between the antagonists. The chapter is question (21) could serve with honor in any saga.

Aside from this chapter, it is not until the last six chapters that the narrative acquires saga dimensions and saga rhythm. In the three chapters preceding the last six, no fewer than eighty-six new characters are introduced, but in the final six chapters we find not a single new character. Instead there are a vivid confrontation between Þorbjǫrg and Sturla, high tension, and a much larger proportion of dialogue. The author appears to have exchanged the role of chronicler for a new role as dramatist.

The last-minute literary reprieve does not, however, do much to alter the effect of the text as a whole. It remains predominantly a registration of regional conflicts centered at Staðarhóll and Hvammr. The author makes little use of the strategies that have made the sagas famous, the economy of detail designed to focus on a particular outcome, the escalation of tensions, the creation of memorable personalities, and the tantalizing deferral of the finale. On the other hand, the battle on Sælingsdalsheiðr and the last chapters make it clear that these literary strategies were already in the air and available for use.

Guðmundar saga dýra

Guðmundar saga dýra takes place in north central Iceland rather than in northwestern Iceland, but chronologically it is a continuation of *Sturlu saga*. The action begins in 1184–85 and carries down to 1212 when Guðmundr dýri dies. It is shorter and simpler than *Sturlu saga* but has much in common with it structurally. It begins obliquely with the family of Guðmundr Eyjólfsson in Reykjadalr. When Guðmundr retires at Munkaþverá, his property passes to his son Teitr, but Teitr is lost at sea. The inheritance is subsequently disputed by his father Guðmundr and Guðmundr's two brothers Halldórr and Bjǫrn.

Guðmundr tries to extricate himself by selling the property at half price to Eyjólfr Hallsson at Grenjaðarstaðir, on the understanding that Eyjólfr will take responsibility for the legal problems. Halldórr and Bjǫrn appeal to their respective chieftains, Þorvarðr Þorgeirsson at Mǫðruvellir in Hǫrgardalr and Ǫnundr Þorkelsson at Laugaland. The two chieftains then take over the land at Helgastaðir. As the dispute between Eyjólfr and the two chieftains heats up, Guðmundr dýri at Bakki in Øxnardalr remains neutral and works to keep the contending parties apart. The matter is eventually referred to the *alþingi*, where Þorvarðr and Ǫnundr mount no defense and are considered to be outlawed. When an attempt is made to confiscate the property at Mǫðruvellir and Laugaland, Guðmundr dýri again intervenes to prevent fighting and is finally able to settle the matter through a marriage alliance.

This narrative occupies the first three chapters and concludes with the comment that Guðmundr "got great honor" from the case. The author might well have added, in the style of *Sturlu saga*, that this was the first case in which Guðmundr was involved—a case involving an inheritance dispute, as happens so often in *Sturlu saga*. What follows is in any event a serial account of Guðmundr's legal dealings in ten chapters (4–13), all leading up to the great burning at Langahlíð:

1. Guðmundr mediates a case arising from the slaying of a man in Ǫnundr Þorkelsson's camp, perpetrated by three men from Fljót.
2. Guðrún Þórðardóttir at Arnarnes has a complicated marital life and ends up marrying a certain Hákon Þórðarson after he kills her second husband, Hrafn Brandsson. Guðmundr dýri, who is Hákon's uncle, settles the case with Hrafn's family (chapters 5–6).
3. Þorgerðr Þorgeirsdóttir quarrels with her lover Ingimundr, and Ingimundr is slain by men in the employ of Þorvarðr Þorgeirsson and Ǫnundr Þorkelsson. Guðmundr dýri has no role in this tale.
4. Guðmundr dýri successfully prosecutes Brandr Ǫrnólfsson and his helpers for the slaying of a certain Sumarliði.
5. Þorfinnr Ǫnundarson (Þorkelssonar) woos Guðmundr dýri's daughter Ingibjǫrg but is rejected because Guðmundr claims that the kinship is too close. Þorfinnr eventually forces Guðmundr to agree, but the bishop declares that the offspring of the marriage will be illegitimate.
6. Þorvarðr Þorgeirsson's son Ǫgmundr sneis returns from abroad and wreaks havoc with married women at Draflastaðir and Laufás. The second incident precipitates an armed confrontation in which Ǫgmundr is nearly killed. In the subsequent litigation a settlement is reached, with Jón Loptsson supporting Ǫgmundr. Guðmundr dýri is charged with turning over the payment but fails to do so. Ǫgmundr then declares the settlement null and void.
7. One of the parties to a quarrel over trespassing cattle (that also has an overtone of sexual tension) takes refuge with Guðmundr dýri. Guðmundr's kinsman Þorfinnr Ǫnundarson offers to mediate but finds against Guðmundr's interests and incurs general dissatisfaction.
8. A certain Runólfr Nikulásson from Mjóvafell wounds a man during a horse match and is exiled from the district in proceedings managed by Guðmundr dýri and Kolbeinn Tumason (in Skagafjörður). Runólfr tries to placate Guðmundr with a gift of horses, but he later retracts the gift, thus doing a good deal of damage to Guðmundr's reputation. The quarrel continues at the residence of Guðmundr's kinsman Þorvaldr at Bægisá and is complicated by visits paid to a mother and daughter (both named Birna) at Efri-Langahlíð by Þorvaldr and his hired man Guðmundr

Tassason. The matter ends with the wounding of Þorvaldr, who is taken in by Guðmundr dýri.

9. Guðmundr gathers a force of ninety men against Ǫnundr Þorkelsson (the leader of the opposition) and surrounds his house at Langahlíð. Ǫnundr elects to keep his fifty men inside the house.

The burning at Langahlíð is clearly the high point of the saga and is described with epic detail pertaining to the igniting and progress of the fire, the dialogue between those within and those without, and the fate of a number of individuals as they either succumb in the house or try to escape. The style of this narrative is not dissimilar from (though considerably less full than) the account of the burning of Njáll and his household at Bergþórshváll in *Njáls saga*. What follows (chapters 15–23) recounts the aftermath of the catastrophe. We learn how Jón Loptsson takes charge of an enormous settlement but dies the next year; how Ǫnundr Þorkelsson leads a raid against Hákon Þórðarson, Guðmundr's nephew and one of the burners; how Hákon mounts a pursuit but is himself trapped; how Ǫnundr seeks help from Jón Loptsson's sons in the south; how Ǫnundr's son-in-law Þorgrímr alikarl is wrongly rumored to be advancing from the south; how Guðmundr captures and threatens to disgrace Ǫnundr's daughter but is prevented by Kolbeinn Tumason; how attempts at settlement alternate with bloodless confrontations; how Jón Loptsson's son Þorsteinn organizes a major attack on Guðmundr but is turned back; and, finally, how Guðmundr recruits six hundred men, corners Þorsteinn's men at Grund, and forces his surrender. The remaining three chapters tell of three minor disputes involving Guðmundr before he retires to the monastery at Þingeyrar and dies in 1212—"ok andaðisk þar ok lagði svá metorð sín" [and he died there and brought to an end his (worldly) honors].

The saga as a whole consists of an introduction with a moderate amount of genealogical matter, a sequence of largely unrelated incidents on Guðmundr dýri's dealings with others (most notably but by no means exclusively Ǫnundr Þorkelsson), the dramatic apogee at Langahlíð, a fairly prolonged account of the aftermath of Langahlíð, and three detached episodes at the very end. This structure is quite reminiscent of what we find in the classical sagas with their neutral introductory material, gradually mounting conflicts, dramatic climaxes, and sometimes rather detailed epilogues. The chief deviation from this pattern lies in the less effectively organized sequence of conflicts, a number of which have nothing to do with the confrontation at Langahlíð. Indeed, half the chapters in this central section (chapters 5, 6, 8, 10, and 12) have little or no bearing on the antagonism between Guðmundr and Ǫnundr. The section as a whole could just as well be characterized as a record of Guðmundr's public life or as an account of regional conflicts during his life. The focus is on Guðmundr's record of success, with intermittent failures. The narrative centers on his *metorð* (honor), which is put in perspective at the end of his life when he retires to Þingeyrar.

The author gives the impression of being very close to the events but has not been able to abstract them into drama and personality to the same degree as in the classical sagas. We have in fact very little sense of Guðmundr's personality and none whatever of Ǫnundr's. The author seems not to have reflected on the persons of his tale, on the underlying issues, even on the tragedy at Langahlíð: in short, on all those matters that distinguish literature from chronicle and invite us to ponder politics, ambitions, social relationships, and the human lot. *Guðmundar saga dýra* offers no key to how these concerns became so central in the classical sagas.

Mid- and Long-Term Traditions: *Þorgils saga ok Hafliða*

Our third text, *Þorgils saga ok Hafliða,* narrates events from around 1120 and could have been written down as early as around 1220. The dating of the saga has been assessed differently, with estimates ranging from 1160 to 1237. As we will see below, the case for ca. 1220 rests on evidence that the author of *Ljósvetninga saga* inserted a passage from *Þorgils saga.*[27] There is some reason to believe that *Ljósvetninga saga* dates from the 1220s, in which case *Þorgils saga* would have to be a little earlier.[28] Thus there is a period of about a century that lies between the events described in *Þorgils saga ok Hafliða* and the writing of the saga.

Like the previous sagas, *Þorgils saga* begins with genealogical matter explaining the family connections and friendship bonds of both Hafliði Másson at Breiðabólstaðr in Vestrhóp and Þorgils Oddason at Staðarhóll (Einarr Þorgilsson's farm in *Sturlu saga*) in Saurbœr. The key figure in the first phase of the story is Hafliði's nephew Már Bergþórsson, who is promptly described as unpopular and ill natured. He is given in fosterage to a poet named Þórðr, who lives on Þorgils's land in Hvammsdalur. Már gives an ill return for good treatment and ends up wounding his foster father. We are told that there is a long story about the litigation that ensues and that this was the beginning of the trouble between Hafliði and Þorgils, but it is interesting that none of the story is told. The author does not aspire to the sort of overall regional news coverage that we found in *Sturlu saga* and *Guðmundar saga dýra*. Instead, the next six chapters focus on the further problems caused by Már.

These difficulties begin with the arrival at Þorgils's farm of another unsavory character in the person of Óláfr Hildisson. Þorgils advises him to take employment at Strandir, where he falls in with Már Bergþórsson. The two of them quarrel, and Óláfr inflicts a superficial wound. Már in turn abuses his host Hneitir, as well as Hneitir's daughter, and finally contrives to have Hneitir killed. As a result Hafliði prepares to prosecute Óláfr Hildisson, while Þorgils moves to prosecute Már. The upshot is that Óláfr is outlawed and free for the killing unless he is in Þorgils's company or on Þorgils's property. In response Þorgils lures Már into a trap and forces him to take to his heels with a humiliating loss of dignity.

From this point on the tension is shifted away from Már and Óláfr and is played out more directly between Hafliði and Þorgils (chapters 10–32). At the wedding at Reykjahólar, famous for an interesting record of literary activity, the most distinguished guests are Þorgils and Hafliði's son-in-law Þórðr Þorvaldsson from Vatnsfjörður. The festive high spirits take the form of mockery aimed at Þórðr, a mockery not encouraged but also not discouraged by Þorgils. When Þórðr then discovers the presence of Óláfr Hildisson at the feast, he protests, and when his protest is ignored, he departs with his men (chapter 10).

Sometime later a certain Grímr Snorrason is roughly treated by Óláfr on the playing field and appeals to Hafliði, who promises unspecified help. Grímr then contrives to kill Óláfr (chapter 11). In the next episode Þórðr Rúfeyjarskáld takes a fancy to Þorgils's ax, but Þorgils avers that he himself has good use for it (chapter 12). Accordingly he dispatches a man named Ketill to kill one of Hafliði's men (chapter 13). Hafliði finds that the corpse of the victim has been improperly buried and prepares a legal case, while Þorgils counters by preparing a case for the killing of Óláfr Hildisson. At the *alþingi* Hafliði offers Þorgils the price of eight cows out of deference to his standing, but not as a legal fine. As a result no settlement can be reached (chapter 15).

One morning, as the contending forces confront one another, Þorgils has half a mind to attack, but Bǫðvarr Ásbjarnarson urges him to refrain out of respect for St. Peter's feast day. Later it emerges that this is a purely rhetorical appeal, the real reason being that Þorgils is hopelessly hemmed in and therefore in imminent peril (chapter 16). Back at Reykjaholt Þórðr Magnússon has a prophetic dream that suggests there will be great dissension at the thingmeeting (chapter 17). In a press of people the next day Þorgils sees Hafliði's ax raised and reacts with a blow that severs Hafliði's middle finger. As a result he is outlawed, but makes no move to go into exile. Instead he gathers four hundred men to block access to the district and prevent Hafliði from convening a confiscation court (chapter 18). Accordingly the confiscation is thwarted, and Hafliði is able to seize only part of a timber cargo that Þorgils fails to secure (chapters 19–20).

In the remaining twelve chapters the focus shifts to the culmination of the quarrel at the meeting of the *alþingi* in 1121. Hafliði arrives first and destroys Þorgils's thingbooths, then lies in wait for his arrival with a force of twelve hundred men, despite the remonstrations of the priest Ketill Þorsteinsson and Bishop Þorlákr. Þorgils approaches with a body of seven hundred men but is urged to exercise reason and is finally deflected by a dinner invitation. The impression arises that Þorgils's advance scouts may have been captured by Hafliði's forces, and Þorgils refuses to abandon them. Two of the scouts return to report on the destroyed thingbooths and the hostility in Hafliði's camp, but Þorgils persists in his advance. Bishop Þorlákr gains a day's reprieve and Ketill Þorsteinsson delivers an exemplum on humility from his own experience, by which Hafliði is deeply moved. A huge monetary settlement is finally agreed upon and is funded by Þorgils's friends. Thereafter Þorgils and Hafliði live in good harmony.

The narrative outline of *Þorgils saga ok Hafliða* is quite straightforward: three chapters of introduction, six chapters on the troublemakers Már and Óláfr, eleven chapters on the mounting tensions between Hafliði and Þorgils, and twelve chapters on the climactic confrontation at the *alþingi*. The simple outline is enhanced by a radically simplified cast of characters. There are a few more names than can be retained in the first three chapters, but thereafter the action concentrates on Már, Óláfr, Hafliði, and Þorgils. Other characters are clearly arranged on one side or the other of the contest. The consequence of this simplification is that the reader has little difficulty in keeping the dramatis personae and the drift of the plot in mind. Another principle brought into play is relevance: no loose ends and no incidents tangential to the central conflict burden the reader's memory. The reader expends no energy in a fruitless effort to relate a particular detail to the plot as a whole.

The details are furthermore ordered hierarchically, with the lesser characters and incidents accounted for first and then cleared away to make room for the emergence in high relief of the protagonists Hafliði and Þorgils. Any lack of clarity or direction at first is only for effect, because it is later understood that whatever the reader is told has explanatory force in leading to the outcome. There is in addition a regular progression from matters of lesser to matters of greater import. The mockery of Þórðr at the wedding feast and Grímr Snorrason's rough treatment by Óláfr in a game do not seem like insurmountable frictions, although a reader of the classical sagas knows from experience that such things are often more fateful than they appear at first. It is therefore not a complete surprise when they lead to the killing of two relatively insignificant men, Óláfr Hildisson and Steinólfr (chapter 14). The experienced reader also knows that, once the killings have begun, the plot is on an irreversible course. The next phase involves the elaborate preparation of cases and a direct legal confrontation between the principals. When one of them is actually wounded, the climax has been reached, and it requires an almost superhuman effort to restore peace.

The building of the climax makes obvious use of certain symmetries, killing and counterkilling, case and countercase, but also a regular shifting of narrative focus from one camp to the other. This last feature becomes increasingly emphasized in the final phases as the contending parties gather intelligence from one another, view each other from afar, then close in on each other. These are practices abundantly attested in the classical sagas, and they are supplemented by hints of foreknowledge. When Þorgils suggests in chapter 12 that he cannot make a gift of his ax because he may have use for it, we may be sure that armed conflict is in the offing. When a man at a great distance from the *alþing*i has a foreboding dream about dissension, we know that calamity is in store. The architecture of *Þorgils saga ok Hafliða* is thus more self-conscious, more compact, and more conceptual than that of *Sturlu saga* or *Guðmundar saga dýra.* The transition has been made from loose chronicle to contrived narrative.

The differences of form are not limited to matters of narrative architecture but apply equally to portraiture. It is a common feature of *Sturlu saga* and *Guðmundar saga dýra* that they reveal almost nothing about the character of their protagonists. There is one startling moment at the burning of Langahlíð when Guðmundr professes that it would make no difference to him whether his daughter, who is married to one of his enemies, is in the house or not, but the moment is so isolated that we do not know whether it is characteristic of Guðmundr or not.

By contrast, *Þorgils saga ok Hafliða* is quite revealing about personality. When Þorgils's ally Bǫðvarr seeks to deter him from an attack by arguing that it is a holy day, we learn that Þorgils has a religious streak and that he may be susceptible to religious arguments. When Bǫðvarr later admits that religion was not the issue at all and that the real reason for not attacking was Þorgils's imminent peril, we learn further that, however susceptible Þorgils is on the score of religion, he is not susceptible to intimidation or a threat to his personal safety, and he would not have responded to representations on this front. In the same sequence we learn of his loyalty to his followers, whom he categorically refuses to abandon. Hafliði shares Þorgils's religious scruples, as he demonstrates when he is deeply affected by Ketill Þorsteinsson's parable on humility. In addition, Hafliði is prescient, foreseeing that a man is about to be killed and may turn out not to be properly buried. In short, the narrative episodes in this saga are not exclusively selected with an eye to registering tradition but also with a view to revealing the character of the protagonists.

Þorgils saga ok Hafliða thus offers a more complex view of the characters that populate its pages. They are people with ingrained principles and sentiments, who act on the basis of abstract convictions. The saga does not simply state what people do but explores how and why they do it. An inner life comes into view behind an otherwise neutrally observed sequence of events. That is tantamount to replacing an observation of events with an observation of the people who motivate the events; such a shift produces a moral backdrop.

The moral stance is not necessarily complicated. In *Þorgils saga ok Hafliða* in particular there is a rather simple opposition between the villains (Már and Óláfr) and the principled gentlemen (Hafliði and Þorgils). It is tempting to think of the opposition as a social statement contrasting commoners and chieftains, but Már is after all Hafliði's nephew and therefore in a chieftainly family. The issue is not social but moral, as is illustrated by the occasion on which Hafliði heaps reproaches on his nephew (chapters 5–6). Here too there is a larger and more abstract issue on the author's mind: the notion that trouble is caused by bad character and resolved by good character. There are to be sure a number of villainous characters in *Sturlu saga* and *Guðmundar sage dýra* as well, but there is no thematic contrast between them and their betters. Nor are the villains invested with a capacity for evil that threatens to engulf the social order.

This understanding of *Þorgils saga* has sometimes been associated with a religious vein, and, as we have seen, both Þorgils and Hafliði exhibit religious principles. The hardened saga reader might be tempted to regard Ketill Þorsteinsson's sentimental *dæmisaga* (exemplum) at the critical final stage of the negotiations as intrusive and superimposed on the feud action, but it might also be understood as the logical culmination of a conflict not so much between Þorgils and Hafliði as between good and evil. It abstracts the principle that some concession in the interest of peace is superior to an uncompromising pursuit of personal honor. That too is a feature quite often found in the classical sagas, not infrequently as an underlying moral of the story.

To sum up the contrast between *Þorgils saga* and the two preceding sagas, it is hardly an exaggeration to say that the former is for all intents and purposes a classical saga, while the latter two are not. If the action of *Þorgils saga* had been set in the Saga Age (930–1030), there is no doubt at all that it would have been classified among the classical sagas. Only because it postdates the Saga Age by a hundred years and is transmitted in *Sturlunga saga* has it been classified among the contemporary sagas. In point of fact it is located at almost the exact midpoint between Saga Age and the age of saga writing. It therefore occupies a crucial position and may provide hints about the nature of the transmissions from both earlier and later times.

Implications

We have referred to three subtypes of the sagas written about events in medieval Iceland: two sagas of the late twelfth century, a saga of the early twelfth century, and the sagas of the Saga Age. The first were written in all probability between twenty-five and perhaps sixty years after the events they describe; the second was written about a hundred years after the fact; and the classical sagas were written anywhere from two hundred to four hundred years after their historical setting.

In terms of origins, the first category is least mysterious. There can be little doubt that the narrative material is taken fresh from oral tradition. The critical literature offers no speculations on the use of written genealogies or written narrative sources. These sagas seem to be written for readers and listeners who might still be familiar (at least by hearsay) with some of the events that are told. The material itself is arranged chronologically and gives an overview of the political dealings of a particular individual. The narrative is primarily a record of events, although these events are certainly formulated in such a way as to redound to the protagonist's credit. Such sagas do not formulate larger problems or moral perspectives, nor do they develop character sketches.

In the absence of any indications to the contrary, we may assume that *Þorgils saga ok Hafliða* also capitalizes on living traditions, but the events lie in the more distant past. And yet, when it comes to an analysis of literary characteristics, *Þorgils saga*, which reports events a hundred years or more later than the Saga Age, is clearly aligned with the classical sagas. How should we explain this alignment?

One explanation might be that the author of *Þorgils saga* had the same sort of tradition available as the authors of *Sturlu saga* and *Guðmundar saga dýra* but was literarily more skilled and imaginative. The religious undertone could suggest a cleric with a habit of moral reflection; however, the religious perspective does nothing to explain the structural and dramatic affiliation of *Þorgils saga* with the classical sagas. We could perhaps imagine that the author of *Þorgils saga* was familiar with oral versions of the classical sagas and imitated their style, but we are not as comfortable as we once were with the supposition that there were full-blown oral precursors to the written classical sagas. It seems more likely that the author of *Þorgils saga ok Hafliða* and the authors of the classical sagas drew their compositional practices from a common tradition of oral narrative. The rhetorical devices appear to be more a matter of inherited style than of literary imitation. If there was such a style, it had not yet been elevated to a literary plane at the time *Þorgils saga* was written around 1220. At that time there were relatively few classical sagas on parchment. The narrative practices must therefore have been oral.

Our task is, as it has been for more than a century, to assess the oral antecedents from which such a saga style might derive. *Sturlu saga* and *Guðmundar saga dýra* surely tell us much about the nature of the tradition in the short term. They tell us that there was an extraordinary knowledge of names and family relationships, that half a century after the events people (at least in the same region) knew the genealogies well and even knew the names of lesser persons connected only marginally with the action.

To know so many names implies a knowledge of the events in which the persons were involved, and indeed these sagas suggest a quite intricate knowledge of such events. They also suggest that the events could be ordered in roughly chronological fashion, that people in a given region knew the sequence of local events. But the material at hand, though abundant, was also somewhat chaotic. There is no indication that it was cast in literary form. It looks rather as though the incidents were strung together with very little sense of narrative economy. Such is not the case in *Þorgils saga ok Hafliða*. If we choose not to explain the compositional superiority of *Þorgils saga* by resorting to the argument of literary genius, what are the alternatives?

The three sagas under study were probably written at approximately the same time as nearly as we can tell. The difference of style is therefore not accounted for by a difference in the time of writing or the stage of literary evolution. The more significant difference seems to be the date of the events reported, the events in *Þorgils saga* being forty to seventy-five years older than the events in the other sagas. The stylistic discrepancy may therefore be a matter of transmission rather than literary refinement. The transmissions from the early twelfth century seem to have passed through some preliterary filter that reorganized and focused a particular tradition, simplified the genealogies, narrowed the antagonisms, and dramatized the conflict.

That traditions could be shaped by transmission is no new insight into the operations of oral narrative. The process was outlined by Liestøl and accepted by Heusler.[29] But these scholars did not see that we have such an accurate measure of the evolution—that traditions only fifty years old remain disorganized, whereas traditions a hundred years old have acquired form and depth. What does this transformation suggest about a possible long form at the oral stage? There is not much doubt that Clover is right to think that individual incidents could be told separately; the so-called *þættir* are a sufficient warrant of this option. But is she right to believe that the "immanent saga" was not realized until a writer gathered the incidents together on parchment? *Þorgils saga ok Hafliða* certainly makes it appear that the whole story of the conflict between these chieftains was known and could be reproduced. A number of the rhetorical devices—such as unity, symmetry, alternation, relevance, and dramatic intensification—are contingent on the whole story rather than individual episodes. They could not be learned and practiced by singling out this incident or that. They constitute an art of the whole—an art of the saga, not just of the episode. Hence there is reason to believe that the assembling and organizing of incidents began at the oral stage and that the "immanent saga" was not merely potential; it was also practiced.

We need not assume that every saga was orally preconditioned, as *Þorgils saga ok Hafliða* seems to have been. Some sagas (e.g., *Egils saga*) subscribe to a more biographical pattern (and therefore also to a chronological pattern) that lies closer to the kings' sagas or the bishops' sagas. Other sagas partake of the chronicle style we have observed in *Sturlu saga* and *Guðmundar saga dýra* (e.g., *Eyrbyggja saga* or *Vatnsdœla saga*). But the preponderant style among the classical sagas is dramatic and akin to what we find in *Þorgils saga ok Hafliða*. This style is likely to have been cultivated in the oral transmission of whole sagas such as those of Gísli, or Kjartan and Bolli, or Hrafnkell, or Gunnarr and Njáll. The style of the written plot that eventually emerged was in all likelihood preconditioned by a well-articulated oral plot.

The study of oral rhetoric has for the most part been confined to matters of phraseology in the "oral formula" and the construction of individual "type scenes," although the more overarching principle of "envelope structure" has also been invoked.[30] What I suggest here (as in 1967) is that the saga as a whole was characterized by rhetorical features that are so pervasive in the written sagas as to imply oral precedents, not just of the individual scene but of the total composition. Thus the saga as a whole is more often than not constructed around a dramatic high point that all the preliminary scenes are designed to profile. The preliminary scenes do not have independent or evenly weighted status, only a subsidiary function in pointing toward the climax. That climax may be the killing of a hero (Bjǫrn Hítdœlakappi, Kjartan Óláfsson, Gísli Súrsson, Grettir Ásmundarson, Þorgeirr Hávarsson, Helgi Droplaugarson, or Gunnarr Hámundarson). It may be the burning in of a protagonist (Blund-Ketill Geirsson or Njáll and his family), the unexpected expulsion of a chieftain (Hrafnkell Hallfreðarson or Víga-Glúmr Eyjólfsson), or the execution of a long-deferred vengeance (as in *Heiðarvíga saga* or *Hávarðar saga Ísfirðings*), but in each case there is a central event that focuses the action of the remaining narrative and guides the reader's attention. That attention is not randomly dispersed over a series of scenes or episodes but is controlled by a dénouement that lends meaning to all the lesser episodes. This persistent pattern suggests that readers (and, by extension, listeners at the oral stage) were accustomed to a dénouement highlighted and set in relief by a greater or lesser series of episodes, all contrived to underscore the central drama.

The preliminary episodes can be managed in several ways. They can be ordered as independent occurrences that have no immediate connection with each other but are all prefatory to and suggestive of the central conflict. Or they can be carefully linked in a chain of causation that leads inexorably to the climax. The exact relevance of a particular incident may not be apparent at first but becomes increasingly clear as the sequence unfolds. In this arrangement each link presupposes the previous one and provokes the following one, a technique that produces a pleasing narrative tightness. Finally, the preliminaries may be structured as a sequence of miniature dramas, with points of departure that are separate from but always anticipatory of the major conflict and understood to be adumbrations of the outcome.

Typically these opening sequences intensify the conflict gradually. Minor tensions yield to more perilous confrontations and ultimately to overt collisions. Verbal encounters give way to deliberate provocations, which in turn give way to hotly contested litigation, armed conflict, and bloodshed. The sequence is spread over time and shapes the eventual climax with calculated deliberateness. The paradoxical effect of this deliberateness is to retard the action artificially and, at the same time, to quicken the reader's interest as the outcome comes into view with increasing clarity.

The most traditional anticipatory device is the dream, which reveals the outcome quite explicitly. Other foreshadowings take the form of portents, predictions, or premonitions. Such signals are apt to occur quite early in the story. Akin to the dramatic buildup of the plot, they serve to fix the end point of the action firmly in the reader's mind while at the same time exciting interest in the details that lead up to the foreordained end point. In addition, the culmination of the plot is also signaled by a manipulation of pace, a marked deceleration and an accumulation of detail as the end approaches. For example, if the end takes the form of an armed confrontation, the dramatic moment is framed with details on the gathering of men, the route leading to the battle site, and the words spoken by the protagonists. The effect can be doubled when both parties are tracked as they proceed to a showdown, with the focus sometimes shifting between the two.

What these narrative devices have in common is that they are predicated on a long story, not a brief episode. Foreshadowing, gradual intensification, and the manipulation of narrative pace and density are rhetorical tricks that presuppose the "long prose form." These devices are so ubiquitous from the very outset of saga writing in Iceland—most prominently in the native sagas but also in the kings' sagas—that they must have been part of the preliterate oral repertory of story techniques. There is no latitude for foreshadowing, retardation, or an alternation between two armed camps in the episodic short form. Thus the fully evolved presence of these strategies suggests that they must traditionally have been put to use in longer stories. Exactly what narrative length they imply is hard to calculate, but even the shorter or middle-length sagas (such as *Hœnsa-Þóris saga* or *Gísla saga*) make full use of such strategies. It is therefore not impossible that oral tellings may have been equivalent to forty- or fifty-page written sagas.

Residues of an Oral Saga

One of the passages sometimes cited in connection with oral saga telling is found in *Fóstbrœðra saga*.[31] The scene is set in Greenland, where Þormóðr Bersason has arrived on a secret mission to take revenge against the killers of his foster brother Þorgeirr Hávarsson. One day during a thingmeeting Þormóðr is asleep in his booth but is awakened by a certain Egill to be informed that he is missing out on something:

> At that moment Egill rushed into the booth and said: "You're really missing some good entertainment." Þormóðr asked: "Where are you coming from and what's up in the way of entertainment?" Egill replied: "I was at Þorgrímr Einarsson's booth, and most of the people at the thing are there too." [Þorgrímr Einarsson is one of Þorgeirr's killers.] Þormóðr asked: "What is the entertainment there?" Egill replied: "Þorgrímr is telling a saga (i.e., a story)." Þormóðr asked "Who is the subject of the saga he is telling?" Egill answered: "I'm not quite sure whom the saga is about, but I do know that he is a good and entertaining teller. A chair has been set out for him by the booth and people are sitting around listening to the saga." Þormóðr said: "Maybe you can name a character in the saga, since you seem to think it affords so much amusement." Egill said: "Some Þorgeirr is a great hero in the saga, and I get the impression that Þorgrímr himself was somewhat involved in the story and cut quite a figure on the attack, as might be expected. I wish you would go there too and listen to the entertainment." "I might do that," said Þormóðr.

This brief passage tells us rather a lot about oral delivery. In the first place, storytelling is not just a matter of casual conversation but something approaching a formal exercise. The teller is seated apart, presumably in front of a crowd of listeners, perhaps seated in a semicircle. They constitute an official audience, not unlike a modern audience for an author's reading. In the second place, the passage is quite insistent in emphasizing how well the story is told and how entertaining it is. The word *skemmtan* (entertainment) or *skemmtiliga* (entertainingly) is used five times and the word *gaman* (fun) once. In fact, the style of telling seems to overshadow the content, because

Egill is not quite sure who the characters in the story are. The effect of the story is correspondingly great since almost everyone at the thingmeeting crowds around to listen, to the extent that Þormóðr is conspicuous by his absence.

The subject matter is also defined to a certain extent. Þormóðr asks not "what" the saga is about but "whom" it is about, suggesting that such a story might typically center on a particular individual. The incident reported by Egill is by no means indifferent but centers on the famous warrior Þorgeirr, presumably the circumstances of his death and the events leading up to that moment. If there were no preparatory narrative, the incidents would not be substantial enough to constitute a story. Indeed, the narrative dimensions seem to be considerable because Egill is able to absent himself for a time with no apparent concern that he may lose the thread of the story. The nature of the tale is clearly martial, a tale of heroic confrontation. Þorgeirr is described as a *mikill kappi* (a great champion) and Þorgrímr credits himself with having cut quite a figure on the attack ("gengit mjǫk vel fram").

The actual killing of Þorgeirr has been recounted earlier in the saga (ÍF 6:206–10), though clearly more to Þorgeirr's advantage than to Þorgrímr's. It forms the first high point in *Fóstbrœðra saga*, and Þorgrímr's retelling illustrates how such a dramatic moment, no doubt set off with some account of the prefatory conflict, could have been perpetuated in oral tradition. A separate question is whether an episode such as Þorgrímr's storytelling could have been maintained in tradition. It may well have been, because it too is part of a dramatic high point, the revenge taken by Þormóðr for Þorgeirr's killing, which plays out as follows.

Þormóðr proceeds with Egill to Þorgrímr's booth, the site of the storytelling. We must understand both that he has kept his vengeful intentions secret and that he is fully aware of the identity of the Þorgrímr who is telling the story. As Þormóðr arrives, the sky begins to cloud over, and he forms a plan of attack. Inspecting the sky above and the ground under his feet, he warns Egill that something momentous is about to happen and that if Egill should hear a great crash, he should take to his heels as fast as he can. At this point the rain begins to come down and the audience scatters. Þormóðr approaches Þorgrímr, gives him an oblique intimation of what is about to happen, and buries his ax in his skull. When Egill hears the crash, he duly runs off, and

Þormóðr calls back the scattering crowd with the fiction that some unidentified man has killed Þorgrímr. They see Egill running at top speed and, assuming that he is the unknown culprit, they set out in pursuit, thus giving Þormóðr time to escape.

This culmination of Þormóðr's mission is cast not so much in terms of heroic confrontation as in terms of an exaggeratedly ingenious stratagem. Þormóðr cannot merely face off against his antagonist Þorgrímr; he must kill him without allowing the crowd of people around them to realize what has happened. That he is able to do so on the spur of the moment by capitalizing on a change in the weather and a witless decoy is what makes the scene memorable and likely to have been fashioned in and preserved by tradition. Thus there is evidence that ingenuity, no less than drama, was a crucial factor in maintaining oral transmissions.

The use of this incident to shed light on oral storytelling in Iceland is of course problematical. Whether traditional or not, it certainly cannot be assumed that the incident is historical. If it were historical, it would have the disadvantage of shedding light only on how stories were told in the early eleventh century, not in the thirteenth century. But it is finally more credible that the storytelling scene in *Fóstbræðra saga* reflects contemporary practice familiar to the readers of the saga in the thirteenth century. Though the scene cannot be shown to be historically true, it must have been culturally true, because the author would not have devised a situation that contemporaries would have found implausible. The scene suggests therefore that stories about the Saga Age could still be performed orally in the era of the written sagas. How long such sagas might have been we cannot know, but they were long enough to induce a crowd to come together as a formal audience and listen attentively.

Conclusion

The present chapter returns to the long-standing debate on the oral antecedents of the Icelandic sagas. In her full-scale inquiry Carol Clover concluded, on the basis of analogous prose traditions around the world, that the prose performances of medieval Iceland are likely to have been episodic. On the one hand, a survey of the international evidence on prose transmission makes it improbable that there were long oral performances with dimensions approximating those of the longer written sagas. On the other hand, the performers of episodic narratives in Iceland were aware of how their short recitations fitted into a larger narrative whole, which Clover referred to as the "immanent whole." But she maintained that at the oral stage the "immanent whole" was only potential and was not realized until the saga writers of the thirteenth century undertook to assemble fuller narratives on parchment.

Most studies of the problem have confined themselves to the classical sagas, which deal largely with events in the Saga Age (ca. 930–1030) when the Icelandic state was newly established. The underlying assumption was that the record of events from this period must have been passed down orally through the generations and that at some point during the transmission the narratives took on a shape very similar to the written sagas as we know them. I depart from this precedent by shifting the focus from the classical sagas to three sagas that narrate events from the twelfth century, a hundred or two hundred years after the Saga Age. Two of these sagas (*Sturlu saga* and *Guðmundar saga dýra*) cover the period 1150–1212; both seem to have been written early in the thirteenth century. Both have a great wealth of personal names and genealogical information, quite beyond a modern reader's powers of retention. Unlike the classical sagas, both report regional conflicts in a largely nondramatic, serial, chronicle-like narrative style. The narrative details are recapitulated in much simplified form but nonetheless at some length in this chapter in order to show to what degree the sagas in question differ from the dramatically stylized narrative of the classical sagas.

The third saga under study here, *Þorgils saga ok Hafliða,* was probably written approximately at the same time as the other two (ca. 1220), but it relates events from a century earlier (ca. 1120). It is not overburdened with names and genealogical connections and is told very much in the economic and dramatic style of the classical sagas. The difference cannot be accounted for by supposing that the three sagas represent differing stages in the literary evolution of saga writing, because all three seem to have been written roughly at the same time. The argument advanced here is therefore that the stylistic difference should be explained by the differing length of time between the actual events and the time of writing. It appears that recent events, within the memory of the listeners or readers, were set down in superabundant detail. On the other hand, older events that had receded in memory and had passed through a period of narrative refinement in the oral tradition acquired a leaner, simpler, and more dramatic style.

A number of the most prominent characteristics of this "oral" style—escalation, foreshadowing, contrived symmetries, gradually mounting tensions, expanded dialogue, and so forth—are appropriate not to brief, episodic tales, such as those envisaged by Clover, but to full-length, highly articulated, almost meditative narratives such as are exemplified in *Þorgils saga ok Hafliða* and the best of the classical sagas. The most likely source of this stylistic development is oral refinement over time—an oral refinement that presupposes the telling of a long prose form that provided the necessary latitude for practicing those larger rhetorical patterns and strategies, which define the style that ultimately emerged in the written sagas.

CHAPTER 2

The Prehistory of the Kings' Sagas

For almost a hundred years now, that is to say for almost as long as saga research has existed as an autonomous field, there has been what might strike the outsider as an obsessive interest in the prehistory of the sagas, the period before the sagas actually reached parchment. The first half of the twentieth century witnessed a vigorous, albeit somewhat oblique, debate between the advocate of fully evolved oral sagas, Andreas Heusler, and the various representatives of the "Icelandic School," notably Björn M. Ólsen, Sigurður Nordal, and Einar Ól. Sveinsson, who emphasized the creative and literary role of the saga authors.[1] A strong voice on the oral side of the debate was the Norwegian folklorist Knut Liestøl, whose book was translated into English and probably reached a larger audience than the Icelandic and Swiss contributions.[2] My own summary of the research became largely a critique of the Icelandic School.[3] At the same time Lars Lönnroth was publishing his dissertation serially.[4] Rather than considering the sagas in the context of the native Icelandic tradition, he explored possible European roots, but his emphasis remained literary in the tradition of the Icelandic School. More recently the indigenous Icelandic tradition has come to the fore again in Daniel Sävborg's compendious book from 2007.[5]

The question of literary versus oral origins was quiescent for the last decades of the twentieth century, with the notable exception of Óskar Halldórsson's small but transformative book on *Hrafnkels saga*.[6] It was a counterthrust to Sigurður Nordal's epoch-making monograph on the same saga, which was translated into English and thus became the international voice of the Icelandic School.[7] That voice became less audible in the wake of Óskar's book. In the meantime Else Mundal compiled an extensive anthology, in 1977, of many of the key contributions to the debate, and Carol Clover surveyed the field in 1985.[8] As we saw in the last chapter, Clover also contributed a broadly conceived paper in 1986 suggesting that the sagas are in some sense conglomerates of shorter oral stories.[9] I replied in 2002 with a paper that tried to assemble the evidence that there were long oral stories as well as short ones.[10] But the field did not really move until the appearance of simultaneous books by Gísli Sigurðsson and Tommy Danielsson in 2002.[11] Gísli worked with saga variants that seem quite likely to be oral and therefore presuppose stories that we might refer to as oral sagas. Danielsson's approach was more panoramic, but it focuses once again on *Hrafnkels saga*. The combined effect of these books was to put oral sagas back in the center of the discussion.

It may be noted, however, that throughout this long-standing debate very little has been said about the kings' sagas. The only exception to this was Siegfried Beyschlag, who tried to show that the synoptic histories inherited their uniformity from oral tradition.[12] This thesis appears not to have gained adherents. We are therefore in the anomalous position of believing that there were full-blown stories about Saga Age Icelanders but no stories about Norwegian kings. Scholarly silence on this question has been as curious as it has been universal, and the silence was broken only in the last ten pages of Tommy Danielsson's second volume. The body of the book is devoted to a long series of specialized king's saga problems, but, almost as an afterthought, the author opens large horizons in the conclusion (pp. 385–95). Here he surveys the evidence that the Norwegian kings also lived on in memory and tradition. He reminds us of the prominent place occupied by the Norwegian kings in *Laxdœla saga* and other predominantly Icelandic sagas, then goes on to review the meetings of prominent Icelanders with Norwegian monarchs, particularly in the short, self-contained stories called *þættir*. These contacts could have served as the point of departure for the Icelandic interest in the kings and the growth of oral narrative.

Danielsson also reviews the named Icelandic bearers of royal tradition: Þorgeirr afráðskollr, Oddr Kolsson, and Hallr Þórarinsson, all of whom were among Ari Þorgilsson's sources at the beginning of the twelfth century. Included as well is the young Icelander who learned the story of Haraldr harðráði's early adventures from Halldórr Snorrason and performed it at Haraldr's court (see below). We do not know the exact form of such transmissions, but Danielsson takes due note of the comments made by Theodoricus and Saxo indicating that the Icelanders were well known for cultivating rich traditions, a reputation confirmed by the prologues in *Heimskringla* and by the *þættir* in *Morkinskinna*.[13] This narrative material is generally assumed to have provided a rough basis for the written accounts later shaped by writers, but Danielsson asks whether this quite loose and general assumption is adequate and whether the underlying narrative could not have been in the form of fully developed storytelling (p. 392: "ett ytterst avancerat berättande"). Such stories do not surface in the early period because there would have been no reason for Ari or Sæmundr or the later synoptic historians to reproduce stories that everybody knew.

At about the same time as these stories were circulating, domestic Icelandic sagas would have been evolving on the basis of legal disputes and feud stories, as Danielsson argues in his first volume. A likely venue for the exchange of such stories would have been the Icelandic thingmeetings, just as the young Icelandic storyteller in *Morkinskinna* learned the story of Haraldr harðráði at thingmeetings over a series of summers. The evolution of royal stories is perhaps less easy to grasp than the evolution of native stories, but Danielsson suggests several possibilities. There could have been a tradition of comparing kings, or the kings could have been of ongoing and central importance to the Icelanders, or there could have been a concretization of royal stories analogous to the *þættir*. The kings' sagas could also have been modeled on the agonistic patterns of the evolving Icelandic sagas. In turn, the growth of the kings' sagas into large books could have paved the way for the large Icelandic sagas such as *Laxdœla saga* and *Njáls saga*.

The central issue in this argument is the existence of fully developed kings' sagas in oral tradition. This is indeed a new perspective on the kings' sagas, and we may ask ourselves why it has not been aired before. One reason is surely that the very idea of an oral saga fell out of favor in Icelandic circles throughout the twentieth century. A leading project of the Icelandic School was to diminish our faith in the existence of full oral sagas about early Iceland, and it was only to be expected that the generations engaged in this project would not contradict themselves by advocating oral kings' sagas. On the contrary, they focused on the development of the sagas as a purely literary enterprise, perhaps ultimately based on scattered oral traditions but carried out exclusively with quill and ink. Naturally the same assumption would have carried over to the kings' sagas.

But an analogy with the native Icelandic sagas is not the only justification for believing in the piecemeal literary composition of the kings' sagas. Our information about the latter begins in fact almost a century earlier than the information on the native sagas and gives every appearance of suggesting a gradual literary evolution from smaller written denominations to larger denominations. The process began with Sæmundr and Ari early in the twelfth century and culminated in the Norwegian synoptics at the end of the century, Theodoricus's *Historia de Antiquitate Regum Norwagiensium, Historia Norwegiae,* and *Ágrip af Nóregs konunga sǫgum.* That this was a literary sequence is supported by what seems to be a growing consensus that there is a continuity between the early epitomes and the later ones. Despite Theodoricus's protestations that he based himself not on "visa" but on "audita," it seems likely that he also used written sources and that these sources are most likely to have been Sæmundr and Ari.[14]

The picture that emerges from the twelfth century is therefore a puzzling together of information, including oral sources, but collected by writers who converted what they could learn into little digests and summaries, not stories. This picture is reinforced by the shape of the first full-length kings' sagas, Oddr Snorrason's *Óláfs saga Tryggvasonar* and the *Oldest Saga of Saint Olaf* largely represented by the *Legendary Saga.* To be sure, these are full-blown biographical stories, but they are quite awkwardly composed.[15] They do not suggest authors recording flowing narratives but rather writers who are trying to fit and join scraps of tradition. That might lead us to believe that writers in the twelfth century began by condensing the main points provided by the oral transmissions and ended by trying to expand these early indications somewhat artificially into real books, an entirely literary project. The tacit assumption might then go on to stipulate that when the master narratives appear, largely in *Morkinskinna* and *Heimskringla*, they again perfect the form of the older written narratives using strictly literary methods.

How does Tommy Danielsson's suggestion of ready-made, full-fledged oral narratives about the kings comport with this picture of writers struggling to achieve a literary form for the royal biographies from scattered traditions? If the first biographers were faced with the simple task of setting down well articulated oral stories in writing, why did they perform the task so poorly? Perhaps an analogy will help us out of this dilemma. Since the publication of Gísli Sigurðsson's and Tommy Danielsson's books no one seems any longer to have difficulty with the idea that there were fully developed sagas about early Iceland, but we must remind ourselves that these sagas also had an awkward beginning.

The question of which *Íslendingasögur* came first is of course a subject of dispute, and I can only offer my own view. I think that *all* the skald sagas, including *Gunnlaugs saga*, were early, and to that group of four I would add *Fóstbrœðra saga, Víga-Glúms saga,* and *Reykdœla saga.*[16] What these sagas have in common is that they are not gracefully composed, unlike the great sagas of the next generation, *Egils saga, Gísla saga,* and *Laxdœla saga.* The early sagas are in some cases quite short and in other cases rather mechanically constructed around skaldic stanzas. They are not ranked among the saga masterpieces.

Accordingly we find both among the sagas about early Iceland and the kings' sagas a prefatory period of experimental and rather problematical composition before the perfected form emerges. There can now be little doubt that the domestic Icelandic sagas were drawn from oral tradition. It therefore seems clear that the transposition from oral stories to written stories was by no means straightforward. It required practice. By analogy we can suppose that oral kings' sagas would have been no easier than the *Íslendingasögur* to convert smoothly into written sagas at the first attempt. That means that the awkward first biographies of Óláfr Tryggvason and Óláfr Haraldsson do not exclude the possibility that there existed full oral sagas about these and other kings. It was only a question of learning to recast these oral prototypes into written sagas.

Nor should we forget that there were stories intermediate between the domestic sagas and the kings' sagas, to wit the *þættir*, in which equal space is given to the Norwegian kings and the Icelandic adventurers. The *þættir* are very much at the center of Tommy Danielsson's discussion and are at least one secure key to the operations of oral transmission, inasmuch as they can hardly be explained by any other conveyance. They provide information on the kings and their attitudes, character, and politics, as well as on their contacts with Icelanders. The warrant that they were circulated in the earliest period of saga writing (1200 to 1220) is the preservation of thirteen examples in *Morkinskinna.*[17] Their focus is the Icelandic experience of the outside world, and they must therefore have been handed down in Iceland, perhaps in the families of those who experienced them. The dual focus on kings and Icelanders assures us that at least some memory of the kings would have stayed alive in Iceland.

As Tommy Danielsson points out, they also illustrate the general Icelandic preoccupation with Norwegian kings. In the early twelfth century, both Sæmundr and Ari directed their attention to the neighboring kings in Norway. If their books had been preserved, the task of understanding Icelandic thinking about the Norwegian kings would perhaps have been facilitated, but even the bare existence of these books tells us something. The kings seem to have been Sæmundr's sole preoccupation, and though we may be apt to think of Ari's "konunga ævi" as a supplement to his *Íslendingabók*, simply because we have one and not the other, the situation may have been reversed. Perhaps the "konunga ævi" were the primary undertaking, and perhaps we should consider *Íslendingabók* as the supplement. In either case the Norwegian kings were a dominant factor when the Icelanders first began to write.

We are not told much about the interaction between the Norwegian kings and Iceland under the early kings down to 995, but after the advent of the conversion kings the interaction becomes charged. Óláfr Tryggvason appears to have been an energetic proselytizer well beyond the shores of Norway, and that may perhaps understate the case. He was credited with the conversion of five lands, and texts such as Ari's *Íslendingabók*, Oddr Snorrason's *Óláfs saga Tryggvasonar*, *Kristni saga*, and *Laxdœla saga* lead us to believe that he exerted strong pressure on the Icelanders to convert.[18] Whether or not Óláfr's efforts at proselytizing were really so effective, later writers thought they were, and they must have believed that Óláfr applied pressure on the Icelanders to convert. In their minds this was the point at which Norway becomes a real, not to say a menacing, factor in the political life of Iceland.

The threat materializes palpably under Óláfr Haraldsson, who, according to *Heimskringla*, not only tries to cajole the Icelanders into making him a gift of the island Grímsey, but later holds distinguished Icelanders hostage to increase his leverage.[19] Subsequently Haraldr harðráði is said to have been a great friend of the Icelanders, but given his record of deceitfulness and his aggressive foreign policy, we would like to know what motivated his friendship.[20] Adam of Bremen states that Haraldr extended his rule as far as Iceland.[21] This corresponds to nothing in the indigenous sources, but we may well wonder where Haraldr's contemporary Adam may have gotten the idea. Could it signal that Haraldr indeed had designs on Iceland? In the twelfth century the Norwegian kings were sufficiently preoccupied with other matters that they did not pose much of a threat, but the very fact that the Icelanders had such a clear memory of Norwegian aspirations under two proselytizing rulers indicates that they must have had a watchful eye on Norway. Add to this that, whatever the actual history of immigration to Iceland may have been, the Icelanders clearly thought of themselves as kin to the Norwegians by lineage and culture.[22] The national umbilical cord seems not to have been severed, and Norway remained much more than just a horizon.

We can be in no doubt that information on Norway was plentiful in Iceland, but the question to be dealt with is not one of information but of literary form. The Icelanders could of course have known a great deal about Norway without ever casting anything in narrative form. That they did think in terms of literary form is sufficiently demonstrated by the *þættir* with their identifiable morphology,[23] but the oral existence of short *þættir* may not justify the assumption of longer sagas. Even so, the evidence for oral kings' sagas is rather better than the evidence for oral sagas about the early Icelanders. This evidence resides largely in the *útferðarsaga* of Haraldr harðráði that Halldórr Snorrason teaches to a young Icelander, who in turn recites it at Haraldr's court.[24] Tommy Danielsson refers to this recital in both of his volumes, but it may lend itself to further exploitation. At the very least the episode suggests that such stories were formally composed with enough detail so that they had to be learned, that they were formally recited to a large group, and that they were long enough to be presented for two weeks. They were formal stories, not just random accounts.

Not only that, but the story of Haraldr's adventures in the Mediterranean, as they are told in *Morkinskinna* and by extension in *Heimskringla*, constituted a highly dramatic story of intrigue in the Byzantine court, military prowess and ingenuity, and the accumulation of fabulous wealth, a thirteenth-century counterpart to *The Count of Monte Cristo*. The oral version that held the attention of King Haraldr's court for two weeks must have shared some of these qualities; it too must have been a rousing tale of daring and high romance.

I have indicated that there seems to be a tacit assumption that the evolution of the kings' sagas from notes and summaries in the twelfth century to epic canvases in the thirteenth century was a strictly literary process. That is to say, people simply learned to write better and better and more fully as time went on. At the same time, we have evidence that there were full-blown, dramatic tales in oral form. The awkward formulations in the twelfth-century epitomes and the first attempts at biography teach us that the ostensibly simple option of transcribing oral stories was not adopted. The first efforts at duplicating what may have been rather good oral stories fell short and converted good stories into not very successful books. The art of capturing good stories on parchment was a gradual process, learned slowly and a little painfully. It seems to have combined a knowledge of stories with a faltering acquisition of writing skills.

Vésteinn Ólason has recently used the word "imitation" to describe this process and refers to Preben Meulengracht Sørensen's earlier use of the same term: "The narrative style and technique of the sagas shows every sign of being an imitation, conscious or unconscious, of oral narrative."[25] "Imitation" may well be as close as we can get to a resolution of this problem. Vésteinn uses it with reference to the *Íslendingasögur,* but, following Tommy Danielsson, I have no difficulty in extending the usage to the kings' sagas as well. Indeed, it seems to me that the kings' sagas reveal the nature of the imitation more clearly and more fully by making the stages in the development more palpable. The first stage was to skim the high points by way of a summation. The second stage was to add detail in order to approximate at least the length of the oral sagas. The third stage was then to imitate the narrative style as well as the narrative dimensions of the oral stories.

The progress from brief summary of the main points in the oral transmission to a fuller recapitulation in the first biographies and finally to a recreation of the dramatic story line is clearer in the kings' sagas than in the *Íslendingasögur*, but the same line can also be detected, though more tentatively, in the latter. The famous summary of *Hœnsa-Þóris saga* found in Ari's *Íslendingabók* is analogous to the epitomes on the Norwegian kings and represents the first stage in the narrative development. The second stage is more difficult to match because the differences in the quality of composition among the early *Íslendingasögur* are less pronounced than in the kings' sagas. We can nonetheless make it plausible that the earliest *Íslendingasögur* were less well assembled than the later masterpieces. If we were to choose one *Íslendingasaga* to illustrate the original defects of composition, it might be *Kormáks saga*, a saga that does not so much tell the story as it extracts the main moments of the biography from a large collection of stanzas. Dialogue and drama are largely missing.

There is also a good match in the chronology of these developments. If *Egils saga* was written as early as the 1220s, we might infer that the third stage in the *Íslendingasögur* was reached in the same time frame as the culmination of the kings' sagas in *Morkinskinna* and *Heimskringla*. These were the high points in both genres and they represent a level seldom attained again.

It may therefore be reasonable to suppose that there was not only a significant similarity between *Íslendingasögur* and kings' sagas at the literary stage in the thirteenth century but also that there must have been a real similarity at the oral stage as well. To imagine that the king's saga masterpieces (*Morkinskinna* and *Heimskringla*) acquired their art by imitating written *Íslendingasögur* is not practicable because the early *Íslendingasögur* were not well put together and cannot have stood model for *Morkinskinna* and *Heimskringla*. Both types are more likely to have acquired their narrative art from an increasingly skillful imitation of oral storytelling. Their affinity to this narrative tradition explains the much-praised uniqueneess of the *Íslendingasögur*, but it also explains why the best, though less frequently praised, kings' sagas are the most readable chronicles of the Middle Ages.

CHAPTER 3

The First Written Sagas of Kings and Chieftains

In his monograph *Fyrsta sagan* Bjarni Guðnason preempted the title of "first saga" for Eiríkr Oddsson's **Hryggjarstykki*, a lost text referred to and paraphrased in *Morkinskinna* and *Heimskringla* and written sometime in the middle of the twelfth century.[1] This text is difficult to reconstruct even in outline and may have been narrowly focused on the ill-fated pretender Sigurðr slembir (died 1139), as Bjarni Guðnason thought. If he is right, **Hryggjarstykki* was a contemporary saga in the style of *Sturlu saga* or *Guðmundar saga dýra* rather than a historical narrative with an oral prefiguration. Another saga with a claim to be "first" was the saga of King Sverrir Sigurðarson (died 1202), *Sverris saga*, which appears to have been begun by Abbot Karl Jónsson of the northwestern Icelandic monastery of Þingeyrar in the late 1180s but may not have been completed until a good many years later.[2] It too was a contemporary saga.

If we cast about for the "first saga" in the sense of a long traditional narrative with biographical proportions, the choice might well fall on the so-called *Oldest Saga of Saint Olaf* or on Oddr Snorrason's (originally Latin) *Óláfs saga Tryggvasonar*. At one time there was a solid consensus that the former antedated the latter. Gustav Storm dated the *Oldest Saga* to 1155–1180, and Sigurður Nordal not much later (1160–1185).[3] Oddr Snorrason's saga is most often dated ca. 1190, but the priority is nonetheless difficult to resolve. In more recent years the antiquity of *The Oldest Saga* has been doubted, and neither saga is extant in the original form. We have six quite brief fragments of the

Oldest Saga, but the text as a whole is preserved only in the so-called *Legendary Saga of Saint Olaf*, a somewhat abbreviated redaction with at least two substantial interpolations. Oddr's Latin original is also lost and survives only in three differing redactions of an Icelandic translation of uncertain date.[4] Although Oddr's original is commonly dated around 1190, a looser estimate of 1180–1200 would be considerably safer.[5] At the same time, the work of Jonna Louis-Jensen and Jónas Kristjánsson has shaken the early dating of the *Oldest Saga*. The latter scholar believes that a date "around 1200" is more likely.[6]

In sum, then, it is difficult to determine which came first, the *Oldest Saga* or Oddr's *Óláfs saga Tryggvasonar*. Yet there are several points of convergence, suggesting that one may have referred to the other. The Stockholm manuscript of Oddr's saga in fact refers in so many words to the person who "made the saga" (scil. of Óláfr Haraldsson), indicating that the writer of this redaction had access to a text of the saga of Saint Óláfr.[7] But Bjarni Aðalbjarnarson judged that the reference is not attributable to Oddr's original and may allude to *Heimskringla*.[8] We are therefore thrown back on the wording of the texts in any attempt to ascertain whether the writer of one saga was familiar with the other.

A good point of departure is one of Konrad Maurer's epic footnotes.[9] Without recapitulating the details, we may simply note that Maurer found enough similarity between Oddr's *Óláfs saga Tryggvasonar* and the saga of Saint Óláfr that later became known as the *Oldest Saga* that he regarded both sagas as the work of Oddr Snorrason.

Sigurður Nordal rejected Maurer's idea that Oddr authored a saga about Saint Óláfr, but he found it tempting to believe that he knew such a saga and was inspired by it to write his own saga about Óláfr Tryggvason.[10]

Finnur Jónsson differed with Nordal's general view of *The Oldest Saga* largely to the extent that he believed it to have been much more extensively interpolated in the process of being transformed into the *Legendary Saga* than Nordal supposed.[11] Among the interpolations he identified were two important passages that will be discussed below: Saint Óláfr's encounter with a prophetic hermit and the episode in which Einarr þambarskelfir's bow bursts from his hands and metaphorically signals the loss of Norway.[12] Since Finnur Jónsson believed the versions in the *Legendary Saga* to be interpolations, he could not make use of them in assessing the relationship between the *Oldest Saga* and Oddr's *Óláfs saga Tryggvasonar*. Nonetheless, he states elsewhere that it is reasonable to think that Oddr knew the *Oldest Saga* and was led by his reading of it to write his biography of Óláfr Tryggvason.[13] Bjarni Aðalbjarnarson's detailed study of the relationahips among the kings' sagas did not add anything new because he considered that Nordal had adequately clarified the relationship of the texts pertaining to Saint Óláfr, but he too was prepared to believe that Oddr was familiar with the *Oldest Saga*.[14]

Without commenting on the textual priorities, Lars Lönnroth argued that narrative material belonging originally to Saint Óláfr was later transferred to Óláfr Tryggvason.[15] Thus the *Legendary Saga* (chapter 19), Theodoricus, and *Ágrip* agree that when Saint Óláfr came to Norway, he landed on an island with the auspicious name Sæla (= Selja). In Oddr's account Óláfr Tryggvason is also said to have landed on an island off western Norway, Mostr.[16] (Mostr is, however, well to the south of Selja, and these landing traditions may be entirely separate.) Similarly, the report of Saint Óláfr's visit to a prophetic hermit (discussed below) is slightly closer to Gregory the Great's anecdote about King Totila's attempted deception of Saint Benedict, which stood model for the tale (Lönnroth, pp. 60–61). An analogous anecdote is attributed to Óláfr Tryggvason in *Ágrip* (ed. Driscoll, 30) and the *Historia Norwegiae* (MHN, 114), but the phrasing in these texts is slightly expanded and may therefore be secondary.

The anecdote about Einarr þambarskelfir and his bow is also attached to both Óláfrs, but Lönnroth argues that it is more likely to belong originally to Saint Óláfr because Einarr þambarskelfir figures prominently in his reign and because it seems unlikely that Einarr, who fell victim to Haraldr harðráði's treachery sometime after 1046,[17] would have been old enough to participate in the Battle of Svǫlðr in the year 1000. Lönnroth describes these transfers in terms of tradition rather than as textual borrowings, but the old idea persists that the narrative of Saint Óláfr is anterior to that of Óláfr Tryggvason.

More recently, however, Lönnroth has revised his point of view. Noting the current dating of the *Oldest Saga* around 1200, he suggests that the earliest long prose narrative must have been Oddr's saga from around 1180, and he goes on to say that he had probably underestimated the importance of Oddr's biography for the development of saga writing.[18] A few pages later he is even more explicit: "When the *Legendary Saga* (or *Oldest Saga) of Olav the Saint* was written around 1200, its most important model was probably Odd's Latin biography of Olav Tryggvason—or perhaps its Icelandic translation since the *Legendary Saga* was written in Old Norse and not in Latin."[19] It is this proposition that stands to be tested below.

The major break leading to Lönnroth's reversal of the old priorities came in 1970 when Jonna Louis-Jensen raised questions about the early date traditionally assigned to the *Oldest Saga* (see note 6). Her work was quickly followed up by Jónas Kristjánsson, who at first thought it was quite likely that Oddr knew an early version of the saga about Saint Óláfr.[20] A few years later, however, he considered the problem in greater detail and came to the conclusion that there was no strong reason to believe that the *Oldest Saga* was written earlier than ca. 1200.[21] His weightiest reason for this view is his rejection of Nordal's arguments that the *Legendary Saga* was interpolated with excerpts from *Ágrip*.[22] He therefore found no reason for thinking that these excerpts were not already part of the *Oldest Saga*.[23] Hence the *Oldest Saga* must be later than *Ágrip* (ca. 1190). As a result, he finds it difficult to settle on a chronological priority of one Óláfr saga over the other:[24] "Perhaps they were written at about the same time, but in different parts of Iceland, and in fact they are very unlike in construction—and moreover one of them is in Icelandic while the other was originally composed in Latin."

Since there are no external criteria to guide our decision on priorities, we are obliged to make a close comparison of the texts if we wish to identify possible echoes of one in the other. In doing so I will cite Guðni Jónsson's normalized texts for uniformity and ease of reference, bearing in mind that the comparison is more motival than textual because we have the *Oldest Saga* only in the altered reflection of the *Legendary Saga* and Oddr's saga only in the approximation of an Icelandic translation.[25]

The Infancies of Óláfr Tryggvason and Óláfr Haraldsson

The first suggestion of a correspondence is that both Óláfrs begin life in a little (or an old) shed:

> Ok er hon vissi, at nálgaðist sú stund, er hon mundi barn fæða, kómu þau til vatns, er Rönd heitir, ok þar váru þau í litlu nausti, ok þar fæddi hon barn, ok var þat sveipt klæðum ok var nafn gefit ok vatni ausit ok kölluðu Óláf sveininn. (Oddr, p. 9; ÍF 25:131)

> [And when she realized that the time was at hand when she would give birth to a child, they came to a lake called Rönd and stayed in a little boatshed, and there she gave birth to a child, and it was wrapped in clothing and given a name and sprinkled with water and they called the boy Óláfr.]

> Engu kemr öðru við en barnit verðr út at bera. En þar hafði verit áðr forn skemma ok af ræfrit. Þangat var sveininn færðr ok settr niðr í gröf eina. (*Helgisaga*, p. 207)

> [There was nothing for it but that they were obliged to carry the child out. There used to be an old shed there with the roof gone. The boy was taken there and put in a hollow.]

The situations are quite different. In Oddr's account the mother takes refuge in a "lítit naust" to give birth. In the *Helgisaga* the child has already been born (under magical circumstances) and is exposed in a "forn skemma," but in both cases the birth is associated with a shed. Oddr's version is close to Luke's story of Jesus's birth and is clearly modeled on it. The *Helgisaga* has no reminiscences of Luke. Furthermore, in this latter account the "skemma" seems quite unmotivated because children in Icelandic literature are not exposed in nearby sheds but in the wilds.[26] Oddr's version is not a story of exposure and is thus not modeled on the *Helgisaga*. If there is a connection, it is that the author of the *Helgisaga* vaguely remembered something about a shed in Oddr's narrative. Because of Oddr's deliberate use of Luke, the correspondence cannot be a case of transferred tradition but only of a textual transfer.

The following chapter 7 in the *Legendary Saga* (and presumably the *Oldest Saga*) deals with the death of Saint Óláfr's father Haraldr grenski at the hands of Sigríðr stórráða, whom he has had the temerity to woo. The author gives the following information on Sigríðr.

> En í þann tíma réð fyrir Svíðþjóð Sigríðr in stórráða, er átt hafði Eiríkr inn ársæli. Hon var dóttir Sköglar-Tósta . . . ok margir segja hana fyrir Gautlandi hafa ráðit, fyrir því at konungr mátti eigi bera hennar ofsa. (*Helgisaga*, p. 209)
>
> [At that time Sigrid the Imperious ruled Sweden, who had been married to Erik Harvestluck. She was the daughter of Sköglar-Tósti . . . and many people say that she ruled Gautland because the king could not endure her arrogance.]

The formula "many people say" can imply an oral transmission, but it can also refer to a written text. Such a written text is provided by Oddr in chapters 5 and 32. The first passage reads as follows:

> Þá váru skilið ráð þeira Sigríðar stórráðu, dóttur Sköglar-Tósta [scil. ok Eiríks konungs]. En þat bar til at sumra manna sögn, at hon var stórráð ok þó ráðgjörn, en konungr vildi eigi hafa ofsa hennar. (Oddr, p. 16; ÍF 25:138–39)
>
> [Then Sigrid the Imperious, the daughter of Sköglar-Tósti, and King Erik were separated. According to some people that was brought about because she was imperious and willful, and the king would not stand for her arrogance.]

Essentially the same information is repeated in chapter 32:

> Eiríkr konungr átti Sigríði ina stórráðu, ok var þeira sonr Óláfr sænski. Þat segja menn, at konungrinn vildi skilja við Sigríði dróttningu ok vildi eigi hafa ofsa hennar ok ofmetnað ok setti hana dróttningu yfir Gautlandi. (Oddr, p. 90; ÍF 25:225–26)
>
> [King Erik was married to Sigrid the Imperious, and their son was Óláfr the Swede. People say that the king wanted to separate from Queen Sigrid and would not stand for her arrogance and excessive pride, and he made her queen of Gautland.]

These passages share the report formulas "margir segja," "at sumra manna sögn," and "þat segja menn" as well as the phrasing "mátti eigi bera hennar ofsa" or "vildi eigi hafa ofsa hennar." In addition, they share the information that Sigríðr reigns over Gautland, but whereas Oddr gives a full account of the divorce, including variant versions, the author of the *Legendary Saga* does not explain the divorce and does not make it clear how Sigríðr ended up in Gautland. Therefore, assuming that the *Legendary Saga* reproduces the *Oldest Saga* at this point, Oddr's account probably does not represent a borrowing from the *Oldest Saga*. On the other hand, the passage in the *Legendary Saga* could perfectly well be an abbreviated reference to the information in Oddr.

When the *Legendary Saga* goes on to recount how Sigríðr burned her two unwanted suitors Haraldr grenski and Vissivaldr in their separate halls, we might consider this too to be a borrowing from Oddr, who reports the burning in chapter 32. Sigríðr has an important role in *Óláfs saga Tryggvasonar* as one of the fomentors of the plot against Óláfr. She is at home in this saga, whereas her role in the *Legendary Saga* is confined to the killing of Haraldr grenski. On the other hand, the author of the *Oldest Saga*, judging by the evidence of the *Legendary Saga*, either elaborated the episode freely or had access to a separate tradition about the burning of Haraldr grenski, because he provides a more dramatic version of the event. It includes an initial wooing of Haraldr by Sigríðr (chapter 1) and a drinking contest she stages between her competing suitors to make them more vulnerable to her designs.

If Dietrich Hofmann was correct in vindicating the attribution of *Yngvars saga víðfǫrla* to Oddr, there is a further indication that the information on Sigríðr was primarily Oddr's literary property. *Yngvars saga* begins with the following passage:[27]

> Eiríkr hét konungr, er réð fyrir Svíþjóðu. Hann var kallaðr Eiríkr sigrsæli. Hann átti Sigríði ina stórráðu ok skildi við hana sakir óhægenda skapsmuna hennar, því at hon var kvenna stríðlyndust um alt þat, er við bar. Hann gaf henni Gautland.

> [Erik was the name of the king who ruled Sweden. He was called Erik the Victorious. He was married to Sigrid the Imperious and separated from her because of her difficult disposition, for she was most contentious about whatever happened. He gave her Gautland.]

This looks like a contracted version of the fuller account that Oddr gives in *Óláfs saga Tryggvasonar*, but whether it is primary or secondary, it would seem to suggest that the story is well anchored in Oddr Snorrason's writing and more likely to have radiated from that source into the *Oldest Saga* than vice versa. If the verbal echo "mátti eigi bera hennar ofsa" ("vildi eigi hafa ofsa hennar") is significant, the transfer may have come from the Icelandic translation of Oddr's text rather than the Latin original, as Lönnroth suggested.[28]

The echoes persist in chapter 8 of the *Legendary Saga*, directly after the burning of Haraldr grenski. Here the author reports how the child Óláfr Haraldsson was baptized by Óláfr Tryggvason:

> En í þann tíma kemr Óláfr Tryggvason í land ok boðar þegar trúna. Ok er hann kemr á Upplönd, þá kristnar hann þar. Ok sjálfr helt hann nafna sínum undir skírn . . . . Þá var hann fimm vetra gamall. (*Helgisaga*, p. 210)
>
> [At that time Óláfr Tryggvason came to Norway and immediately preached the faith. And when he came to Upplönd, he brought Christianity there. And he himself held his namesake for baptism . . . . At that time he was five years old.]

In his prologue Oddr makes a programmatic comparison of Óláfr Tryggvason and Óláfr Haraldsson, emphasizing the former as the forerunner of the latter:

> Ok á inu fimmta ári hans ríkis helt Óláfr konungr nafna sínum undir skírn ok tók hann af þeim helga brunni í þá líking sem Jóan baptisti gerði við dróttin, ok svá sem hann var hans fyrirrennari, svá var ok Óláfr konungr Tryggvason fyrirrennari ins helga Óláfs konungs. (Oddr, p. 3; ÍF 25:125)
>
> [And in the fifth year of his reign King Óláfr held his namesake for baptism and raised him from the holy font just as John the Baptist did with the Lord, and just as the latter was His forerunner, so too was King Óláfr Tryggvason the forerunner of King Óláfr the Saint.]

There is a misunderstanding or a misconstruction in this second passage. If the sense is that Óláfr Tryggvason stood godfather to Óláfr

Haraldsson in the fifth year of his reign, the construction should have been "á inu fimmta ári *síns* ríkis." The original text may therefore be distorted at this point, and the intention may have been to refer to the child's age rather than the chronology of the king's reign.[29]

The passage would then be in line with the *Legendary Saga*, a significant correspondence inasmuch as other sources, notably Theodoricus and *Heimskringla*, make the boy three years old. There is also a match in phrasing between "sjálfr helt hann nafna sínum undir skírn" and "helt Óláfr konungr nafna sínum undir skírn." Where the priority lies is not obvious, but the information is more conspicuously located in Oddr's prologue, a location that would have been immediately obvious to the author of the *Oldest Saga*. The match in phrasing might again suggest that the author of the *Oldest Saga* already had the Icelandic translation of Oddr's book in hand. If Oddr is the source and the *Oldest Saga* is the borrower, it appears that the author of the latter made drafts on Oddr in three consecutive chapters (6–8) that pertain to the most important moments in Óláfr Haraldsson's early life, his birth, the death of his father, and his baptism.

The Transition to Kingship

The next sequences of echoes also appear in clusters, in chapters 16–19 of the *Legendary Saga* and chapters 12–14 of Oddr's saga. In chapter 16 of the former the young Óláfr Haraldsson gains victory in fifteen battles that may well have been commemorated in skaldic stanzas and would have been accessible in that form. At the conclusion of this sequence Óláfr finds himself off Ireland on yet another viking expedition, but this time his ships are stranded by the outgoing tide and he faces a great host of militia gathering on land. Responding to an appeal from his men, he settles on a solution through the efficacy of prayer:

> Ef þér vilið mitt ráð hafa, þá heitum nú allir á almáttkan guð ok látum af hernaði ok ránum ok hverfi hverr nú heðan í frá til þess, er guð hefir hann látit til berast, ok leiti nú hverr við at varðveita sína herferð með réttendum. (*Helgisaga*, p. 233)

> [If you wish to follow my advice, let us all call on Almighty God and desist from raiding and plundering, and from now on let each man turn

> to what God intended him for, and let each man seek to conduct his raiding with righteousness.]

All his men agree and clasp hands to confirm their vows. No sooner do they do so than their ships are refloated and they are able to make their escape out of the clutches of the Irish.

This episode, which, unlike the preceding ones, seems not to be based on skaldic authority, has a strong functional resemblance to the episode in Oddr's saga in which Óláfr Tryggvason and his men are raiding in Denmark and suddenly find themselves at the mercy of a gathering multitude. Óláfr addresses the emergency:

> "Ek veit," sagði hann, "at sá er máttugr guð, er himnunum stýrir, ok þat hefi ek heyrt at þat sigrmark á hann, er mikill kraftr er með, ok er þat kallat kross. Köllum nú á hann sjálfan, at hann leysi oss, ok föllum allir til jarðar ok lítilllætum oss sjálfir. Tökum nú tvá kvistu ok leggjum í kross yfir oss. Gerið nú svá allir sem þér séð mik gera." (Oddr, p. 37; ÍF 25:161)

> ["I know," he said, "that He who rules heaven is a powerful God, and I have heard that He possesses a victorious icon endowed with great power, and that is called a cross. Let us call on him to release us, and let us all fall to the ground and humble ourselves. Let us take two branches and lay them in the shape of a cross over us. Now you should all do as you see me do."]

The vastly outnumbered men now become miraculously invisible, and after a repetition of the device for emphasis they make good their escape from the Danes. The functional similarity lies in the transition from a pagan (or viking) stage to a truly Christian way of life. In Oddr's saga there is no indication that Óláfr Tryggvason has a prior experience of Christianity; for him the episode constitutes a sort of anticipatory revelation. In the case of Óláfr Haraldsson, the chieftain is a Christian of long standing. For him the miracle does not serve the purpose of conversion. Instead it marks the passage from an unfettered viking life to an acknowledgment of Christian values. Both Óláfrs begin their adult lives as viking leaders, and both authors are confronted with the problem of explaining how they reform their ways. Both authors hit on the same solution, one premonitory of conversion and the other admonitory to better conduct. Whether these miracles were hit on independently or interdependently is the question. But if one miracle is dependent on the other, it seems more likely that Oddr led the way because a premonitory conversion miracle is more convincing than a miracle conducive to marginal moral improvement. Indeed, the idea of "righteous raiding" in the *Legenday Saga* seems peculiarly awkward and contradictory.

In chapter 17 of the *Legendary Saga* Óláfr Haraldsson and his men encounter a pagan seeress. Óláfr's companion Sóti asks permission to consult her, and, although Óláfr is quite averse, he finally yields. In response to Sóti's inquiry the seeress is reticent, but she does make the following pronouncement about Óláfr:

> Hann er svá mikils máttar ok dýrligs, at þar er mér fátt leyft at ræða, ok gagnstaðrligr er várr kraftr. Ógn er mikil yfir honum ok birting ok ljós. (*Helgisaga*, p. 234)

> [He has such great and glorious power that I am not allowed to say much; our powers are opposed. There is great awe and brightness and light over him.]

This prophecy marks the end of Óláfr's viking years and the beginning of his royal mission:

> Nú lætr Óláfr af öllum hernaði ok renndi hug sinum til ættlanda sinna, hversu hann skyldi hana með sæmd sækja eða öðlast. En hversu margt sem sagt er í frá víðlendisferð Óláfs, þá kom þegar aftr, er guð vildi opna ríki fyrir honum. (*Helgisaga*, p. 234)

> [Now Óláfr ceased all raiding and turned his mind to his ancestral lands, how he might honorably reach and acquire them. And however much is told of Óláfr's travels abroad, he returned immediately when God wished to make the realm accessible to him.]

Óláfr Tryggvason is also initiated into his new life prophetically, by a voice from above and a vision of heaven and hell. He is commended for scorning the heathen gods and admonished to go to Greece for further instruction. Here he is duly primesigned before returning to the north to convert the Russian king and queen (Oddr, chapter 13). The conversion sequence makes sense in Oddr's saga because Óláfr Tryggvason grew up at a pagan court and must be guided toward Christianity. Why Óláfr Haraldsson's Christianity must be reconfirmed is less clear; the narrative at this point may be no more than a pale reflection of the more crucial conversion experience in Oddr's *Óláfs saga Tryggvasonar*. Óláfr Haraldsson's reluctance to consult a pagan seeress is in fact also reminiscent of Óláfr Tryggvason's visit with a prophetic Lapp, who advises him on how to rid himself of Þórir klakka in chapter 19. Like his namesake, Óláfr Tryggvason is also very reluctant to consult a pagan, though he finally accedes.[30]

The emblematic miracles do not, however, complete the full Christian accreditation of either king. The final step is accomplished in interviews with specially empowered men of God. In chapter 18 of *The Legendary Saga* Óláfr Haraldsson encounters a prophetic hermit in England and resolves to test his powers:

> Óláfr vill reyna, hvat hann veit, sendir til hans þjón sinn einn vel búinn ok vegliga með konungs búnaði. Fór sá á fund hans . . . ok fannst munkinum ekki um hann ok mælti: "þat ræð ek þér, góðr maðr," sagði hann, "at leggja niðr þenna búnað, því at eigi samir hann þér. Ver heldr hlýðinn lávarði þínum." (*Helgisaga*, p. 235)

> [Óláfr wishes to test what he knows and sends to him one of his servants decked out in royal garb. He went to meet with him . . . but the monk did not like the look of him and said: "I advise you, my good man," he said, "to take off that costume, because it does not become you. You should rather be faithful to your lord."]

Convinced of the hermit's prophetic powers, Óláfr now visits him in person and learns that he is destined to be not only a temporal king but an eternal king as well.

This episode corresponds to chapter 14 of Oddr's saga, in which Óláfr Tryggvason encounters a distinguished abbot on the Scilly Isles:

> Þess er getit, at Óláfr heyrði sögur frá einum ágætligum manni, er var í eyju nokkuri, er Syllingar heita; þat er skammt frá Írlandi. Sjá var prýddr gift mikilli ok spáleiksanda almáttugs guðs. (Oddr, p. 41; ÍF 25:166)
>
> [It is recounted that Óláfr heard reports about a distinguished man who lived on a certain island known as the Scilly Isles; that is not far from Ireland. This man was endowed with a great gift and the power of prophecy of Almighty God.]

It is, however, the function of this abbot not to prophesy Óláfr's impending royal status but rather to effect the final conversion of him and his men and to baptize them. Nor does the abbot exercise his "spáleiksandi" by seeing through the deception of a messenger disguised in royal garb. There is no sign of that motif in Oddr's account, but it does turn up in the biography of Óláfr Tryggvason recorded in *Ágrip*:[31]

> . . . þá gørðisk svá til of síðir at hann lendi þar við í einum stað í Englandi sem var einn mikill guðs vinr ok sá einsetumaðr ok frægr af góðum vísendum ok margfróðum. Ok fýstist Óláfr at freista þess ok gerði einn sinn þjónustumann í konungs búnaði hans hjálpræða at leita sér undir konungs nafni, ok fekk þessur ansvǫr: "Eigi ertu konungr, en þat er ráð mitt attu sér trúr konungi þínum."
>
> [It eventually came about that he landed at a place in England where there was a great friend of God, who was a hermit and famous for his good and great wisdom. Óláfr was eager to test this and sent one of his servants dressed in his royal garb to seek out his counsel under the king's name, and he received this answer. "You are not a king, but it is my advice that you be faithful to your king."]

Sigurður Nordal offered detailed arguments for believing that the *Legendary Saga* was interpolated from *Ágrip*, while Jónas Kristjánsson believed that the interpolations were already present in the *Oldest Saga* (notes 22–24 above). But this uncertainty is not the only problem that besets a comparison of the prophetic episodes. If the *Legendary*

Saga or the *Oldest Saga* is interpolated from *Ágrip* at this point, the interpolator not only borrowed the anecdote but also transferred it from Óláfr Tryggvason to Óláfr Haraldsson.

Oddr Snorrason used a source close to Theodoricus for the early part of his saga.[32] Accordingly Oddr's account of Óláfr's encounter with the abbot is very close to what we find in Theodoricus.[33] If the author of the *Oldest Saga* referred to Oddr, he would not have found the deception motif there, but he could have found it in *Ágrip* and availed himself of it to dramatize the story of Óláfr Haraldsson. Oddr clearly did not borrow the motif from *Ágrip*, the source of *Ágrip*, or the *Oldest Saga*. He retained the account found in the common source he shared with Theodoricus.[34]

This is a case in which Oddr Snorrason could not have borrowed from the traditions of Óláfr Haraldsson, but it is possible that the author of the *Oldest Saga* was inspired by the encounter of the earlier Óláfr with a prophetic abbot on the Scilly Isles to devise a premonitory event for Óláfr Haraldsson before he returned to Norway. Oddr's abbot is "prýddr gift mikilli ok spáleiksanda" only in the sense that he foresees the arrival of Óláfr Tryggvason. The author of the *Oldest Saga* may have fastened on the word "spáleiksandi" to create a much more far-reaching prophecy pertaining to Óláfr Haraldsson's royal and saintly destiny.

The gist of the argument here is that chapters 16–19 in the *Legendary Saga* show traces of modeling on chapters 12–14 in Oddr's *Óláfs saga Tryggvasonar*. Oddr is concerned with Óláfr Tryggvason's conversion to Christianity in the period between his youthful exploits and his claiming of the Norwegian throne. A preliminary miracle involves crosses that make him and his men invisible to the enemy during a viking raid, a revelation of heaven and hell, some initial conversion activity on Óláfr's part, and a formal conversion by a clairvoyant abbot on the Scilly Isles. The equivalent sequence in the *Legendary Saga* (and presumably the *Oldest Saga*), also covering the period between Óláfr Haraldsson's youthful viking activity and his return to Norway, passes through similar stages: miraculous salvation in response to a vow to abandon viking raids, a pagan seeress's glimpse of brightness and light over Óláfr (the future saint), and a visit with a prophetic hermit who foresees Óláfr's destiny.

In all probability Oddr took this sequence from a source on Óláfr Tryggvason's youth, as Theodoricus's matching report of the conversion on the Scilly Isles most clearly shows. The author of the *Oldest Saga* may not have had such clear narrative guidelines. He had Sigvatr's "Víkingarvísur" on Óláfr's viking years and he had a quantity of stanzas on later events, but he may not have had much on the transition between the years of roaming and Óláfr's royal career. It is conceivable then that he bridged the gap with an imaginative reworking of the equivalent period in Óláfr Tryggvason's life as he found it in Oddr's biography.

Further Considerations

There is one correspondence between the sagas of the two Óláfrs in which the verbal echo is palpable. It is found in the episode in which Einarr þambarskelfir's bow breaks and signals the "bursting" of Norway from the ruler's grasp. In the *Legendary Saga* (*Oldest Saga*) the anecdote is connected with the Battle of Nesjar, in which Sveinn jarl Hákonarson defends his claim to rule Norway against the invading Óláfr Haraldsson. Einarr puts his prowess with the bow in Sveinn's service and takes aim at Óláfr. The first two arrows miss the mark, and Óláfr, reluctant to wait for the third shot, wishes that someone would knock the bow away. That does not happen, but as Einarr prepares to shoot the third arrow, he becomes disoriented:

> En er hann dró bogann, þá brast hann í sundr í tvau fyrir honum, ok vissi eigi, hví sætti. Þá mælti jarlinn: "Hvat er nú, Einarr, eða brast bogi þinn?" Einarr svarar: "Eigi brast bogi, heldr allr Noregr ór hendi þér." (*Helgisaga*, p. 247)

> [When he drew his bow, it broke apart in two pieces in his grip, and he did not know what caused that. The jarl said: "What now, Einarr, did your bow burst?" Einarr replied: "The bow did not burst, but rather all of Norway burst from your grasp."]

The episode is duplicated in a passage found in Oddr's account of the great Battle of Svǫlðr, which is both the centerpiece and the culmination of *Óláfs saga Tryggvasonar*. Here Einarr is in the service of Óláfr Tryggvason and takes aim at Eiríkr jarl Hákonarson, who is trying both to avenge his father and wrest Norway from Óláfr's grip. Einarr misses with his first two arrows. Eiríkr then echoes Óláfr Haraldsson by stating that he is not eager to wait for the third shot. Finnr af Herlǫndum, a great archer in his own right (as chapter 72 in Oddr's saga confirms), responds by saying that he will not shoot Einarr but will try to disable his bow:

> Ok nú vildi Einarr skjóta inni þriðju ör ok dró nú bogann. Fiðr skaut þá á bogann Einars með bíldör, ok kom á þinurinn, ok brast í sundr boginn Einars. Óláfr konungr mælti, er hann heyrði brestinn: "Hvat brast?" Einarr svaraði: "Noregr ór hendi þér, konungr," segir Einarr. (Oddr, p. 180; ÍF 25:343)

> [And now Einarr was about to loose the third arrow and drew his bow. Fiðr took aim at Einarr's bow with a leaf-shaped arrow and struck the bowpiece, and Einarr's bow burst apart. When King Óláfr heard the bursting sound, he asked: "What burst?" Einarr replied: "Norway burst from your grasp, lord," said Einarr.]

Lars Lönnroth argued that the episode is original in the *Oldest Saga*, noting that Einarr has an important political role in the story of Saint Óláfr but is mentioned only here in *Óláfs saga Tryggvasonar*.[35] In addition, Einarr would have been very young to be in Óláfr Tryggvason's service at Svǫlðr fifteen years before the Battle of Nesjar. How and where the anecdote originated is hard to fathom, but, as the texts stand, the *Legendary Saga* (*Oldest Saga*) appears to be the borrower. In the first place, the episode is the culminating moment in the highly dramatic finale of a battle that Oddr himself describes as "the most famous battle in northern lands" (p. 183). The verbal exchange was surely part of the popular tradition that circulated about the battle and on which Oddr built his account. The monumental phrasing belongs in this context and not in the context of the lesser Battle of Nesjar and the very considerably lesser Sveinn jarl Hákonarson. For Óláfr Tryggvason the anecdote signals the end, but for Sveinn Hákonarson it signals no more than a retreat from battle.

Furthermore, the *Legendary Saga* (*Oldest Saga*) suggests its indebtedness with a blind motif. Sveinn Hákonarson asks that someone knock away Einarr's bow, but nothing comes of that request. Finnr's Robin Hood shot, which is a crucial part of the mini-drama in the story of Óláfr Tryggvason, is lost in the *Legendary Saga*. Instead, Einarr becomes disoriented and his bow bursts spontaneously. We are no doubt meant to understand that Óláfr Haraldsson is protected against the third shot not by human agency but by a miracle. This is one of the legendary moments in the *Legendary Saga*. That it is supervenient is suggested by the fact that it leaves Óláfr's wish for mortal intervention, carried over from Oddr's version of the episode, exposed as a pointless motif.

Oddly enough, the episode echoes a second time in the *Legendary Saga* (*Oldest Saga*) at the moment when Áslákr Fitjaskalli kills Erlingr Skjálgsson (chapter 64). Óláfr understands that this killing dooms his chances of winning acceptance among the northern chieftains, and he reproaches Áslákr with the following words (*Helgisaga*, p. 324): "Högg allra manna armastr. Nú hjótt þú Noreg ór hendi mér" [that was a most wretched blow—now you have struck Norway from my grasp].[36] The author may simply have liked the phrase well enough to use it twice.

Two chapters after the episode of the burst bow, in chapter 27, there is another correspondence, perhaps not of great significance, but tangible enough to have been noted by Konrad Maurer.[37] We are told that Óláfr Haraldsson was the first to gain sole rule of Norway after Haraldr hárfagri:

> Óláfr leggr nú allan Noreg undir sik, ok var hann nú til konungs tekinn í öllum Noregi. Óláfr eyddi öllum fylkiskonungum í landinu ok hafði nú einn allan Noreg undir sik lagðan næst eftir Harald inn hárfagra frá Ægistaf norðan ok alt til Elfar austr. (*Helgisaga*, p. 249)

> [Olaf now subjected all of Norway to his rule and he was taken as king in the whole of Norway. Óláfr displaced all the petty kings in the country and had now placed the whole of Norway under his rule for the first time after Haraldr hárfagri from Ægistafr from the north to Gautelfr (Götaälv) to the east.]

This particular way of describing the extent of Norway echoes chapter 22 in Oddr, a chapter that provides a general topography of Norway:

> Noregr er vaxinn með þrem oddum. Er lengd landsins ór útsúðri í norðrætt frá Gautelfi ok norðr til Viggistafs . . . . (Oddr, p. 72; ÍF 25:203)

> [Norway is shaped with three promontories. The length of the land from the southwest northward is from the Gautelfr [Götaälv] north to Veggistafr.]

As in some of the previous correspondences, the passage in Oddr is full and detailed and could have stuck in the memory of another writer interested in conveying topographical information. Furthermore, Oddr's chapter bears some similarity to the topography in the *Historia Norwegiae* and could have been taken over from a related geographical source.[38]

By contrast the passage in the *Legendary Saga* (*Oldest Saga*) amounts to no more than a brief note in passing, hardly memorable enough to have been inserted into Oddr's geographical overview.

There is one final passage in the *Legendary Saga* (chapter 67) that looks as though it might be an echo of Oddr. Among the supernatural accounts in Oddr's biography is a long chapter (60) in which two of Óláfr Tryggvason's men overhear a conclave of trolls complaining about the ill treatment meted out to them by Óláfr. The treatment is described in some detail and involves Óláfr's burning grip as well as blows resulting in broken heads.[39] In the *Legendary Saga* there are no trolls, only a ghostly visitation. As Óláfr is making his way over the mountains to escape from Norway, he spends the night in prayer:

> En um nóttina, er menn váru komnir í svefn, þá kvað við áskrámliga úti ok mælti: "Svá brenna mik nú bænir Óláfs konungs," sagði sú in illa vættr, "at ek má nú eigi vera at hýbýlum mínum, ok verð ek nú at flýja ok koma aldrigi á þenna stað síðan." (*Helgisaga*, p. 330)

> [And at night when the men had fallen asleep, there was a frightful noise outside and these words were spoken: "King Óláfr's prayers now burn

> me," said the evil demon, "that I cannot stay inside my dwelling and I am obliged to flee and never return to this place again."]

The burning sensation and the flight of the ghostly creature echo Oddr's trolls. As in the previous instance, Oddr's passage comes from a full story, whereas the passage in the *Legendary Saga* is a fleeting allusion. The priority, if we may speak of one, is therefore more likely to lie with Oddr.

We may conclude with a more general consideration. In chapter 52 of the *Legendary Saga* Óláfr attempts to convert the Gautish jarl Valgarðr, but the jarl refuses:

> Hann segir eigi þat munu verða ok eigi þess leita. Konungr segir, at svá mun sýnast sem hann hafi vald at neyða hann til, en eigi segist hann þat munu gera, segir þat mest týja, at eigi hafi guð nauðga þjónustu, lætr Valgarð á braut fara. (*Helgisaga*, pp. 290–91)

> [He said that that would not happen and not to attempt it. The king said that it might appear that he had the power to force him but that he would not do it; he said that the best thing would be that God not have forced service, and he let Valgarðr depart.]

The proposition that it is best for God not to have "forced service" is a striking departure from Oddr's *Óláfs saga Tryggvasonar*, in which conversion atrocities are a notable feature.[40] There are no such atrocities in the *Legendary Saga*, and, presumably, there were none in the *Oldest Saga*. Óláfr Haraldsson's opposition to forced service looks as though it might in fact be a conscious rejoinder to the policy of conversion at swordpoint pursued by Óláfr Tryggvason. It is also difficult to imagine how Oddr Snorrason could have attributed such an unselfconsciously sanguinary policy to Óláfr Tryggvason if he had been familiar with the salutary principle that "the best thing would be that God not have forced service."

In summary, it seems quite likely that the famous replique about the bow's bursting out of Einarr þambarskelfir's hands was transferred from Oddr Snorrason's *Óláfs saga Tryggvasonar* into the *Oldest Saga/Legendary Saga*. In addition, there are some indications that *The Oldest Saga/Legendary Saga* made use of Oddr in fashioning the story of Óláfr

Haraldsson's birth and childhood. It is particularly the information on Sigríðr in stórráða, who assassinates Óláfr's father, that seems more securely anchored in Oddr's account and more likely to be original in that version. There are also several moments in Óláfr Haraldsson's transition from viking exploits to the throne of Norway, including the visit with a prophetic man of God, that appear to be influenced by Óláfr Tryggvason's precedent. Finally, tacit revulsion against conversion atrocities may suggest a response to Oddr's narrative.

Implications

It has been argued above that the balance of the textual evidence suggests that Oddr's *Óláfs saga Tryggvasonar* preceded and influenced the composition of the *Oldest Saga of Saint Olaf* (as represented by the *Legendary Saga*). That proposition is quite hypothetical; the correspondences can, and no doubt will, be argued in the opposite sense. Or the criteria may be judged inadequate to support any connection at all between the two texts. If, however, Oddr is granted precedence, we may ask whether this ordering of the texts has any importance for our understanding of the earliest evolution of saga writing. As long as the *Helgisaga* was given precedence, there could be a tacit understanding that the first impulse for the writing of kings' sagas came from Norway, where there were accounts of Óláfr Haraldsson's sanctity and Latin synopses of kings' lives.[41] This impression could then be reinforced by the prologue to *Sverris saga*, which tells us that King Sverrir supervised the beginning of his own biography written by Karl Jónsson. Karl Jónsson appears to have gone to Norway in 1185 and returned to Iceland before 1188.[42] If we date Oddr's composition to 1190 or a little later, we might imagine that Karl Jónsson, having undertaken a royal biography himself, returned to Þingeyrar and passed the impetus along to Oddr Snorrason.[43] Oddr's saga would then in some sense have been inspired by the royal auspices under which Karl Jónsson worked.

But a different sequence of literary events is equally possible. If Oddr Snorrason composed his saga in the early 1180s, Karl Jónsson could have brought with him to Norway a tradition of saga writing already under way. King Sverrir's patronage would then not have constituted a royal initiative as much as a capitalizing on the new biographical activity in Iceland, which Karl Jónsson would have been in a position to bring to King Sverrir's attention. The *Oldest Saga of Saint Olaf*, with its heavy dependence on Icelandic skalds and traditions, would similarly not have been spurred by Norwegian interests so much as by the newly initiated biographical school at Þingeyrar. In short, to put Oddr first is to reemphasize the Icelandic primacy in the emergence of saga writing. Oddr Snorrason's *Óláfs saga Tryggvasonar* should, under these circumstances, not be viewed as an Icelandic response to the Norwegian celebration of Saint Óláfr, as has sometimes happened,[44] but rather as the true inception of king's saga writing in Iceland.

An Antiroyalist Saga: **Hlaðajarla saga*

We will see in the next chapter that kings' sagas were not necessarily adulatory and that Icelandic writers could take a mixed view of Norwegian monarchs. This ambivalence is already apparent in the surviving texts of the sagas about the Orkney Islanders and the Faroe Islanders, the former most recently dated ca. 1190 and the latter ca. 1215.[45] It is a subtheme in both these sagas that the island chieftains felt pressured by the Norwegian kings, who wished to reduce their territories to fiefdoms subject to taxation by the crown. The chieftains' opposition to this arrangement is more pronounced in *Orkneyinga saga* than in *Færeyinga saga*, but we have the former only in later versions. It is therefore difficult to assess just how important opposition to royal hegemony was in the original. Such opposition may have been most palpable in a lost saga known as **Hlaðajarla saga,* which can only be hypothetically reconstructed from later compilations of kings' sagas that appear to have made use of it.

Finnur Jónsson seems to have been the first to speculate on the existence of a saga about the jarls of Hlaðir in Þrœndalǫg.[46] He surmised that this lost text began with Hákon gamli Grjótgarðsson in the days of King Haraldr hárfagri, or perhaps even earlier, with a legendary preface based on Eyvindr skáldaspillir's "Háleygjatal." Such a preface might, he thought, explain the tale of Hersir jarl in chapter 12 of *Ágrip* (ÍF 29:18). The narrative would then have passed on from Hákon gamli to his son Sigurðr Hlaðajarl, accounting for his dealings with King Hákon Aðalsteinsfóstri and Haraldr gráfeldr. It would also have narrated the career of Hákon jarl and, in conclusion, the story of Hákon's son Eiríkr jarl, who is referred to as the subject of a saga in *Fagrskinna* (ÍF 29:138) and *Grettis saga* (ÍF 7:62). Finnur suggested further that *Hákonar saga Ívarssonar*, of which we have only fragments, was a continuation of the lost saga of the jarls.

Gustav Indrebø undertook a much fuller inquiry in his study of *Fagrskinna*.[47] His point of departure is the relationship between *Fagrskinna* and the various redactions of *Jómsvíkinga saga*. He argued that the author of the redaction in AM 510, 4to used two redactions of the saga, the redaction in AM 291, 4to and a shorter redaction, which he referred to as the oldest *Jómsvíkinga saga* and which he maintained was also used by the author of *Fagrskinna* (pp. 60–80). But this author had in addition some narrative material over and above the oldest *Jómsvíkinga saga*, and Indrebø reasoned that this extra material came from the same source that provided the main body of the narrative before and after the Jomsviking interlude (p. 80). This source he identified with Finnur Jónsson's lost saga of the jarls and called "Ladejarlssaga" (pp. 58, 81). It covered chapters 37–49 (pp. 58–80) in Finnur Jónsson's edition of *Fagrskinna* (= ÍF 29:103–21) on Hákon jarl and the subsequent narrative on Eiríkr jarl (ed. Finnur Jónsson 114–40 = ÍF 29:146–67). Indrebø (p. 83) also believed that this source provided Snorri's account of the dealings between Sigurðr Hlaðajarl and Hákon góði in *Heimskringla* (ÍF 26:167–73). Characteristic of this source were a special knowledge of Þrœndalǫg topography (pp. 117–20, 268, 271) and a strong bias in favor of Hákon jarl (pp. 81, 145). Toralf Berntsen pursued the inquiry and focused particularly on the battles of Hjǫrungavágr and Svǫlðr.[48] For the description of both he conjectures a common source used in *Fagrskinna* and *Heimskringla*, because the similarities between these two texts cannot, in the case of Svǫlðr, be explained as derivative from Oddr Snorrason's *Óláfs saga Tryggvasonar.* They must go back to a different source. In both battles Eiríkr jarl is the central figure. Berntsen therefore prefers to entitle the lost text not **Jarlasaga* (in Finnur Jónsson's coinage) but **Eiríks saga jarls*. Berntsen agreed with Indrebø that this text underlies chapters 37–49 (pp. 58–80 minus 69–74 in Finnur Jónsson's edition = ÍF 29:103–21 minus 111–16) and 65–67 (pp. 104–7 in Finnur Jónsson's edition = ÍF 29:137–39). That is, it covered four generations: Hákon gamli, Sigurðr Hlaðajarl, Hákon jarl, and Eiríkr jarl, with whom the saga probably concluded. Berntsen also thought that the lost saga must have been Norwegian.

The next scholar to attack the problem was Johan Schreiner, who disagreed with Berntsen almost point by point.[49] He denies that a second source is necessary to explain *Fagrskinna*'s version of the Battle of Svǫlðr and holds that the account in *Fagrskinna* can be explained by the use of Oddr Snorrason and an occasional admixture of oral tradition (pp. 25–26). Similarly, the differences between *Fagrskinna* and AM 510, 4to in the account of the Battle of Hjǫrungavágr can be explained on the basis of differing oral transmissions (p. 28). Schreiner counters Berntsen's argument that *Fagrskinna* and *Heimskringla* used a common source on the Battle of Stafanessvágr by insisting that Snorri is directly dependent on *Fagrskinna* (p. 42). He denies further that Snorri's account of Hákon góði's dealings with Sigurðr Hlaðajarl is based on a **Hlaðajarla saga* and considers it to be Snorri's own creation, with perhaps some recourse to Þrœndalǫg tradition (pp. 42–49). Schreiner also rejects Indrebø's view that Oddr's *Óláfs saga Tryggvasonar* could have drawn on **Hlaðajarla saga* (p. 51). Finally, he argues that the story of Hákon jarl's stratagem to win Norway in *Fagrskinna* was taken from oral tradition, not from **Hlaðajarla saga* as all previous critics had agreed (pp. 53–54). Schreiner does concede that there may have been some narrative supplement available to the authors of *Fagrskinna* and *Heimskringla* on matters pertaining to the sons of Gunnhildr, Hákon jarl, Eiríkr jarl, and Óláfr Tryggvason, but he traces the supplement to Ari's *konunga ævi* (p. 58).

When Bjarni Aðalbjarnarson reviewed the problem ten years later in 1936, he was just as decisively opposed to Schreiner as Schreiner had been to Berntsen.[50] He reverted in the main to Indrebø's view of **Hlaðajarla saga*, judging that most of the narrative on the jarls of Hlaðir that cannot be traced to other known sources must come from **Hlaðajarla saga* (pp. 216–17). He argues against Schreiner's view that Hákon góði's dealings with Sigurðr Hlaðajarl are Snorri's innovation by analogy to Óláfr Tryggvason's conversion activity in Þrœndalǫg, noting that Snorri would not have committed such a blunder as to suppose that Óláfr's conversion initiative would duplicate Hákon's (p. 219). He also vigorously disputes Berntsen's view that **Hlaðajarla saga* was primarily about Eiríkr jarl (pp. 220–21). If we are to identify a central figure, it would surely be Hákon jarl.

Unlike Schreiner, Bjarni Aðalbjarnarson agrees with Indrebø that Hákon's stratagem to win Norway is attributable to **Hlaðajarla saga* and is indicative of the artistic quality of the text (p. 223). Lastly, he disagrees with Schreiner's view that Snorri's description of the Battle of Hjǫrungavágr is predicated on *Fagrskinna*. He believes rather that it is not possible to work out the textual relationships in this section satisfactorily (pp. 223–24).

There is general agreement, at least among Finnur Jónsson, Gustav Indrebø, Toralf Berntsen, and Bjarni Aðalbjarnarson, that a saga about the jarls of Þrœndalǫg from the early thirteenth century must have existed. The assumption is based first of all on the mention of a saga about Eiríkr jarl, son of Hákon jarl Sigurðarson, in *Fagrskinna* (ÍF 29: 139): "Þetta er talit et fyrsta fra<ma>verk Eiríks jarls [scil. the killing of Tíðenda-Skopti] í hans sǫgu" [This is counted Jarl Erik's first great deed in his saga]. Gustav Indrebø (p. 81) pointed out that such references in *Fagrskinna* consistently imply a written source. The second reason for assuming the existence of such a saga is a cluster of well-told episodes bearing on the jarls of Þrœndalǫg and not otherwise accounted for in the repertory of kings' sagas.

There is a consensus that the lost saga probably began with notes on Hákon jarl's ancestry, his grandfather Hákon gamli at Hlaðir (ÍF 29:65) and his father Sigurðr Hlaðajarl (ÍF 29:66, 80, 101). The main narrative then centered on Hákon jarl and his son Eiríkr jarl. There is, however, no consensus on how the saga may have ended: "There is no way of knowing what **Hlaðajarla saga* told about Jarl Sveinn and Jarl Hákon Eiríksson, or how it concluded."[51] The argument that will be advanced here is that **Hlaðajarla saga* (or a sequel) carried over into the next generation and included the life of Einarr þambarskelfir, who figures prominently at the beginning of *Morkinskinna* and is the last great leader of Þrœndalǫg. The justification for this proposal is that Einarr is already conspicuous in the earlier narrative, and it would make little sense to drop him in mid-career. Furthermore, it is generally agreed that we are dealing with a regionally partisan narrative, and the true extent of that partisanship does not emerge until Einarr's career is in full swing.

We will begin with a recapitulation of what I theorize to have been the content of **Hlaðajarla saga*:[52]

Jarl Hákon gamli asks Haraldr hárfagri for the fief of Sygnafylki but falls in a battle at Fjalir in Stafanessvágr, as recounted in "Háleygjatal" (*Fsk* 65–66). His son Sigurðr becomes King Haraldr's jarl (*Fsk* 66). Sigurðr maintains his father's heathen sacrifices at Hlaðir (*Hkr* 167–68). King Hákon urges the acceptance of Christianity at the Frostathing but is roundly rejected. Only the intercession of Jarl Sigurðr preserves the peace (*Hkr* 169–71). At a sacrificial feast at Hlaðir the farmers press the king to participate. Again Sigurðr finds a way to avert hostilities (*Hkr* 171–72). At a Yule sacrifice at Mærin the king is forced to participate, and Sigurðr warns him not to wage war in Þrándheimr, "er mestr styrkr er landsins" [which is the power center of the country] (*Hkr* 172–73). The sons of Eiríkr blóðøx kill Sigurðr at Ǫgló, as attested by Eyvindr skáldaspillir (*Fsk* 101; *Hkr* 207).

Sigurðr Hlaðajarl's wife was Bergljót, the daughter of Þórir þegjandi and Álof, daughter of Haraldr hárfagri. After Sigurðr's death their son Hákon goes harrying but spends the winters with Haraldr Gormsson (blátǫnn) in Denmark (*Fsk* 103). The author provides a physical and psychological portrait of Hákon. Haraldr Gormsson's nephew Gull-Haraldr arrives at court. At this point Hákon either falls ill or appears to fall ill (*Fsk* 104). Gull-Haraldr claims part of his uncle Haraldr's realm, and Hákon drives a wedge between them by appearing to side with each in turn (*Fsk* 105). Hákon suggests that Haraldr Gormsson should unleash Gull-Haraldr against Norway. He then recovers from his (alleged?) illness, and long discussions ensue (*Fsk* 106).

Haraldr Gormsson invites Haraldr gráfeldr, who is now ruling Norway, to Denmark (*Fsk* 107). Gull-Haraldr ambushes him in the Limfjord (*Fsk* 108). Haraldr gráfeldr falls in the ensuing battle, and Hákon then manages to turn Haraldr Gormsson against Gull-Haraldr (*Fsk* 109). It is settled that Hákon will get Norway. He meets, defeats, and kills Gull-Haraldr. Haraldr Gormsson then establishes him in Norway (*Fsk* 110). where he reinstates paganism (*Fsk* 113). Warm friendship prevails between Hákon jarl and Haraldr Gormsson (*Fsk* 116).

The king tries to compel Hákon to convert, but Hákon fails to comply (*Fsk* 118). Sometime later he ceases to pay tribute in the north (Þrœndalǫg) and makes Vík into a war zone (*Fsk* 120). Haraldr

Gormsson undertakes a punitive expedition as far north as Staðr, then turns back (*Fsk* 121). At this point there must have been a substantial account of the events leading up to the Battle of Hjǫrungavágr, the battle itself, and the aftermath, but the details are hard to extract from *Fagrskinna*, *Heimskringla*, and the various redactions of *Jómsvíkinga saga* (*Fsk* 121–37; *Hkr* 272–86).

Hákon jarl's first son, later Eiríkr jarl, is born when his father is only fifteen years of age. Later Hákon marries Þóra, sister of Tíðenda-Skopti, and Tíðenda-Skopti himself marries Hákon's daughter Ingibjǫrg (*Fsk* 137). Hákon and Þóra have a son Sveinn and a daughter Bergljót, later married to Einarr þambarskelfir. After a quarrel over a mooring Eiríkr kills Tíðenda-Skopti (*Fsk* 138). Hákon and Eiríkr are enemies henceforth. Hákon begins to feel so confident in his position that he becomes arrogant and a womanizer, with the result that he is killed. In the meantime Eiríkr goes to Sweden (*Fsk* 139) and ultimately joins the alliance against Óláfr Tryggvason (*Fsk* 147). At the Battle of Svǫlðr it is Eiríkr who observes Óláfr's advancing fleet and finally identifies Ormr inn langi (*Fsk* 148–51). Óláfr singles out Eiríkr as his worthy (Norwegian) opponent among the attackers (*Fsk* 153). Eiríkr closes in on Óláfr (*Fsk* 155). He boards Ormr inn langi (*Fsk* 158). Among other survivors Einarr þambarskelfir gets quarter from Eiríkr (*Fsk* 159).

As a result of the battle Eiríkr is allotted rather more than a third of Norway, but King Sveinn (tjúguskegg) of Denmark continues to control Vík (*Fsk* 163). The far north is ceded to Óláfr, king of the Swedes, who places it under the governorship of Sveinn Hákonarson. Of the two sons of Hákon, Eiríkr is described as the more powerful. His deeds are summed up, and it is noted that they figure in Eyjúlfr dáðaskáld's "Bandadrápa" (*Fsk* 164–65). Christianity prevails on the coast but paganism inland. Eiríkr does not maintain Óláfr Tryggvason's foundation at Niðaróss, but he does keep up the residences at Hlaðir as during Hákon's lifetime. He also builds a town at Steinker. The jarls marry their sister Bergljót to Einarr þambarskelfir and he becomes their confidant. All the *lendir menn* are well disposed toward Eiríkr except Erlingr Skjálgsson (*Fsk* 166). Eiríkr joins King Knútr (the Great) in his English campaign, leaving his son Hákon to rule in Norway. After returning from Rome he dies in England (*Fsk* 167).

Hákon jarl Eiríksson is surprised and captured by Óláfr Haraldsson in Sauðungssund. He swears not to oppose Óláfr and is allowed to take refuge with Knútr in England. Óláfr tries to surprise Sveinn jarl Hákonarson at Steinker, but Einarr þambarskelfir warns him and enables him to escape. The local population acknowledges Óláfr as king (*Fsk* 170–73). Óláfr does battle with Jarl Sveinn at Nesjar and defeats him, but Sveinn escapes again with the aid of Einarr þambarskelfir (*Fsk* 174). He is well received by King Óláfr of Sweden and subsequently dies in Russia. After his death Einarr þambarskelfir returns to Sweden and spends time alternately in Sweden, Norðhelsingjaland, and Denmark (*Fsk* 177–78).

King Knútr sets out from England with Hákon jarl Eiríksson. He proceeds from Denmark to Norway, has himself proclaimed king in Agðir and Þrándheimr, and places Norway under the rule of Jarl Hákon (*Fsk* 190–93). Hákon organizes the coastal defenses against Óláfr Haraldsson, seizes his ships, and forces him to leave Norway (*Fsk* 196–97). Hákon then travels west to England to fetch his betrothed, but on his return he falls victim to a storm at sea. King Knútr now offers Eggjar-Kálfr (Árnason) the same position that Hákon jarl held under Haraldr Gormsson, but the upshot of the offer is not clear (*Fsk* 198).

Óláfr Haraldsson falls in the Battle of Stiklarstaðir (*Fsk* 200). After his death King Knútr's son Sveinn and Sveinn's mother Álfífa come north to Norway and subdue the country (*Fsk* 201). Sveinn Álfífuson defeats and kills Tryggvi, son of Óláfr Tryggvason, but at a subsequent thing meeting at Niðaróss Einarr þambarskelfir speaks out against Sveinn and Álfífa. Sveinn reads the writing on the wall and retreats south. King Knútr asks Eggjar-Kálfr to have Norse axes fashioned for him, but Kálfr replies that he will send him none, though he will supply his son Sveinn with enough to make him think that he has a great plenty. Kálfr and Einarr þambarskelfir subsequently go to Russia to repatriate Magnús Óláfsson (*Fsk* 206–7).

Morkinskinna harmonizes this initiative with a countervailing initiative clearly derived from a different source. According to this latter version King Jarizleifr (Yaroslav the Wise) dispatches Karl vesæli to Norway to explore the possibility of repatriation (ÍF 23:6–18). At the same time *Morkinskinna* is also fuller on the Þrœndalǫg initiative led by Einarr þambarskelfir, and that version is quite in line with the emphases of **Hlaðajarla saga*. Einarr þambarskelfir acts as a spokesman but is seconded by Rǫgnvaldr Brúsason, who has become a military leader at the Russian court. King and queen are doubtful about the fidelity of the Norwegians, but the queen notes that Einarr was not in Norway when Óláfr Haraldsson fell. Einarr then accomplishes his mission by agreeing to swear an oath of twelve with his followers. Magnús and Rǫgnvaldr Brúsason return to Norway with him. In Norway Kálfr and Einarr become foster fathers and advisers to Magnús (ÍF 23:23), with the implication that the reunification this time proceeds from Þrándheimr, in unstated contrast to the unification under Harald Fairhair, which proceeded from south to north (*Hkr* 97–99).[53]

There follow three scenes from the life of Einarr þambarskelfir, the first introduced with the words "nú er þess við getit" [now it is reported], perhaps suggesting a written source. It tells how Einarr insisted on his regular seat next to King Magnús by sliding down into it from behind, thus forcing the king and Kálfr, who has usurped his prerogative, apart. The second anecdote tells how Einarr observed Kálfr tying a sword to his sword hand at the approach of unidentified men. In the third episode Einarr deflects the task of showing King Magnús the battle site at Stiklarstaðir onto Kálfr (ÍF 23:29–30). As a result of this compromising task Kálfr feels obliged to flee to Orkney, where he stays with his brother-in-law Þorfinnr jarl (ÍF 23:30).

King Magnús now becomes harsh toward the Þrœndir, who were after all responsible for the death of his father. The Þrœndir respond with an expression of patriotic outrage, citing the position of their province as the "heart of Norway" ("hǫfuð Nóregs"; ÍF 23:31 = *Fsk* 212). An uprising is prevented only by Sigvatr Þórðarson's mediation in the form of his "Bersǫglisvísur" (ÍF 23:26–30 = *Fsk* 212–15). Magnús now mends his ways. He also establishes Rǫgnvaldr Brúsason as jarl in Orkney, with a resulting outbreak of hostilities between Þorfinnr and Rǫgnvaldr "sem segir í jarlasǫgum" [as is told in the sagas of the jarls] (ÍF 23:43 = *Fsk* 215). Magnús also takes Kálfr back into his good graces provided he will support Rǫgnvaldr.

When Magnús appoints Sveinn Úlfsson as jarl in Denmark, Einarr þambarskelfir comments that he is "ofjarl" [too much jarl] (ÍF 23:51 = *Fsk* 219). Prior to the Battle of Hlýrskógsheiðr Einarr accompanies

Magnús in disguise to scout the enemy. Together they visit a farmer, at whose cottage Magnús has an auspicious dream. Magnús recounts the dream to Einarr. Just before the battle Einarr facilitates the approach of a man who gives the king strategic advice (ÍF 23:61). This mysterious adviser later appears at Magnús's court (ÍF 23:132–33). Haraldr Sigurðarson (harðráði) approaches Magnús with a proposal to divide the realm, but Einarr rejects the idea (ÍF 23:138). Einarr's son Eindriði accepts a gift of horses from a certain Þorsteinn Hallsson, who has done business in Dublin without King Magnús's consent. Einarr has the very difficult task of making peace between his son and King Magnús (ÍF 23:140–43).

Sometime later Magnús falls ill and Einarr expresses apprehension (ÍF 23:167–68). After the king's death Einarr proclaims that he would rather accompany Magnús dead than Haraldr alive (ÍF 23:173 = *Fsk* 248). Accordingly he escorts the body home for burial, stopping on Samsø on the way. Here a poor blind man approaches the king, is given a little gold ring once in the king's possession by Einarr, and miraculously regains his sight (ÍF 23:175). The naval cortège now returns to Niðaróss, where Magnús is buried in Christchurch (ÍF 23:176 = *Fsk* 249).

Subsequently Einarr competes with King Haraldr in Þrœndalǫg, to the extent of protecting a thief against him (ÍF 23:207 = *Fsk* 262). Haraldr tests the fidelity of his district chieftains with ostensible bribes from Denmark, and Einarr responds by vowing to defend Norway. King Haraldr approves his words (ÍF 23:212–13).

Einarr is invited by King Haraldr to a feast, where he is mocked by the king's relative Grjótgarðr. He retaliates by killing Grjótgarðr, much to the king's chagrin. A settlement is initiated, but Haraldr lures Einarr into a dark room and kills both him and his son Eindriði (ÍF 23:214–16 = *Fsk* 263).

It remains to be tested whether this outline represents a single continuous narrative. Should that be the case, the shape of the narrative is political. It traces the rise and fall of political fortunes in Þrœndalǫg. The story may have begun at a low ebb with the subjugation of Þrœndalǫg by Haraldr hárfagri and the continued subjection under Haraldr's sons. Jarl Hákon gamli tries to ally himself with Haraldr but falls in the Battle of Stafanessvágr. His son Sigurðr Hlaðajarl also allies himself with Haraldr but is eventually killed by the sons of Eiríkr blóðøx. Sigurðr's son Hákon (Hákon jarl) therefore looks elsewhere for support and is able to manipulate the Danish king Haraldr Gormsson so cleverly that he regains Þrœndalǫg and is able to contest the whole of Norway with Denmark. Eiríkr jarl follows in his father's footsteps for a while but ultimately abandons Þrœndalǫg in favor of following King Knútr of England.

That leaves Norway to Óláfr Tryggvason and, following a Danish interlude, Óláfr Haraldsson. But after Óláfr's fall at Stiklarstaðir the magnates of Þrœndalǫg reassert themselves under the leadership of Einarr þambarskelfir and Kálfr Árnason by repatriating and sponsoring Óláfr's son Magnús. There ensues a period of political tension between the new king and the Þrœndir, but Magnús learns to respect the ancestral autonomy of Þrœndalǫg. After his death the tension is renewed in a contest between royal privilege advocated by Haraldr harðráði and regional autonomy pressed by Einarr þambarskelfir. The death of Einarr and his son Eindriði at the hands of Haraldr marks the end of Þrœndalǫg's independent aspirations.

This tale of alternating political fortunes is predicated on the assumption that **Hlaðajarla saga* did not conclude with the death of Eiríkr jarl or some brief account of his brother Sveinn and son Hákon. It must rather have continued down into the days of Magnús góði and Haraldr harðráði, as related in *Morkinskinna*. As far as I know, it has never been suggested that the author of *Morkinskinna*, as well as the author of *Fagrskinna*, referred to **Hlaðajarla saga* in constructing this part of the narrative, but the possibility is worth exploring. The key to the continuity is the figure of Einarr þambarskelfir, who enters the story during the life of Eiríkr jarl (*Fsk* 138) and controls much of the narrative down to the days of Haraldr harðráði. He was not technically a "jarl" and therefore has not found entry into a text speculatively entitled **Hlaðajarla saga*, but he did marry into the house of Hlaðir and became a more dominant figure in the political tale than any of the jarls in the dynasty with the exception of Hákon jarl.

If *Fagrskinna* and *Morkinskinna* are combined, they produce the following narrative of Einarr's life:

1. He is destined to be married to Hákon jarl's daughter Bergljót (*Fsk* 138).
2. He is given quarter by Eiríkr jarl at the Battle of Svǫlðr (*Fsk* 159).
3. Eiríkr and Sveinn marry their sister Bergljót to him (*Fsk* 166).
4. He enables Sveinn to escape from Óláfr Haraldsson (*Fsk* 172).
5. He enables Sveinn to escape a second time from the Battle of Nesjar (*Fsk* 174).
6. He accompanies Sveinn to Sweden and Russia (*Fsk* 177–78).
7. He speaks out against Sveinn Álfífuson and his mother (*Fsk* 206).
8. He goes to Russia to repatriate Magnús Óláfsson (*Fsk* 207).
9. He acts as spokesman in Russia (ÍF 23:6–18).
10. Together with Kálfr Árnason he becomes foster father and adviser to Magnús (ÍF 23:23).
11. He interacts with Kálfr in three episodes, ending with Kálfr's flight to Orkney (ÍF 23:29–30).
12. He opposes Magnús's appointment of Sveinn Úlfsson as jarl (ÍF 23:51 = *Fsk* 219).
13. He accompanies Magnús on Hlýrskógsheiðr (ÍF 23:59–60).
14. He opposes a division of the realm with Haraldr harðráði (ÍF 23:120–21 = *Fsk* 240).
15. He warns Magnús against Haraldr's encroachments (ÍF 23:137).
16. He makes peace between his son Eindriði and Magnús (ÍF 23:142–43).
17. After Magnús's death he returns his body to Niðaróss for burial with the comment that he would rather accompany Magnús dead than Haraldr alive (ÍF 23:173 = *Fsk* 248–49).
18. He competes with Haraldr for authority in Þrœndalǫg (ÍF 23:207 = *Fsk* 262).
19. He is tested by Haraldr and demonstrates his Norwegian patriotism (ÍF 23:212–13).
20. He avenges himself by killing Haraldr's relative Grjótgarðr and is subsequently ambushed and murdered, together with his son Eindriði, by Haraldr (ÍF 23:215–16 = *Fsk* 263).

Most scholars would probably agree that at least the first part of the narrative was located in **Hlaðajarla saga*, perhaps items 1–6 ending with Sveinn Hákonarson's death in Russia. At this point Einarr is already well integrated into the story of the Þrœndalǫg jarls. He has married Hákon jarl's daughter, has reached an accommodation with Eiríkr jarl Hákonarson, and has twice saved the life of Sveinn Hákonarson, whom he accompanies in exile. He has clearly established himself as the right-hand man of the jarls of Hlaðir, a role that comes to fruition under King Magnús.

Are we to imagine that the dramatic story of Einarr's staunch service to Þrœndalǫg was dropped in midcourse? Did it stop with the death of Sveinn Hákonarson in Russia? That would be something of an anticlimax. We would have to imagine a story that reached its high point in the career of Hákon jarl and then petered out slowly in the decreasing successes of Eiríkr jarl and Sveinn Hákonarson.

If, on the other hand, we conceive of a saga that carried down to the murder of the last great defender of Þrœndalǫg autonomy, a broad political canvas unfolds. It leads from the submerging of Þrœndalǫg independence in the days of Haraldr hárfagri to the brilliant, albeit pagan, revival under Hákon jarl, through a second decline under Danish and Olavian rule, and ultimately to a second revival in which the monarch Magnús Óláfsson góði is for all intents and purposes the creation of the magnates of Þrœndalǫg, particularly Einarr þambarskelfir. One of the problems in the reconstruction of **Hlaðajarla saga* thus far has been the lack of a clear dramatic line, but a culmination in the death of the last defender of Þrœndalǫg autonomy would provide both a dramatic and a historically momentous conclusion.

This reading is attractive because it correlates the beginning with the end of the story. At the beginning the great unifier Haraldr hárfagri advances from the south and puts an end to an autonomous Þrœndalǫg, but at the end Þrœndalǫg, led by Einarr, fashions a new king, a reunifier, who this time advances from north to south to reassemble the splintered realm. This time Þrœndalǫg is not the victim of monarchical ambition but the originator of a new enlightened monarchical policy. As *Fagrskinna* (212) and *Morkinskinna* (ÍF 23:31) both state, Þrœndalǫg is the "hǫfuð Nóregs," the heart of Norway. This idea, like all dreams of empire, is illusory, but it was no doubt seen in retrospect as the proudest moment in Þrœndalǫg history.

We may ask ourselves what the alternative might be to a

**Hlaðajarla saga* reconstituted as a panoramic sweep from Haraldr hárfagri's conquest to Einarr's death in Haraldr harðráði's darkened council chamber. We could imagine that the saga ended with Eiríkr jarl's straw death in remote England or Sveinn Hákonarson's straw death in remote Russia, but neither provides a vivid finale. We could imagine that **Hlaðajarla saga* just happened to end where *Morkinskinna* began, but we could also imagine that **Hlaðajarla saga* continued for some time and provided the basis for the remarkably Þrœndacentric presentation at the beginning of *Morkinskinna*. The sources for this part of *Morkinskinna* are a mystery. Finnur Jónsson thought it was based on a separate independent saga of Magnús and Haraldr, but later scholars have been in doubt.[54] A **Hlaðajarla saga* stretching down to the death of Einarr þambarskelfir would have the advantage of explaining the Þrœndalǫg bias in *Morkinskinna* and providing a narrative backbone for roughly 40 percent of the text. (Much of the narrative material on Haraldr harðráði would still require explanation.)

One question posed above is why a text such as **Hlaðajarla saga* would have established an important role for Einarr þambarskelfir only to foreshorten it. The same question might be posed about Kálfr Árnason. A combination of *Fagrskinna* and *Morkinskinna* provides the following account:

1. King Knútr offers Kálfr the same position that Hákon jarl had under Haraldr Gormsson (*Fsk* 198).
2. King Knútr asks Kálfr for some Norse axes and receives an acid reply (*Fsk* 206–7).
3. Kálfr participates in the repatriation of Magnús Óláfsson and becomes his foster father and adviser (ÍF 23:23).
4. He occupies Einarr's seat next to King Magnús and is forced aside (ÍF 23:28).
5. Faced by an advance of unidentified men, he ties his sword to his sword hand (ÍF 23:28).
6. He explains the battle site at Stiklarstaðir to Magnús and feels sufficiently imperiled that he flees to Orkney (ÍF 23:29–30).
7. Magnús offers to restore him to favor if he will support Rǫgnvaldr Brúsason in Orkney (ÍF 23:43).

There is a good chance that the first scene at least was taken over from **Hlaðajarla saga* because it refers to an episode that is virtually guaranteed for the saga, the account of how Hákon jarl became Haraldr Gormsson's deputy in Þrœndalǫg. Kálfr's response to King Knútr's request for axes is also likely to have been in **Hlaðajarla saga* because it deals with the conflict between Danish overlordship and Þrœndalǫg autonomy. Whether one believes that the remaining five items derive from the lost saga depends entirely on a decision about the extent of the saga and whether it included the Þrœndalǫg sponsorship of King Magnús. If, however, we believe that the story of Einarr þambarskelfir was carried down into the time of Magnús, Kálfr must have figured prominently in the continuation as well.

Of particular interest are the last two items on Kálfr in Orkney, where he takes refuge with his brother-in-law Þorfinnr jarl. Magnús later sends Rǫgnvaldr Brúsason to replace Þorfinnr as jarl, but Rǫgnvaldr is not a chance candidate. He is presumably being rewarded for faithful service going back to the time when he and Magnús were in Russia and he supported Einarr's mission to bring Magnús to the Norwegian throne. If that mission was part of **Hlaðajarla saga,* Rǫgnvaldr's reward in Orkney might logically also have been reported in the lost text.

Rǫgnvaldr's arrival in Orkney naturally precipitates a conflict with Þorfinnr, and this conflict is referred to explicitly in *Msk* 31 (ÍF 23:43) and *Fsk* 215. The passage in *Msk* is as follows:

> Magnús konungr kom Rǫgnvaldi Brúsasyni til ríkis vestr í Orkneyjum ok gaf honum jarls nafn. Ok um hans daga síðan gørðisk ófriðr mikill í milli Rǫgnvalds jarls ok Þorfinns jarls, fǫðurbróður hans, ok urðu þar um mǫrg stórtíðendi, sem segir í Jarla sǫgum.
>
> (King Magnús brought Rǫgnvaldr Brúsason to power to the west in Orkney and gave him the title of jarl. Later during his time there was great conflict between Jarl Rǫgnvaldr and Jarl Þorfinnr, his uncle, and there were many momentous events, as is told in the sagas of jarls.)

The wording in *Fsk* is practically identical.

The reference here to "Jarla sǫgur" [sagas of jarls] is normally taken to apply to some version of *Orkneyinga saga.* in which the battle between Þorfinnr and Rǫgnvaldr at Rauðabjǫrg is described.[55] It is, however, difficult to establish any written link between *Orkneyinga saga* and *Morkinskinna/Fagrskinna*.[56] If, on the other hand, we suppose that **Hlaðajarla saga* included Rǫgnvaldr jarl's role in returning Magnús to Norway and his eventual reward in Orkney, then his conflict with Þorfinnr could have been mentioned in **Hlaðajarla saga* and the reference to "jarlasǫgur" could be to that text.

There is in fact the possibility of a third reference to this written source. If, once again, we assume that **Hlaðajarla saga* included the career of Einarr þambarskelfir, it would also have included the interaction between Einarr and Kálfr Árnason. In *Msk* (ÍF 23:28) this interaction is prefaced with the words:

> Nú er þess við getit, þá er þeir váru á einni veizlu báðir, Kálfr Árnason ok Einarr þambarskelfir með Magnúsi konungi, en þetta var í Vík austr.

> (Now it is reported that both Kálfr Árnason and Einarr þambarskelfir were at a banquet with King Magnús, and that was east in Vík.)

The verb *geta við* need not but can imply a written source, as the phrasing in the reference to "jarlasǫgur" in *Fsk* 215 suggests: ". . . gørðisk missætti milli Rǫgnvalds ok Þorfinns fǫðurbróður hans, sem getit er í Jarla sǫgunum" [. . . there was dissension between Rǫgnvaldr and his uncle Þorfinnr, as is reported in the sagas of the jarls]. These three source references can, therefore, all be explained by a **Hlaðajarla saga* that included the career of Einarr as well as the jarls of Hlaðir.

We may now recapitulate briefly the outline of this hypothetical text. It seems to have begun with the suppression of Þrœndalǫg independence in the days of Haraldr hárfagri, continued with a political reemergence of the region in the days of a still religiously and morally flawed Hákon jarl, declined again under Danish and Olavian rule, and culminated under the model rule of Magnús góði, who is both the religious and moral counterpoise to Hákon jarl. Magnús is also the political foil to Haraldr hárfagri because, under the tutelage of the Þrœndalǫg magnates, he learns the necessary respect for regional law and custom. When his rule spreads south, as Haraldr hárfagri's rule once spread north, it is presumably informed by a new outlook, characterized by the true faith, moral rectitude, and respect for local law. The saga may therefore have had a pleasing structural and historical symmetry. If it pursued the story down to the death of Einarr þambarskelfir, it must also have had a sense of political promise and ultimate failure.

In literary terms the author seems to have had an unusual capacity for scenic design. The dramatization of Hákon jarl's machinations to win Norway was suitably praised by Gustav Indrebø.[57] There must have been effective scenes from the Battle of Hjǫrungavágr and the Battle of Svǫlðr, although the details are difficult to disentangle from the accounts in *Jómsvíkinga saga* and Oddr Snorrason's *Óláfs saga Tryggvasonar*. If the saga went further, it must have included a full council scene at the Russian court, a tense depiction of the strain between Magnús and the magnates finally mediated by Sigvatr Þórðarson, a dramatic prelude to the Battle of Hlýrskógsheiðr, a mournful narrative of King Magnús's death underscoring Einarr's fidelity, and finally King Haraldr's treacherous murder of Einarr and his son in a darkened room. There seem to have been comic scenes as well: Hákon jarl's "diplomatic illness," Sveinn Álfífuson's discomfiture, Einarr's outmaneuvering of Kálfr Árnason, and the trick played by Grjótgarðr on an aging Einarr. The evidence suggests that **Hlaðajarla saga* was both a lively and dramatic text, which deservedly attracted the attention of other writers and underlies some of the best scenes in *Fagrskinna* and *Morkinskinna*.

The lost saga envisioned here seems not only to have had a certain literary distinction but also to have embodied a well-defined historical viewpoint, an antiroyalist and pro-regional perspective. Its focus is on the jarls of Þrœndalǫg and their attempts to free themselves from the control of kings, Danish kings as well native Norwegian kings in the persons of Haraldr hárfagri, the succession of Óláfr Tryggvason and Óláfr Haraldsson, and their reincarnation in Haraldr harðráði. They ultimately fail but there is not much doubt about where the author's sympathies lie. **Hlaðajarla saga* could therefore be described as an opposition saga, a corrective to the earlier celebrations of the two conversion kings as Christian heroes. It can of course be objected that this historical construction is predicated on a text we do not have, but the bias is perfectly clear in the surviving texts of *Morkinskinna* and *Fagrskinna*. It must therefore have derived, if not from **Hlaðajarla saga*, then from some equivalent source. We will see in the next two chapters that a spirit of opposition to royal, or quasi-royal, autocracy was by no means isolated.

That was one strand of public opinion, but there would have been mixed views in Iceland. We have seen above in this chapter that Toralf Berntsen (1923:216) assumed that **Hlaðajarla saga* was Norwegian, although the evidence that any king's saga was written in Norway is thin. Norwegian origin has most frequently been weighed for *Ágrip af Nóregs konunga sǫgum* and *Fagrskinna*, but in both cases the issue is quite uncertain. On the whole saga writing is very predominantly Icelandic, and there is a strong probability that **Hlaðajarla saga* is also Icelandic. If, as I have argued here, it was drawn on by the authors of both *Morkinskinna* and *Fagrskinna,* it is most likely to have been written before 1220, but the question of where it was written and who the author might be has not been broached.

The Icelandic family in which the jarls of Hlaðir are most likely to have been remembered and cultivated is the distinguished lineage at Oddi. This lineage goes back to the colonist Ketilbjǫrn Ketilsson, who was married to Æsa, the daughter of the original jarl of Hlaðir, Grjótgarðr, and the sister of his successor Hákon gamli.[58] Six generations later the family produced Sæmundr Sigfússon at Oddi, one of the founders of Icelandic literature in the early twelfth century. Sæmundr's son Loptr married a certain Þóra, who, according to the *Hauksbók* version of *Landnámabók,* was the daughter of King Magnús berfœttr of Norway (ÍF 1.2:341). Loptr and Þóra were the parents of Jón Loptsson (died 1197), who is routinely referred to as the greatest chieftain in Iceland and whose commanding role we observed in Chapter 1 in connection with *Sturlu saga.* In a land very much preoccupied with genealogy, the family at Oddi is unlikely to have forgotten or downplayed its ancestral association with the jarls of Hlaðir.

We know in fact that ancestral distinction was prized in Jón Loptsson's family. Their hereditary pride emerges with all possible clarity in an anonymous poem titled "Nóregs konunga tal" and composed by an unknown poet between 1184 and 1197. It celebrates Jón Loptsson and retraces his royal ancestry through his mother Þóra back to Hálfdan svarti and Haraldr hárfagri, forefathers of the Norwegian royal dynasty.[59] The existence of this poem may have provided an impulse to celebrate Jón's descent from jarls as well as kings and thus have inspired **Hlaðajarla saga.* Jón's son Páll became a bishop and is duly memorialized in *Páls saga biskups*, which, it is assumed, was composed shortly after Páll's death in 1211.[60] We therefore know that there was ongoing literary activity attached to Jón's family, and the period between 1211 and 1220 is precisely the span in which **Hlaðajarla saga* must have fallen.

In "Nóregs konunga tal" Jón Loptsson was firmly connected to the Norwegian monarchy descended from Haraldr hárfagri, but this is the dynasty against which the author of **Hlaðajarla saga* seems to have reacted. We might therefore ask whether **Hlaðajarla saga* is in some sense a critical response to "Nóregs konunga tal," perhaps an argument to the effect that Jón's descent from the jarls of Hlaðir was as important as, or more important than, his descent from the kings of Norway. Or we could simply assume that the saga serves to supplement the poem and was written by an author with a special partiality for the jarls of Hlaðir. Such speculations no doubt go well beyond what can be deduced from a lost text; the saga could have been written far from Oddi and could have nothing to do with Jón Loptsson or "Nóregs konung tal." Yet the period 1211–1220 is notable for coinciding with the first climax in the contention between kings and jarls in Norway. After the death of King Sverrir's son and successor Hákon in 1204 there is an agreement that holds the succession in suspension between 1208 and 1217, when Hákon Hákonarson succeeds to the throne in the wake of a vigorous dispute. But Jarl Skúli Bárðarson in Trondheim becomes the true power behind the throne and lives in an uneasy power-sharing arrangement with King Hákon right down to his rebellion and death in 1240. Skúli's preeminence in Trondheim could well have given rise to the idea that he was a nostalgic resurrection of the house of Hlaðir and was in competition with the king. Indeed, an alternative to the possible connection with Jón Loptsson suggested above is that the author of **Hlaðajarla saga* was in the service of Jarl Skúli and was charged to promote the jarl's interests. Whatever the precise circumstances surrounding the composition of **Hlaðajarla saga* may have been, it seems clear that the text must in some way have reflected contemporary debates. It may therefore have provided not only the narrative source for the early chapters of *Morkinskinna*; it may also have inspired the political outlook favorable to Einarr þambarskelfir, the last of the powerful Trondheim jarls, as we will see in Chapter 5.

CHAPTER 4

Sources and Attitudes in *Óláfs saga helga* in *Heimskringla*

The prologues to *Heimskringla* and the *Separate Saga of Saint Olaf* famously emphasize the role of poetic sources in reconstructing the early history of Scandinavia. The general prologue to *Heimskringla* argues that these sources are likely to be truthful despite the inherent danger of flattering princes (ÍF 26:5):

> Með Haraldi konungi váru skáld, ok kunna menn enn kvæði þeira ok allra konunga kvæði, þeira er síðan hafa verit í Nóregi, ok tókum þar mest dœmi af, þat er sagt er í þeim kvæðum, er kveðin váru fyrir sjálfum hǫfðingjunum eða sonum þeira. Tǫkum vér þat allt fyrir satt, er í þeim kvæðum finnsk um ferðir þeira eða orrostur. En þat er háttr skálda at lofa þann mest, er þá eru þeir fyrir, en engi myndi þat þora at segja sjálfum honum þau verk hans, er allir þeir, er heyrði, vissi, at hégómi væri ok skrǫk, ok svá sjálfr hann. Þat væri þá háð, en eigi lof.
>
> [There were skalds at the court of King Harald [Fairhair] and people still know their poems, and the poems about all the kings who reigned in Norway later. We have taken our chief support from what is said in the poems that were recited before the chieftains [rulers] themselves and their sons. We consider everything to be true that is found in those poems about their expeditions and battles. It is the custom of skalds to heap the greatest praise on the man in whose presence they find themselves, but no one would dare to recount to his very face deeds that

all the listeners knew to be nonsense and fantasy, even he [the ruler] himself. That would be derision, not praise.]

The prologue to the *Separate Saga of Saint Olaf* (longer version) is fuller and more probing (ÍF 27:421–22):[1]

En síðan er Haraldr inn hárfagri var konungr í Nóregi, þá vitu menn miklu gørr sannendi at segja frá ævi konunga þeira, er í Nóregi hafa verit. Á hans dǫgum byggðisk Ísland, ok var þá mikil ferð af Nóregi til Íslands. Spurðu menn þá á hverju sumri tíðendi landa þessa í milli, ok var þat síðan í minni fœrt ok haft eptir til frásagna. En þó þykki mér þat merkiligast til sannenda, er berum orðum er sagt í kvæðum eða ǫðrum kveðskap, þeim er svá var ort um konunga eða aðra hǫfðingja, at þeir sjálfir heyrðu, eða í erfikvæðum þeim, er skáldin fœrðu sonum þeira. Þau orð, er í kveðskap standa, eru in sǫmu sem í fyrstu váru, ef rétt er kveðit, þótt hverr maðr hafi síðan numit at ǫðrum, ok má því ekki breyta. En sǫgur þær, er sagðar eru, þá er þat hætt, at eigi skilisk ǫllum á einn veg. En sumir hafa eigi minni, þá er frá líðr, hvernig þeim var sagt, ok gengsk þeim mjǫk í minni optliga, ok verða frásagnir ómerkligar. Þat var meirr en tvau hundruð vetra tólfrœð, er Ísland var byggt, áðr menn tœki hér sǫgur at rita, ok var þat lǫng ævi ok vant, at sǫgur hefði eigi gengizk í munni, ef eigi væri kvæði, bæði ný ok forn, þau er menn tœki þar af sannendi frœðinnar. Svá hafa gǫrt fyrr frœðimenninir, þá er þeir vildu sannenda leita, at taka fyri satt þeira manna orð, er sjálfir sá tíðendi ok þá váru nær staddir. En þar er skáldin váru í orrustum, þá eru tœk vitni þeira, svá þat ok, er hann kvað fyr sjálfum hǫfðingjanum, þá myndi hann eigi þora at segja þau verk hans, er bæði sjálfr hǫfðinginn ok allir þeir, er heyrðu, vissu, at hann hefði hvergi nær verit. Þat væri þá háð, en eigi lof.

[But after the time Haraldr hárfagri ruled in Norway people are much better able to tell the truth about the lives of the kings of Norway. In his day Iceland was settled, and there was a great deal of travel from Norway to Iceland. News passed between these countries every summer and it was then committed to memory and passed along in the form of stories. But it seems to me that what is most noteworthy in terms of truthfulness is what is told in plain words in poems and poetic recitation composed about kings and other chieftains in such circumstances

> as they themselves heard them, or in the commemorative poems that the skalds conveyed to their sons. The words in the poems are the same as the original ones if the recitation is correct, even though each man has learned from another, because [the form] cannot be changed. But the sagas [stories] that are told are not understood the same way by everyone. Some people do not remember, as time passes, how they were told, and they often deteriorate greatly in memory, and the stories become unreliable. It was more than 240 years after Iceland was settled before people began to write sagas here; that was a long time, and [it is] unlikely that the sagas [stories] would not have deteriorated in transmission if there had not been poems, both new and old, from which people could take truthful lore. Earlier historians [Ari and Sæmundr?] bent on learning the truth were accustomed to accept as true the words of people who themselves were witnesses to the events or were near at hand. When the skalds participated in battles, their testimony is reliable, and likewise whatever the skalds recited before the chieftains themselves. [The skald] would not dare to ascribe to him deeds when both the chieftain himself and all the listeners knew that he had been nowhere in the vicinity. That would be derision, not praise.]

In the second version the writer distinguishes carefully between mutable prose transmissions and poetic transmissions that are maintained word for word. In one sentence he states that stories would have deteriorated if there had not been poems giving access to the truth. This hints at an interaction between prose and poetry; the latter could perhaps have stabilized the former, but we might wish for more detail. Did tellers of stories combine both so as to authenticate the prose, or were prose stories told and poems recited quite independently so that there were reliable and less reliable traditions in competition with each other? It is the question of independent prose stories that is at the heart of what follows.

The Background

I propose to single out six such stories and explore their roots in oral tradition. The supposition that they are primarily oral rests on several indications. In the first place they are not supported by skaldic stanzas and could therefore not have been extrapolated from such stanzas.

In the second place they all involve Icelanders or were familiar to Icelanders who were present at the time of the events. These Icelanders could have "committed [them] to memory and passed [them] along in the form of stories," just as the prologue to *The Separate Saga* suggests. The avenues of transmission seem quite palpable. Finally, the stories are cast in a style easily reconciled with oral telling; they are dramatically formulated and well told. That they were originally oral stories is of course only a hypothesis, and the reader may object that they could just as well have been the work of a good writer. Such a writer's hand is probably visible in some formal speeches and to some extent in the pointed political outlook. Oral and written features are no doubt intertwined, but I will focus initially on the oral features in the six stories, conscious that an appropriate response would be to emphasize the authorial contribution.

Oral transmission is admittedly difficult terrain, open only to conjecture. It has not been an important topic of discussion in *Heimskringla* studies, for the good reason that so much of *Heimskringla* is based on known or plausibly hypothesized written sources. All of Part III can be traced to *Morkinskinna* and perhaps *Fagrskinna*. In Part I prior versions of *Haralds saga hárfagra* and *Hákonar saga góða* have been surmised. Alongside the main source, Oddr's *Óláfs saga Tryggvasonar*, a version of *Jómsvíkinga saga* and the lost **Hlaðajarla saga* have been thought to underlie *Óláfs saga Tryggvasonar*. *Óláfs saga helga* too has its written precursors, quite likely Styrmir Kárason's version of the saga, perhaps *Fóstbrœðra saga*, and certainly *Færeyinga saga* and some version of *Orkneyinga saga*. But there are no written sources for a number of semi-independent stories in *Óláfs saga helga*. As we will see below, they cannot have been invented from whole cloth because traces of them show up in texts that are unrelated to *Heimskringla*. The only remaining option is therefore the direct use of oral tradition. That concept covers a multitude of matters, from individual names to genealogical relations to random bits of information to memorized stanzas and finally to fully formed stories. It is the final category that I will focus on in the following pages. There can scarcely be any doubt that there were fully formed stories in Icelandic tradition because the sagas and *þættir* are full of them. After surveying the opening sequences in *Óláfs saga helga*, I will turn to six of these stories, review them in some detail, and reflect on their sources.

The Preliminary Narrative

The 412 pages of Bjarni Aðalbjarnarson's edition of *Óláfs saga helga* include 178 full or partial stanzas, but the reader quickly observes that they are unevenly distributed.[2] The first 24 pages (pp. 3–27) on Óláfr's early viking adventures are so densely buttressed by stanzas from Óttarr svarti's "Hǫfuðlausn" and Sigvatr Þórðarson's "Víkingarvísur" that we may wonder whether the author had anything beside these skaldic sources to build on. A short transition passage on the situation in Norway, Jarl Eiríkr Hákonarson's relationship to Erlingr Skjálgsson, and his departure for England and subsequent death, draws on two stanzas by Sigvatr and two others by Þórðr Kolbeinsson, but here the author seems less exclusively dependent on the stanzas; he knows about Erlingr's personal qualities, his family, his resources, and even his slaves. An even shorter passage on Knútr inn ríki's conquest of England and expulsion of King Ethelred's sons draws on a half stanza by Sigvatr, but here too the author seems to have additional sources about Óláfr's alliance with Ethelred's sons and his progress in Northumbria. His return to Norway with two ships and his capture of Hákon jarl Eiríksson in Sauðungssund (pp. 35–39) are underpinned by four stanzas, three by Óttarr and one by Sigvatr. At this point, however, the stanzas are temporarily suspended to allow for a detailed narrative on how Óláfr was received at home and in eastern Norway (pp. 39–54).

The pages in question are rich in particulars and include long speeches by Óláfr, his stepfather Sigurðr sýr, and the petty kings Hrœrekr and Hringr. How would the author have known about these matters, and on what basis would he have devised the speeches? There are no indications of oral sources or any other access to this moment in Óláfr's life. Are we to believe that the author imagined a likely course of events and surmised that the occasion would have called for extended speeches? Can we go further and suppose that the long speeches, which are a special feature of *Óláfs saga helga*, are an earmark of invented narrative? Or should we rather suppose that some account of these events was passed down over time and became the basis of the author's written version? The question is not easily answered. Bjarni Aðalbjarnarson (ÍF 27:XXV) was inclined to believe that the sequence was invented on the basis of what the author knew or could extrapolate about the persons involved.

We must begin by distinguishing between two sections of the narrative, one section on Óláfr's return home and his reception by his mother and stepfather (ÍF 27:39–46) and a second section on his progress to Upplǫnd and as far north as Skaun in Þrándheimr (ÍF 27:46–54). In the course of this march Óláfr is able to gain the submission of the central provinces. Most fully described is his meeting with the petty kings of Upplǫnd. It is Óláfr's stepfather Sigurðr who opens the meeting and to whom the chieftains respond. Hrœrekr is reluctant to accept Óláfr as king of Norway and advocates continued adherence to the Danish king, but his brother Hringr prefers a native Norwegian to a foreign king, and that view prevails. If we ask how the details of this meeting may have come down to the author of *Óláfs saga helga*, we should remind ourselves that Hrœrekr was ultimately exiled by Óláfr and ended his days in Iceland, where he would have had ample opportunity to tell an Icelandic audience his life's story. That could have nurtured an oral transmission maintained and elaborated until it was recorded in writing two hundred years later. We will see that Hrœrekr's story is preserved in even greater detail in later sections of *Óláfs saga helga*.

Such an oral source for Hrœrekr's story does not necessarily account for the vivid domestic scenes in which Óláfr is welcomed home by his mother and stepfather. Hrœrekr was not present during this sequence and would not have had first-hand information about what transpired. It should be pointed out, however, that the domestic scenes and the meeting of the petty kings are cast in the same style to the extent that both are characterized by long speeches delivered by Óláfr and Sigurðr in the first sequence and by Sigurðr, Hrœrekr, and Hringr in the second sequence. The narrative is therefore all of a piece stylistically and is uniformly well told. This narrative style could of course be entirely of the author's making, but it could also be inherited from an oral transmission originating with Hrœrekr. During the meeting of the petty kings, and perhaps later, Hrœrekr could have learned enough about Óláfr's return home to make it part of his eventual narrative in Iceland, although it seems unlikely that he would have devised the political oratory. The latter is more likely to be the author's work.[3]

The subsequent section of the narrative is a continuation of what precedes it by virtue of pursuing the story of Óláfr's conquest and unification of Norway, this time in Þrándheimr. The account is studded by no fewer than eighteen full or half stanzas, fourteen by Sigvatr, three from a *flokkr* by Bersi Skáldtorfuson, and a half stanza by Klœngr Brúsason. The preponderance of Sigvatr's verse makes it logical that this section begins with his arrival in Þrándheimr and his introduction into Óláfr's court.

What follows pertains to the completion of Óláfr's pacification of Norway, his defeat of Sveinn Hákonarson at Nesjar, and Sveinn's escape and mortal illness in Sweden. Sigvatr is said to have been present in the battle; details of the action could have been extrapolated from his verse or could have been circulated as part of a prose transmission in Iceland. Certain particulars about the movements of Sveinn and his troops presumably did not originate with Sigvatr but could well have been part and parcel of Bersi Skáldtorfuson's *flokkr*, of which only three stanzas are set down, either by inference or in a companion story. Bersi was also present at the battle and would have known about the movements in the enemy camp. In this section it is therefore hard to distinguish between genuine tradition and authorial elaboration. There is information about Erlingr Skjálgsson not touched on in Bersi's extant stanzas, but it could have been included in stanzas no longer preserved. Even without skaldic support there was an abundance of tradition about Erlingr underlying other parts of the saga.

With the pacification of Þrándheimr Óláfr's conquest is complete, and the author turns his attention to the king's Christian mission and his territorial dispute with the Swedish king's kinsman Sveinn Hákonarson. This section is again virtually devoid of skaldic stanzas, but we will see presently that the Icelandic sources are fairly transparent. The themes of Christian mission and territorial dispute are intertwined, suggesting that the chronologically meticulous author felt confronted by two long-term issues that could not be ordered in time. After constructing a large hall in Niðaróss and organizing the court, Óláfr devotes himself to a revision of the laws, but he learns that the maintenance of Christianity leaves much to be desired in Iceland, Orkney, Shetland, and the Faroe Islands. In the meantime the Swedish king Óláfr Eiríksson dispatches emissaries to collect taxes in the disputed provinces. They run afoul of King Óláfr, who has one group hanged while another group makes good its escape back to Sweden.

He then turns to the task of mending Christian observances. To begin with he sends for Hjalti Skeggjason in Iceland. At the same time he instructs the lawspeaker Skapti Þóroddsson and the other Icelanders responsible for legal questions to remove from the law those elements most contrary to Christianity. In Norway he devotes himself to extending the rule of Christianity from the coastal areas to inner Norway, where paganism remains firmly rooted. In addition he is able to bring a reluctant Erlingr Skjálgsson into line and force terms on him. Subsequently he also succeeds in imposing his rule in eastern Norway, to some extent by force.

At this point the narrative becomes somewhat fragmented. We learn that Óláfr gains the allegiance of a certain Brynjólfr úlfaldi, on whom the king bestows an estate commemorated in a stanza by Brynjólfr. We also learn that Óláfr appoints a man named Þrándr hvíti to collect taxes, but Þrándr is killed by the agents of the Swedish king. With that the narrative reverts to the conversion theme, informing us that eastern Norway was an easier target for Óláfr's mission because people in that region were more familiar with Christianity. Finally, we learn that Óláfr dispatches Eyvindr úrarhorn to kill the Swedish king's district chieftain and tax collector Hrói skjálgi. The Swedes avenge themselves by killing a certain Guðleikr who is charged with a precious cargo for Óláfr from Russia, but Eyvindr úrarhorn promptly retaliates by killing the culpable Swedes. Apart from two lines of a stanza by Brynjólfr úlfaldi, there is no indication of how these disparate events might have been retained in memory, but they are not sufficiently relevant to the saga as a whole to have been invented ad hoc.

More easily explained is the following sequence. The Swedish jarl Rǫgnvaldr is married to the sister of Óláfr Tryggvason, who harbors ill feeling toward the Swedish king because of his role in her brother's death. At her urging Rǫgnvaldr aligns himself with King Óláfr against his Swedish rival. With the enmity of the contending monarchs at fever pitch, the residents of the border regions between Norway and Sweden become increasingly eager for peace and appeal their case to King Óláfr's lieutenant Bjǫrn stallari. At the same time Hjalti Skeggjason arrives at Óláfr's court and becomes Bjǫrn's close companion. When Bjǫrn urges the peace mission, Óláfr somewhat vindictively puts him in command of the initiative, and Hjalti Skeggjason volunteers to accompany him. They begin by spending some time at the residence of Jarl Rǫgnvaldr, where Hjalti gets a particularly warm reception because his wife is distantly related to Rǫgnvaldr's wife. Hjalti thus becomes a central figure in the subsequent attempts to reconcile the hostile kings. Should we assume that Hjalti is the wellspring of the tradition that grew up about these events in Iceland? We must bear in mind that Hjalti was not the only potential source of information. We are told that Sigvatr also accompanied Bjǫrn (p. 92), and five of his "Austrfararvísur" are recorded. In addition, we have also been told (p. 74) that there were other Icelanders at Óláfr's court. Furthermore, there were Icelanders located at the court of the Swedish king (p. 91), Gizurr svarti and Óttarr svarti. Hence there were multiple sources of information about the dealings between Norway and Sweden.

In this and later passages there seems to be almost enough information about Hjalti to justify our imagining a **Hjalta saga Skeggjasonar*, although no trace of such a saga exists. There may nonetheless have been a considerable tradition. The situation may put us in mind of how Haraldr harðráði's lieutenant Halldórr Snorrason returned to Iceland and instructed a young story-telling Icelander on the subject of Haraldr's Mediterranean adventures. Here too there would have been no written account before *Morkinskinna*, but people would have known a good deal about the events. The point is not, however, to focus on Hjalti as the sole source; the mention of other Icelanders both at Óláfr's court and at the court of the Swedish king suggests an extended Icelandic network. Any number of people in this network could have been important conveyors of tradition. Like the story of Haraldr harðráði, Hjalti's story would have required no supporting stanzas, and indeed the next forty pages of the saga (pp. 95–134) record only three stanzas, all by Óttarr svarti.

Friðgerðar saga

The story of how Bjǫrn stallari, Hjalti Skeggjason, and Rǫgnvaldr jarl conduct complicated, and for a long time abortive, attempts to make peace and arrange a marriage between King Óláfr and the Swedish princess Ingigerðr has been termed a "Friðgerðar saga." In the critical literature it has acquired a semi-independent status and can be broken down into the following phases:

1. The farmers of Vík long for peace between Sweden and Norway and ask Bjǫrn stallari to raise the matter with King Óláfr. Óláfr responds with an ill grace and charges Bjǫrn with the dangerous mission to Sweden. Hjalti joins him.
2. During a sojourn with Rǫgnvaldr jarl, Hjalti travels ahead to the Swedish court to test the waters. The Swedish king rejects any talk of peace.
3. Hjalti and Princess Ingigerðr meet with Rǫgnvaldr and discuss the possibility of her marriage to Óláfr. Rǫgnvaldr relays the plan to the Swedish king, who angrily rejects it.
4. The Uppsala lawman Þorgnýr, to whom Rǫgnvaldr has already appealed, now intercedes and undertakes to support peace at the Uppsala assembly. Under pressure from Þorgnýr and public opinion, the Swedish king accedes but fails to carry out his commitment.
5. A cutting remark by his daughter Ingigerðr causes the Swedish king to cancel the marriage plan and marry his daughter instead to King Jarizleifr (Yaroslav) in Russia. The Norwegians decide not to retaliate.
6. Hjalti, having done what he can, returns to Iceland (p. 128). Sigvatr then assumes his role and is sent to Rǫgnvaldr to test the jarl's loyalty. The Swedish king's second, illegitimate daughter Ástríðr visits at the same time, and new marriage plans are forged. With Rǫgnvaldr's collusion she is married to King Óláfr.
7. The West Gautlanders, caught between the Swedish and Norwegian kings, assemble to discuss their plight. They dispatch the wise man Emundr af Skǫrum to lay the case before the Swedish king. Emundr tells metaphorical stories, which, after his departure, the king's councilors unravel to the effect that the Swedes are about to rebel and that he should make peace. On the point of losing his throne, the Swedish king acquiesces.

This section of the saga has been a particular focus of research, perhaps because the Swedish scene of much of the action has attracted Swedish as well as Norwegian scholars. The special analysis began in 1916 with Oscar Albert Johnsen and Birger Nerman and may be considered to have culminated in Otto von Friesen's very detailed study in 1942.[4] Johnsen emphasized the role of Hjalti Skeggjason as the ultimate source for much of the narrative, but he also allowed for

Snorri's having collected Swedish lore during his visit of 1218–1220. "Friðgerðar saga" subsequently passed through the wringer of Weibullian criticism with the result that only the skaldic stanzas were credited with a residue of history.[5] As a consequence, von Friesen began his study in 1942 with a meticulous review of Sigvatr's stanzas, but he also argued that those parts of the narrative not derivative from skaldic authority have some historical basis and should not be considered Snorri's invention, as some previous critics had held. His arguments are compelling.

Von Friesen levels his criticism in particular against those who concluded that the stories of Þorgnýr (1942:252) and Emundr (1942:266) were Snorri's fictions.[6] They may well have been elaborated and fictionalized in the course of oral transmission, but, he argues, they are nonetheless the residue of historical traditions. Von Friesen leaves latitude for Hjalti Skeggjason's role as a source for what he calls "the first act" of the peace negotiations (1942:244), but Hjalti is no longer as central as he was in Oscar Albert Johnsen's discussion. Indeed, we may observe that Hjalti is a possible source only for parts 1–3 in the synopsis above, not for parts 4–7. We have also seen that there were other Icelanders both in Norway and Sweden; they too could have contributed to the formation of the story.

Sigvatr himself, who seems to have been present at the moment when Ástríðr's marriage to Óláfr was conceived, may have had a more central part in the formulation of the story as a whole than Hjalti. Perhaps we should think of Sigvatr not just as the author of the relevant stanzas but also as a creator of the prose narrative underlying this part of *Óláfs saga helga.*

It is not just the existence of prose narrative that is of interest but the form as well. Both the story of Þorgnýr and the story of Emundr are narrative high points in "*Friðgerðar saga.*" Should we imagine, as Johnsen seems to have done (1916:529, 534–35), that two stray remnants of Swedish lore were converted into particularly brilliant narratives about two wise and authoritative councilors, spokesmen for the people who protected the public weal and saved the king from himself? It seems more likely that they are part of the same narrative concept, twin pillars in one and the same story. If so, "*Friðgerðar saga*" should be considered as a narrative whole, rooted in a rather extended tradition but of course recast and supplemented, especially with oratory, by the author of *Óláfs saga helga*.

The two stories function in tandem, both celebrating the triumph of diplomacy and negotiation. As we have seen, the background is that the farmers of Vík wish to foster peace and urge Bjǫrn stallari to undertake the mission. The Norwegian king is unenthusiastic but agrees to dispatch Bjǫrn at his own risk; Hjalti Skeggjason in turn agrees to accompany him. They take up winter residence with the Swedish jarl Rǫgnvaldr, and Hjalti sets out for the Swedish court in advance. Having ingratiated himself with the king, he raises the topic of peace and the marriage of the king's daughter Ingigerðr to Óláfr of Norway. The Swedish king rejects the project out of hand, but Hjalti is able to engage Ingigerðr's interest. After some account of the Norwegian king's pacification of his eastern realm and some general information on the political divisions and institutions of Sweden the story begins in earnest.

Ingigerðr and Hjalti dispatch messengers to Rǫgnvaldr to let him know that prospects for peace are very dim. Rǫgnvaldr arranges to meet with them in a neutral place, and they come to terms on the marriage project. Rǫgnvaldr now visits his wise old foster father, the lawman Þorgnýr, and decries the difficulties involved in dealing with the Swedish king. Þorgnýr lectures him rather patronizingly on free speech for commoners in the presence of the king, but he agrees to lend his assistance at the Uppsala assembly. Here the scene is set, especially with respect to the impressive attendance of the farmers. Bjǫrn stallari delivers a proposal for peace, only to be silenced by the outraged Swedish king. Jarl Rǫgnvaldr then tries his luck with the marriage proposal, but is rebuked no less severely than Bjǫrn. Now the epic third act is staged, and Þorgnýr rises to say his piece. The scene takes on imposing dimensions as all the farmers stand in unison, creating a great tumult in their eagerness to hear Þorgnýr's words.[7]

When order is restored, Þorgnýr launches into a great address of thirty-three lines, placing the present king in an unfavorable historical light compared to earlier kings and making a clear demand for peace and a marriage alliance. Þorgnýr thus vindicates free speech in the presence of the king in the most uncompromising way. Indeed, he concludes his speech with an outright threat that the farmers will attack and kill the king rather than suffer hostility and lawlessness. The farmers respond with another enthusiastic outburst, and the king is forced to relent and concede the power of public opinion. He agrees to both peace and marriage, allowing Bjǫrn to return to Norway and announce the success of his mission.

This tale is not as adventurous or action-packed as several others, but like all the stories under study here it is artistically and dramatically shaped. It also has in common with the others that it is free-standing and has no support in skaldic verse. In some of these instances there is a fairly prolonged narrative, but Þorgnýr makes only one appearance. There is, however, a certain thematic consistency about the stories; they all dwell on the limits of royal power. Óláfr of Norway must confront unsuspected opposition, while Óláfr of Sweden must acknowledge the power of the people and the power of historical precedent.[8]

The same theme recurs in the second isolable story of "*Friðgerðar saga.*" It is occasioned by King Óláfr's refusal to abide by his promise to make peace and his decision to marry his daughter Ingigerðr to King Jarizleifr (Yaroslav) of Russia instead of King Óláfr Haraldsson. Using Sigvatr and a nephew of Sigvatr's as intermediaries, King Óláfr and Rǫgnvaldr then plan to contract a marriage between Óláfr and the Swedish king's second daughter Ástríðr, without her father's consent. The people of West Gautland consequently worry about their imperiled relationship with the Swedish king in Uppsala and resolve to mend fences. They appeal to the lawman Emundr af Skǫrum, who undertakes the mission and presents himself before the king. Asked what news he brings, Emundr launches into two seemingly trivial and irrelevant anecdotes. The first is about a great hunter who goes out into the forest and collects a large number of pelts, but at the last moment he sees one more squirrel darting among the trees. He sets out in pursuit and persists all day long without bringing the squirrel down. When he finally returns to his original location, the sled full of pelts has disappeared and he is left with nothing.

The second story is about a raider who comes upon five Danish merchantmen loaded with rich booty. He captures four of them, but the fifth escapes. Unable to bear the loss, he pursues the elusive vessel without success and ultimately returns only to find that the other four have been recaptured. He too ends up empty-handed. When the king interrupts Emundr to ask what his business is, he fabricates a legal case in need of resolution. Two men, equal in birth but unequal in wealth and disposition, quarrel over land. The wealthier of the two is found liable, but he pays over a gosling for a goose, a young pig for a mature boar, and, in lieu of a mark of refined gold, only a half mark, the other half being composed of clay and earth. On top of that he utters dire threats. Emundr then asks for the king's judgment, and the king determines that the man who is liable shall make full payment or be subject to outlawry. Emundr thanks him and departs, leaving the court in secret.

The next day the king begins to ponder Emundr's stories with his councilors. He surmises that the two men who quarrel over land are to be understood as the Norwegian and Swedish kings, but he quizzes the councilors on what the forms of payment might mean. They explain that the Norwegian king got the illegitimate princess Ástríðr instead of the legitimate Ingigerðr (a gosling for a goose, etc.) and was nonetheless content with his lot. They go on to explain that the Swedes will rebel if Óláfr does not abide by his agreement to make peace. The king grasps the situation and submits; at a law assembly the gathered delegates work out a compromise according to which Óláfr and his son Jákob (later Ǫnundr) will rule jointly until Óláfr's death. This opens the way for a final peaceful resolution of the conflict between the Norwegian and Swedish kings.

Like the other stories we will explore, the anecdotes involving Þorgnýr and Emundr are straight prose narratives not underpinned by stanzas. Þorgnýr's role may be traceable to Hjalti Skeggjason, but by the time Emundr comes onto the scene, Hjalti has returned to Iceland. We are told that Sigvatr and his nephew are complicit in the marriage of Ástríðr to Óláfr Haraldsson, and perhaps uncle and nephew were the original mediators of the tradition about the final settlement of the conflict. Or there may have been other Icelanders at the Swedish court who were in a position to transmit the tale. In other words, it is perfectly possible that there is a kernel of tradition in the story of Emundr. On the other hand, the narrative is so intricately political and diplomatic that it may have been concocted by a politically minded writer in retrospect. It is not an action story, like some of the others we will review, but a drama of words and metaphors, more a literary than a narrative exercise. It does, however, have in common with all the stories surveyed here that it is about the parameters of royal power and the price of autocracy.

The Story of Hrœrekr

In general terms, everything in *Óláfs saga helga* is a story, but the tale of Hrœrekr, which is inserted between the tales of Þorgnýr and Emundr, is a story in a narrower sense. It is not an essential part of the biography of Saint Óláfr but tangential to it. All the reader really needs to know is that Hrœrekr is one of the five kings Óláfr captured in a single morning; that much is integral to the account of how Óláfr subjected Norway to his rule. But the author goes on to tell the whole of Hrœrekr's story down to his dying day, a narrative that in its final phases has no relevance to Óláfr. It is a private history, not part of the public record with which a royal biography is normally concerned. Nor is it authenticated by any skaldic stanzas, which are the mark of the public record. It is a sort of king's saga within a king's saga since it recapitulates much of Hrœrekr's life.

Stylistically the story has much in common with the Icelandic *þættir*, being of limited scope but rich in deceptively mundane detail with unsuspected implications and resonances.[9] It also shares with many of the *þættir*, and many of the embedded Icelandic stories in general, the theme of wit triumphant. Hrœrekr's case is particularly pointed because the contestants are so unevenly matched. How likely is it that a helpless blind captive will get the better of his captor king? And yet Hrœrekr, blinded after his capture and kept under close guard, very nearly does. That is the gist of the plot and the element that binds the episodes together. Hrœrekr's ingenuity and his psychological discipline are a match even for Óláfr's redoubtable intelligence. But in good saga style, one antagonist is not exalted at the expense of the other; we may think more of Hrœrekr without thinking less of Óláfr.

It is also a concomitant of saga style that the portraits, however brief, are deftly drawn. Óláfr is described elsewhere as being self-contained and not given to overreaction, but nowhere are these qualities so vividly rendered as in this story. The king understands that among the petty kings Hrœrekr is the greatest threat and therefore has him cruelly disabled, but once this measure has been taken, Hrœrekr is well provided for and is the beneficiary of considerable patience. At one point Óláfr's retainers urge him to execute his captive, but Óláfr is proud of his bloodless victory over five petty kings and is reluctant to kill a kinsman. The portrait is one of a decisive but, within the bounds of autocracy, a moderate ruler. The king's character is not compromised by Hrœrekr's extraordinary cunning.

The story of his cunning is briefly as follows. After his blinding, Óláfr assigns a servant to accompany him wherever he goes, but Hrœrekr regularly beats his companion until the man finds it prudent to abandon the task assigned him. The pattern repeats itself with a series of servants, all of whom depart to save themselves. Finally a servant is appointed who is Hrœrekr's kinsman and lets himself be persuaded to make an attempt on Óláfr's life. At the last moment, however, the assassin loses his nerve and throws himself at Óláfr's feet with a plea for mercy.

Óláfr now assigns two loyal retainers to take over the guard duty and supervise Hrœrekr in a separate residence. Since he has an ample supply of money, he makes it a habit to regale his companions with abundant drink. Among these companions is a long- standing servant named Fiðr (Finnr), with whom Hrœrekr holds secret converse. One night Hrœrekr lulls everyone to sleep with drink, then calls his guards to accompany him to the latrine. The guards are cut down by men who have been summoned by Fiðr and who now abduct Hrœrekr in a boat. Sigvatr becomes aware of the escape and awakens King Óláfr so that he can organize a search party. The searchers are able to recapture Hrœrekr, and he is placed under tighter guard than ever. Having failed to enlist successful intermediaries, Hrœrekr now takes matters into his own hands. During a church service he sits next to Óláfr and tries to plunge a knife into his back, but Óláfr's cloak deflects the blow.

The final act of the story is connected with an anecdote about the Icelander Þórarinn Nefjólfsson, who is resident with King Óláfr. One morning Óláfr sees Þórarinn's foot protruding from his bedclothes and comments that it must be the ugliest foot in town; in fact he is willing to make a wager that this is so. Þórarinn accepts the wager and uncovers his other foot, which he claims is uglier than the first because it is missing the big toe. Óláfr counters that the first foot is uglier because it has five ugly toes, not just four. Þórarinn accedes and Óláfr wins the bet. That allows him to make a demand, and he duly requests that Þórarinn transport Hrœrekr to Greenland. The upshot of the story is that Hrœrekr winds up in Iceland, where he stays first with Þorgils Arason and then with Guðmundr inn ríki Eyjólfsson.

The story is both lively and humorous; we are led to ponder whether and how Hrœrekr will outwit Óláfr despite his apparent helplessness. The contrivances emerge gradually, as in the case of the loyal helper Fiðr. The scenes of nocturnal escape and attempted assassination in the church are teased out in vivid detail, and Þórarinn Nefjólfsson has an enduring place in the Icelandic repertory of funny stories. If we ask ourselves how such a tradition originated and was transmitted, three candidates suggest themselves: Hrœrekr, Sigvatr (who discovers Hrœrekr's escape), and Þórarinn Nefjólfsson. As in the case of Hjalti Skeggjason, we should not necessarily assume that a particular individual was the original teller. There may have been no such thing as an "original teller" but rather an accumulation of anecdotes worked together and evolving over time. It is probably simplistic to assume that only one teller is responsible for the narrative form, and perhaps no less simplistic to assume that all the narrative niceties are the property of the final author. More attractive is the idea that the narrative was forged gradually and came to the author as a full-fledged story.

The theme that runs through all the incidents is Hrœrekr's resourcefulness, which develops along the lines of a prison escape drama. Hrœrekr is not only impressively patient and persistent but also a master of deception. The nature of his character is to counterfeit character. We may wonder why at some times he cultivates a harsh manner while at other times he turns cheerful and extroverted. There appears to be no specific reason other than to mask his true designs under assumed moods. Hrœrekr makes a point of never being his true self and is therefore always inaccessible to the observer. His character is to have no ascertainable character, so that he is enabled to operate in complete secrecy. Even the minor players on this stage have character. Sigvatr, as in the well-known scene in which he confers the name Magnús on the king's son, circumvents Óláfr's dislike of being awakened by having the church bells rung prematurely. He too is a man of many remedies. Hrœrekr's kinsman Sveinn is willing enough to help in the mission of vengeance, but unlike the other characters in the story he does not have the requisite discipline, and his character collapses at the sight of Óláfr's penetrating eyes. He is impressionable and succumbs easily to Hrœrekr's flattering recruitment, reinforced by the transparent promise of a jarldom, but he is deluded when he believes that he can execute the plan. He is in fact a foil to Hrœrekr's other helper Fiðr, who is as swift of wit as he is afoot. We learn nothing about him because he operates completely behind the scenes, but that is his strength and the secret of his success.

The personal style of these characters matches the narrative style of the story as a whole. It is one of the characteristics of the sagas that the meaning of the action is not always transparent, or is not revealed until a later point in the story. We do not know at the outset what Hrœrekr is planning, and we cannot readily interpret his actions. This is the narrative strategy that Hallvard Lie labelled "diskresjon" in his elegant book on the style of *Heimskringla*.[10] "Diskresjon" might be rendered freely by "contrived reticence" in English; as in the modern mystery story, the writer does not tell the readers what they really need to know. Thus we are not told why Hrœrekr takes the companions provided by the king off to deserted places to beat them; he could presumably beat them closer to home. The reason seems to be that he is already planning to have in the long run a more collaborative companion. If people are accustomed to his wandering off to a distance, he will then be enabled to communicate in secret with this eventual companion. Similarly veiled is Hrœrekr's second attempt on Óláfr's life. He sits next to the king in church and feels the back of his cloak. He accounts for this gesture by admiring the fine silken material, but by now we know that if Hrœrekr alleges an explanation, it is probably not the true one. The real explanation does not in fact emerge until the end of the story, when the writer reveals that Hrœrekr felt the cloak in order to ascertain whether Óláfr was wearing a byrnie. A feature that elaborates the cloak metaphorically and ironically is the hood. Óláfr is the actor with the unobscured countenance, whereas Hrœrekr is doubly hooded by virtue of being both blind and deceitful. As he stabs Óláfr, the hood falls back, giving the king an extra layer of protection; thus the open countenance survives and the truly hooded antagonist is discountenanced. Hooding and unhooding sum up the story.

The composition of the tale is no less finely wrought than characterization and style. Almost mannered is the threefold repetition of Hrœrekr's machinations, two attempts on Óláfr's life and a foiled escape. The action is insistently retarded by Hrœrekr's repeated mistreatment of his companions and Fiðr's mysterious dodging in and out of the action, only to disappear once and for all at the end of the failed escape. The dialogue is not honed to the point of repartee and is usually limited to a single exchange between two speakers, but the phrasing is crisply formulated. For example, when Sigvatr returns from the latrine with blood on his clothing, there is the following exchange with his attendant: "'Have you hurt yourself, or why are you covered with blood?' He answered: 'I am not hurt, but I think this signals big news.'" It is the big news that stands to be revealed.

At one point the retardative telling transitions into a commonplace pattern that is both opaque and transparent. In one of his expansive moods Hrœrekr provides a great abundance of drink so that his companions fall into a sodden sleep. On the one hand we do not, strictly speaking, know what this drinking portends, but on the other hand we are sufficiently familiar with the intoxication of jailers in Norse literature to suspect immediately that an escape is in the offing. Thus the episode both leaves the reader wondering what will happen next and at the same time clearly suggests a sequel and propels the story forward. For the moment we may simply note that this tale is particularly well told, but we must return to the problem of how it originated and how it was passed down to the thirteenth century in our conclusions.

The Story of Ásbjǫrn Sigurðarson

The patchwork nature of *Óláfs saga helga* emerges with particular clarity in the transition from the dramatic stories of Þorgnýr, Emundr, and Hrœrekr to the somewhat tangled chronicle style of King Óláfr's first dealings with Orkney. The author begins with a brief historical preface on Orkney and then focuses on the contentions among the brothers Einarr, Brúsi, and Þorfinnr Sigurðarsynir over the domination of the islands. The contentiousness is such that first Brúsi and then Þorfinnr appeals to King Óláfr; these appeals allow the king to drive a wedge between the contenders and claim the islands for himself, with the jarls now subordinate to him. The source for this little chronicle is a version of *Orkneyinga saga*, although it is difficult to know exactly what this version contained and what the author of *Óláfs saga helga* adjusted.[11] The style is, however, clearly determined by the written source, not by the sort of oral story that underlies the preceding narrative. The contrast between chronicle style, of which *Orkneyinga saga* is an almost notorious example, and story style is well illustrated by these passages.

The following narrative shows a similar division of labor between chronicle and story style. It gives an account of how Óláfr extended his authority into northern Norway, a region no less remote than the Orkney Islands. Like the previous section, this one begins with a capsule history, this time of Hálogaland, and how Hárekr, the son of Eyvindr skáldaspillir, establishes himself in Þjótta as the most powerful chieftain in the region. Óláfr is in turn concerned with the quality of Christianity in the north and imposes his religion all along the coast to Hálogaland. He also begins to form personal connections, gaining the service of Hárekr, Grankell and his son Ásmundr, and Þórir hundr on Bjarkey.

Having completed his mission in the north, Óláfr turns his attention to rumors of heathen practices in inner Þrándheimr. When verbal admonitions fail, he mounts a punitive expedition to enforce Christianity. At the same time he continues to build his personal network and makes a fast friendship with two sons of Árni Armóðsson, Kálfr and Finnr. He then prosecutes the Christian mission in Upplǫnd, Guðbrandsdalir, Heiðmǫrk, Haðaland, Hringaríki, and Raumaríki. Most of this narrative remains at the informational level, but the story of the conversion of Dala-Guðbrandr is detailed and finely crafted. It is also a self-contained narrative and is found in the *Legendary Saga* in almost identical form. The common assumption is that it was composed as a separate entity and was interpolated into both the *Legendary Saga* and *Óláfs saga helga*. There is no indication of what the ultimate source of the story might be, and there is disagreement about whether it was composed in Iceland or Norway. Since there are no signs of an oral source, and since the story is constructed on the literary model of the so-called thaumaturgic duel, it seems quite likely to be an authorial invention, but it also appears to predate the author of *Óláfs saga helga*.[12]

The point of departure for our next semi-independent story is a famine in northern Norway. Óláfr seeks to protect the south by forbidding the export of grain from Agðir, Rogaland, and Hǫrðaland. The political situation in southwestern Norway is that Erlingr Skjálgsson controls a very large territory, but his domination is threatened when Óláfr installs a certain Áslákr fitjaskalli (second cousin to Erlingr) in this territory and therefore gives rise to frictions in the contested area. Áslákr appeals to Óláfr, who calls Erlingr to account, but mutual friends are able to smooth matters over and leave Erlingr with his authority undiminished.

This is the background for what is perhaps the most polished, as well as the most politically loaded, story in *Óláfs saga helga*, the story of Ásbjǫrn Sigurðarson. He is resident in Hálogaland on the Lofoten Islands and is at the very center of the later tensions between King Óláfr and the great western chieftains of Norway. On his father's side he is the nephew of Þórir hundr, who is destined to desert to King Knútr and oppose Óláfr at Stiklarstaðir; on his mother's side he is the nephew of Erlingr Skjálgsson, whose death in a naval encounter will signal the king's downfall. Ásbjǫrn's story is therefore in some sense the preface to Óláfr's demise at the hands of his chief antagonists.[13]

Ásbjǫrn falls heir to his father's high status on the island of Ǫmð and is eager to maintain his father's level of feasting and hospitality, but Hálogaland is afflicted by harvest failures and a shortage of grain. Ásbjǫrn therefore travels south to purchase the needed supplies and stops at Ǫgvaldsnes on Kǫrmt, a residence in the hands of Óláfr's steward Sel-Þórir. Þórir informs him that the king has forbidden the export of grain to the north and therefore declines to put up any of his own supplies for sale. Ásbjǫrn continues his journey to the residence of his uncle Erlingr Skjálgsson at Sóli. Erlingr evades the king's prohibition by allowing Ásbjǫrn to purchase grain from slaves who stand outside the king's law. On his return north Ásbjǫrn again visits Sel-Þórir, and when Þórir learns of the subterfuge, he enforces the king's prohibition not only by confiscating the cargo of grain but also by seizing Ásbjǫrn's fine sail in addition, substituting a badly worn one in its place. As a consequence Ásbjǫrn must return home empty-handed and disgraced. Once at home he must also suffer the barbs of his uncle Þórir.

Stung by this reception, Ásbjǫrn undertakes a second voyage and lands secretly on the uninhabited outer edge of Kǫrmt. From here he proceeds in disguise to Ǫgvaldsnes, where there is a large gathering in honor of a visit by King Óláfr. In an outer chamber he overhears Sel-Þórir in the main hall recounting the story of his disgrace. Undeterred by the formal occasion, he rushes into the hall and lops off Þórir's head so that it falls at the very feet of the king. Óláfr orders that he be seized and executed, but the son of Erlingr Skjálgsson, Skjálgr, intercedes and pleads for mercy. The king is too furious to be placated, leaving Skjálgr to set out to appeal to his father. In the meantime, Skjálgr leaves word with Þórarinn Nefjólfsson to delay the execution until the following Sunday.

Þórarinn devises three successive ruses (reminiscent of the epic triads in the stories of Hrœrekr and Emundr af Skǫrum) to prolong Ásbjǫrn's life. On Sunday Erlingr Skjálgsson appears in due course with a force of nearly 1500 (1800) men to confront the king. The bishop is able to defuse the situation and salvage a compromise, with the stipulation that Ásbjǫrn is to assume Sel-Þórir's position as the king's steward at Ǫgvaldsnes. When Ásbjǫrn returns home to settle his affairs, however, Þórir hundr convinces him not to become the king's "slave" and he remains on his estate on Ǫmð.

This story once again shares features we observed in the earlier ones. It is told as an independent narrative without recourse to skaldic authority. It is laced with wit and high drama, and there is a clear indication of how it found its way into Icelandic tradition, that is, through the central role in Ásbjǫrn's survival allotted to the same Þórarinn Nefjólfsson who must have contributed to the story of Hrœrekr. Finally, it fixes the limits of royal authority. In this case it illustrates the discountenancing of a king by the hereditary aristocracy.

Other Semi-Independent Stories

The first of the remaining three stories attaches to the same theme. It is organized around a certain Karli í Langey (another island in the Lofoten chain) and his brother Gunnsteinn, who take service with King Óláfr. The king undertakes a commercial venture with them, in which they will be equal partners, although the actual voyage will fall to the lot of Karli and his brother. The destination is Bjarmaland (Permia), but on the way Þórir hundr offers himself as an additional partner. The arrangement is that both Karli and Þórir will rendez-vous with twenty-five men apiece, but Þórir appears at the meeting place with a very large ship and a crew of eighty men. Karli and Gunnsteinn are apprehensive about his intentions, but they are unwilling to turn back and therefore proceed to Bjarmaland substantially outnumbered. At first they engage in profitable trade with the natives, but at the conclusion of these dealings they decide to try their luck with a raid on the sacred precinct of the god Jómali. Þórir stipulates that the idol of the god not be plundered, but he breaks the prohibition himself and seizes a bowl of silver coins from the very lap of the god. Karli then follows suit and cuts a gold torque from the god's neck. In the meantime the natives raise the alarm, and the Norsemen narrowly escape their pursuit as they retreat to their ships.

When the raiders are once more able to assemble, Þórir demands the torque carried off by Karli and insists that the booty be shared out on the spot. Karli replies that half the booty belongs to Óláfr and that Þórir must negotiate the division with him. Þórir turns away to leave, but then calls Karli back and runs a spear through his chest. Gunnsteinn recovers the body and escapes, but Þórir eventually catches up with him, seizes all the booty, and sinks his ship. Gunnsteinn must make his way back to Óláfr's court as best he can.

The story of Karli and Gunnsteinn is now suspended for some fifteen pages while the author turns to other matters: Óláfr's alliance with King Ǫnundr of Sweden, his dealings with the Faroe Islands, his detention of several high-profile Icelanders at his court, his claims on Helsingjaland and Jamtaland, and the escape of one of the Icelandic detainees. At this point the author reverts, without warning, to the story of Karli and Gunnsteinn. The sequel is not only unexpected but managed in an interestingly opaque way. Óláfr summons Finnr Árnason and reveals a plan to raise troops throughout Norway for a campaign against King Knútr. We will come to realize that this is only a pretext and that the real plan is to avenge the slaying of Karli, but that aim is nowhere stated; we can only extrapolate it from the action.

In the meantime Finnr sets out to recruit forces in Hálogaland. When they have all assembled and been inspected, Finnr rises and confronts Þórir hundr with his slaying of Karli and seizure of King Óláfr's booty from Bjarmaland. Þórir finds himself surrounded by overwhelming odds and must yield to Finnr's demand that he pay over thirty gold marks in compensation immediately. Þórir asks for time to borrow the money from his followers, then pays it out in ever decreasing amounts, procrastinating more and more as the day wears on and the assembled forces begin to disperse. Having paid only a fraction of what is owed, he promises the balance at a later date, but as soon as the coast is clear, he sails off to England with his ill-gotten gains largely intact in order to join King Knútr. Finnr returns to Óláfr's court and voices the opinion that Þórir has evaded them and is destined to be a bitter enemy, as indeed the saga will bear out.

This story, like the others, includes no skaldic stanzas and must have survived the generations in prose. There are no identified Icelandic witnesses to transmit the lively scenes in Bjarmaland and Hálogaland, but we should bear in mind that in the intermission between the two parts of the story King Óláfr detained notable Icelanders who would have been on hand to hear the reports brought to court by Gunnsteinn and Finnr Árnason. They were therefore in a position to provide the original formulation of the events. The story as it eventually emerged is also analogous to the others reviewed above in the sense that it illustrates the fragility of royal power. King Óláfr is plundered by Þórir hundr and has his retainer Karli killed with impunity, with no recourse but to accept his defeat. There is indeed a considerable irony in his dispatching of Finnr Árnason to raise troops for an alleged campaign against King Knútr, only to have Þórir hundr desert to Knútr's cause with a substantial share of Óláfr's money.

Even before this story is completed, a new one is broached, the evasion of Steinn Skaptason from Óláfr's court. Steinn is one of the king's Icelandic detainees and, along with his countryman Þóroddr Snorrason, he is very discontent with his lot in captivity. He is not guarded in his pronouncements about the king, and the two of them have a less than friendly exchange. One night Steinn departs without leave for Gaulárdalr, where he takes lodging with Óláfr's steward Þorgeirr. Þorgeirr becomes suspicious about his license to be absent from court, and their confrontation ends in Þorgeirr's death. Steinn then goes on to Gizki in Súrnadalr, the residence of Þorbergr Árnason. Þorbergr is away, but his wife Ragnhildr, who is the daughter of Erlingr Skjálgsson, welcomes him as an old acquaintance with open arms. He had once visited her when she was about to give birth and found herself without a priest to perform the baptism. Steinn had procured an Icelandic priest named Bárðr or Brandr, and there is an interestingly detailed account of the baptism. Steinn becomes the godfather and earns Ragnhildr's fast friendship.

Steinn now calls on her friendship and she commits her full support. When her husband returns home, she appeals for his help, but he knows that Óláfr is in high dudgeon and has already outlawed Steinn. He is unwilling to risk the king's anger and orders her to send Steinn on his way, but she counters that if Steinn leaves, she too will leave, something of a commonplace in the depiction of strong women in the Icelandic sagas. The upshot is that Steinn is allowed to stay during the winter.

In the meantime, Óláfr commands Þorbergr to appear before him. Þorbergr appeals to his brothers Finnr and Árni for help, but they betoken no sympathy, and the meetings end with hard words. Þorbergr next sends for his brother Kálfr, while Ragnhildr sends for help from her father. Finnr and Árni use the time to reconsider their positions and, together with two of Ragnhildr's brothers dispatched by Erlingr, they man large ships. Kálfr and Ragnhildr's brothers are prepared to attack and let fortune take its course, but Þorbergr prefers to give conciliation a chance. A tense negotiation with the king ends with the swearing of loyalty oaths by Árni, Finnr, and Þorbergr, while Kálfr refuses and maintains his full independence. Þorbergr also asks for reconciliation on Steinn's behalf, and the king allows him to go in peace with the stipulation that he not return to his court. Steinn then makes his way to England to join King Knútr, like Þórir hundr before him.

This story is curiously bifocal. On the one hand it is the story of Steinn's escape from his unwelcome captivity, and that tale would surely have lived on among Steinn's descendants. On the other hand, it is also a peculiarly Norwegian story of how tensions arose between King Óláfr and the Árnasynir. There is no particular reason for that story to have been transmitted in Iceland, and we may suspect that the author is making adroit use of an isolated Icelandic tradition to construct a version of the disaffection that led to Óláfr's's downfall. He knew that Steinn had a special relationship with Þorbergr Árnason's wife (and Erlingr Skjálgssson's daughter) and deduced from that tale a personal friction between King Óláfr and the Árnasynir. The other possibility is that the dissension between the Árnasynir and the king could have been maintained in Icelandic tradition just as the personal dealings of Óláfr and Hrœrekr were maintained even though they had no immediate relevance to Iceland and no skaldic warrant.

Whichever option we choose, we may observe the same political thrust as in the previous stories. Steinn escapes Óláfr's clutches despite his killing of the king's steward, and Þorbergr, by dint of having a forceful wife and powerful in-laws, escapes the king's authority even though he has harbored the king's outlaw. The thrust is therefore quite in line with the message we find in many *þættir*, in which the commoner emerges as the moral victor while the king must be satisfied to be a little wiser.

The last of the interlarded stories we will look at is the story of Arnljótr gellini, a bandit with a heart of gold who later returns to the narrative to join the service of King Óláfr at the Battle of Stiklarstaðir. It is the most literary of the tales included in the saga to the extent that it is a variant of the Grendel story.[14] The focus of the narrative is the departure of the second of the malcontents among Óláfr's Icelandic hostages, Þóroddr Snorrason, and the author reminds us, in words similar to the ones used in the case of Steinn, that Þóroddr chafes in his captivity. He therefore volunteers for a dangerous mission in Jamtaland for no other reason than to be at liberty. Once in Jamtaland, he consults with a lawman named Þórarr, who in turn convenes a general assembly. Here it is decided not to become subservient to King Óláfr and to hold his messenger in captivity awaiting the judgment of the Swedish king. Þóroddr thus exchanges one captivity for another.

One evening, when men have drunk deeply, one of the Jamtar lets slip the supposition that the Swedish king will have the Norwegian messengers executed. Þóroddr takes the hint and makes good his escape, but he is recaptured and held under still tighter guard. An excess of drink once more puts the captors off their guard and allows Þóroddr and his companions to escape a second time. They take refuge with a man named Þórir and his wife in a small cottage. During the night a huge man in elegant clothes arrives; this is Arnljótr gellini, with whose name Þóroddr is familiar. He proposes to lead the escapees to safety, but they cannot keep pace and are invited to stand on his extra-long skis while he covers the ground at a great rate of speed. In due course they come to an inn and prepare to sleep in the loft. At the same time twelve traders arrive and, after some revelry, lie down to sleep below. At this moment a great troll woman arrives, makes short work of the traders, and puts them on the fire to roast.

Arnljótr now intervenes and is able to run his great spear through the troll's back; she runs out the door, with the spear projecting, at the same time leaving considerable wreckage behind her. Þóroddr and his companions now part with Arnljótr, who sends his greetings to King Óláfr and goes in search of his spear. Þóroddr finds his way back to King Óláfr and delivers the greetings, which the king receives with a good grace, regretting only that he has not made the acquaintance of such an outstanding man. After spending the winter with Óláfr, Þóroddr gets permission to return to Iceland.

This story exceeds the others in improbability but shares with them the lack of skaldic documentation. Whether it was Þóroddr who had the effrontery to splice his adventure with a folktale or whether subsequent tradition elaborated the tale in this way, we cannot know, but the narrative as we have it represents the furthest stretch of imagination in the saga.[15] It is perhaps the clearest example of a story that can be lifted out of the surrounding narrative without leaving a noticeable gap. The author seems to have indulged himself just this once in story for the sake of story.

But what is the point of the story? Like Steinn Skaptason, Þóroddr feels trapped at the king's court, but unlike Steinn, he emerges from his captivity on good terms with Óláfr. The story does not so much pit Icelander against king as it focuses the individual Icelander's craving for freedom. This is no isolated theme. It is most explicitly embodied in the Icelanders' resistance to King Óláfr's attempted expropriation of Grímsey, but in some way it colors all the stories reviewed here. The stories of Þorgnýr and Emundr argue the independence of the Swedish people from royal tyranny in a highly partisan way. In the story of Hrœrekr the author may seem to favor the dispossessed local king against the dominant overlord. In the story of Ásbjǫrn Sigurðarson the local magnates succeed in freeing themselves from royal authority. Ásbjǫrn does so by refusing to enter the king's service. (According to the *Legendary Saga* [p. 114] he is later killed at the king's orders, but in *Óláfs saga helga* retaliation is only hinted at [ÍF 27:213], never clearly stated.) In the story of Þórir hundr, Þórir evades the king's monetary fine and escapes his orbit altogether by going over to King Knútr. Steinn Skaptason is able to raise a whole clan against Óláfr, and he follows Þórir's example by deserting to Knútr. In all these stories the question is how to maintain independence from royal authority.

Conclusions

In 1914 Sigurður Nordal was able to publish an authoritative book on *Óláfs saga helga* without mentioning oral sources until the last five pages, and then only in passing.[16] This was understandable because it was his mission to work out the filiation of the written versions. Nor does it mean that he was doubtful about the existence of oral stories; his phrasing (p. 199) makes it clear that he believes that much of the narrative derives in the first instance from oral sources. It is this original oral layer that I have focused on.

The argument for the existence of oral stories is not based solely on the observation that lively stories are likely to be oral stories. The six stories studied here can be assumed to have oral roots because the same narrative matter is touched on in other textually unrelated versions, notably the fragments of the *Oldest Saga of Saint Olaf* and the *Legendary Saga of Saint Olaf*. Thus the prior existence of "*Friðgerðar saga*" is shown by a similar but unconnected account in the *Legendary Saga*. The latter does not include the stories of Þorgnýr and Emundr af Skǫrum, but it seems to be generally true that *Óláfs saga helga* expands the narrative material previously recorded. This author is the first to tell the full story of Hrœrekr, but the *Legendary Saga* suggests that some narrative was in circulation when it states (p. 72): "It is told that he [Óláfr] had the one [of the petty kings] named Hrœrekr blinded and sent him out to Iceland to Guðmundr ríki, and that is where he died."

The story of Ásbjǫrn is told in some detail in the *Legendary Saga* (pp. 108–14) and figures at the end of the first fragment of the *Oldest Saga* (pp. 405–7). The killing of Karli is at least mentioned in the *Legendary Saga* (p. 108). Steinn Skaptason is mentioned briefly in the third fragment of the *Oldest Saga*, in words that suggest that there was more to tell (p. 413): "Steinn stayed there [at court] for a short time after that and departed, and it is not told here what he experienced afterwards." Finally, Þóroddr Snorrason's story is alluded to in the *Legendary Saga* (p. 184) when Arnljótr gellini volunteers for service with King Óláfr: "'Lord,' he said, 'I sent you a silver plate with Þóroddr Snorrason as a sign that I wanted to join you and fight for you.'" Here too there would have been more to tell, but the narratives in question did not surface more fully until the composition of *Óláfs saga helga*.

These stories are clearly set apart from the written sources and informational passages by their lively dialogue and dramatic qualities. Most notable among the stories are "*Friðgerðar saga*" (particularly the episodes involving Þorgnýr and Emundr), the story of King Hrœrekr, the story of Ásbjǫrn Sigurðarson, Karli's expedition to Bjarmaland, and Þóroddr Snorrason's adventure with Arnljótr gellini. There is always a close correlation between these stories and identifiable Icelanders who could have put them into circulation. The transmissions seem therefore to be strictly Icelandic, not Norwegian or Swedish, as critics have sometimes thought. Prominent among the informants are Hrœrekr (temporarily resident in Iceland), Hjalti Skeggjason, Sigvatr Þórðarson, Þórarinn Nefjólfsson, Steinn Skaptason, and Þóroddr Snorrason. To the extent that these men were primary sources (rather than other unnamed Icelanders), it should be observed that they are men of some distinction, with the exception of Þórarinn Nefjólfsson. The very fact that Þórarinn is said specifically not to have had a special lineage (ÍF 27:125) may mean that there was an expectation that such traditions were attached to great men. That may mean in turn that the cultivation of these traditions was part and parcel of aristocratic self-promotion.

On the whole, the stories appear to be quite independent of skaldic stanzas, suggesting that such narratives were not necessarily tied to poetic transmissions. Although the author(s) of the prologues to *Heimskringla* and the *Separate Saga* insist particularly on skaldic authority, that may be a moment of historical purism not shared by the body of the saga. *Heimskringla* also has latitude for a man-eating troll, a number of miracles, and stories showcasing wit and ingenuity rather than ascertainable fact. That skaldic verse was not a prerequisite suggests that oral transmission, regardless of content, had a certain authority as well. The author of the prologue to the *Separate Saga* says that the poems are "most noteworthy for truthfulness," but he does not belittle narrative transmissions. Indeed, he states: "News passed between these countries [Norway and Iceland] every summer and it was then committed to memory and passed along in the form of stories." A review of the narrative passages in *Óláfs saga helga* would seem to bear out this assertion.

The evidence of transmitted stories tends to cluster where information about Icelandic informants is particularly palpable. Where we can infer storytellers, there are stories. This is unlikely to be coincidental. Rather, it suggests strongly that the narratives are traditional, not the invention of the writer. If allowance is made for the use of oral stories in *Óláfs saga helga*, it thus appears that everything in the saga has an ascertainable source, whether it be oral tradition, skaldic verse, incidental information, deduction, or miracle tales. It is difficult to see where the latitude for authorial invention might be, apart from the set speeches. Furthermore, if everything in this the fullest of the early sagas is anchored in some form of tradition, the implication may be that there is relatively little authorial invention in any of the early thirteenth-century sagas.

To what extent did the Icelandic traditions color or even determine the political drift of the saga as a whole? We may grant that Óláfr was viewed as a saint and was accordingly honored, but, read against the grain, the saga is also a summary of how his dealings with the magnates of Norway and high-status Icelanders led to their defection and his own downfall. This strand is particularly evident in the narratives that seem to have come down in Icelandic tradition. Hrœrekr's fate follows directly from Óláfr's suppression of the district kings, and his story may be viewed as a determined resistance to tyranny, no less than Egill Skallagrímsson's self-assertion against the Norwegian monarchy. Hrœrekr's stay in Iceland would certainly not have promoted a positive view of Óláfr's political mission, especially when seen in the context of his designs on Iceland. On the contrary, the exiled king would have had an excellent opportunity in Iceland to cultivate the self-image of a forceful and resourceful resistance fighter.

Nor would the inordinate role played by Sigvatr and Hjalti Skeggjason in "*Friðgerðar saga*" have redounded much to Óláfr's credit. Despite the brilliant diplomacy provided by Icelanders, he would have emerged as the lesser king who got the lesser, and illegitimate, Swedish princess. The greater heroes of the story are the local chieftains and wise men Þorgnýr and Emundr, who vigorously defend the rights of the people against autocratic rule.

When the author turns to the story of Óláfr's domestic relations in Norway, the record is also mixed. Most conspicuous is the tale of Ásbjǫrn Sigurðarson, which forms part of the larger story of Óláfr's dealings with Erlingr Skjálgsson. Erlingr is portrayed as a truly great chieftain, with an authority to match the king's. He is in fact able to face the king down and prevent the execution of his nephew Ásbjǫrn. When Erlingr is ultimately slain in battle, Óláfr's cause is already lost; Erlingr's fall signals his own fall, as Óláfr explicitly acknowledges. It is not difficult for the reader to consider Erlingr the greater figure and his local struggle as more admirable than Óláfr's national ambition.

The special Icelandic stake in the favoring of decentralization over centralization comes to the fore when King Óláfr casts his eye on Grímsey. The Icelanders respond at first naively, but the deeply perceptive Einarr Eyjólfsson rises to unparalleled oratorical heights when he lays bare the political implications of giving Óláfr a foothold off the coast of Iceland. What reader would fail to draw an analogy between Óláfr's intrusion into Erlingr Skjálgsson's territory and Einarr Eyjólfsson's stout defence of Iceland's territorial integrity? One way to read the saga as a whole is to conclude that aggression is the mainspring of Óláfr's actions.

The remaining stories are likely to have originated with the Icelandic representatives summoned to Óláfr's court and then held as hostages.[17] A special point is made of their dissatisfaction and eagerness to flee. Two of them, Steinn Skaptason and Þóroddr Snorrason, make good their escape; one of them deserts to King Knútr and the other returns to Iceland. In light of their captivity, it is unlikely that either of them spread positive reports about their detention or about their captor. Either one of them could have circulated the story of Karli's expedition to Bjarmaland, which is politically significant because it is also the story of Þórir hundr's disaffection from Óláfr and defection to Knútr. Steinn Skaptason's escape is also part of the political fabric because it serves to explain in part the alienation of Kálfr Árnason.

The stories brought home to Iceland are therefore not digressions or ornamental additions; they are tightly interwoven with Óláfr's loss of support in Norway and the defection of the magnates to King Knútr. Óláfr's failure to win or retain the loyalty of the Norwegians becomes a major theme in the saga after the feud with the Swedish king is concluded. His shortcomings raise doubts about him, in contrast, for example, to the adulatory tone of Styrmir's *articuli*. Do the relevant stories merely illustrate the crumbling of Óláfr's support, or did their prior circulation in Iceland in fact inspire the author in his formulation of this theme? Are the stories, with their Icelandic bias and underlying anti-monarchism, perhaps the source of the idea that Óláfr's fall was occasioned by a diplomatic failure to maintain cordial relations with the Norwegian magnates? I am inclined to think that the stories are not just a narrative source but also a source for the political viewpoint, which is subtly favorable to the district magnates and discreetly but perceptibly critical of Saint Óláfr.

We must now turn to the essential question of whether there is an underlying and consistent political viewpoint in *Óláfs saga helga* as a whole. The question surfaced in the well-known exchange of views between Halvdan Koht in 1914 and Fredrik Paasche in 1922.[18] Koht argued for a definite conflict between king and aristocracy based on events in Norwegian history just prior to the composition of *Heimskringla*. Paasche found little in the way of political commitment in the text, beyond an alignment with church and king. More recently Sverre Bagge has allied himself more with Paasche on the ground that a political thesis in these early works is anachronistic.[19]

To some extent the discussion is semantic. Paasche entitled his paper "Tendens og syn i kongesagaene," but what exactly is the force of *tendens* and the force of *syn*? *Tendens* is perhaps more active and implies a built-in point of view intended to convey the author's understanding of historical events to the reader. *Syn*, on the other hand, may be more passive; it could be translated "perspective" or "viewpoint," but it does not necessarily imply an effort on the author's part to impose an interpretive framework. The "perspective" could be calculated, but it could also be involuntary, revealing the author's bias but not necessarily signalling a desire on the author's part to make a political argument. The only critic who seems to have conceptualized this problem is Johan Schreiner, who writes as follows:[20] "It is probably not correct to talk about tendency [*tendens*] in the kings' sagas, but in the case of a work like Snorri's *Óláfs saga helga* it cannot be denied that there is a basic point of view [*grunnopfatning*], a total perspective [*totalsyn*], and with this is connected an evaluation [or better: and this is by nature evaluative]." At the end of his study, Schreiner concludes (p. 126) that Óláfr's idea of kingship was fundamentally "anti-aristocratic."

Schreiner tried to read history from the text of *Óláfs saga helga* and therefore concluded with an assessment of the historical Óláfr. If, however, we are content to read the text without reference to the historical Óláfr, we may conclude that the text is more likely to be anti-royal. One problem in the Norwegian discussion of politics in *Óláfs saga helga* is that it is too Norwegian.[21] We must ask ourselves what interest the Icelandic authors of the *Oldest Saga*, the *Legendary Saga*, Styrmir's fragments, *Heimskringla*, and very possibly *Fagrskinna* would have had in an internal Norwegian struggle between King Óláfr and the Norwegian magnates, especially in the political aspects of the struggle. Would the Icelanders have had a great enough interest in this purely domestic matter to formulate a historical thesis about it?

And yet the idea that there was such a conflict seems to be specifically Icelandic. There are traces of it in the fragments of the *Oldest Saga* and in Styrmir's *articuli*, and it is fully present in the *Legendary Saga*. But it may be significant that the oldest source, and the only one certain to be Norwegian, Theodoricus, makes no mention of the conflict and explains Óláfr's demise purely in terms of King Knútr's suborning of the chieftains. This version of events is borne out by *Ágrip*, which may also be Norwegian.[22]

But most eloquent is the silence of the 178 stanzas in *Óláfs saga*. Not a single one of them seems to allude to political tensions between King Óláfr and the Norwegian magnates. A stanza by Sigvatr in praise of Erlingr Skjálgsson (no. 26, p. 29) is placed by the author in the context of his intimidation of Jarl Eiríkr Hákonarson and is not connected with his later contention with King Óláfr. Stanza 59 (p. 106) by Óttarr alludes generally to King Óláfr's suppression of the "kings" of Hedemark but does not identify them. The following stanza, also by Óttarr, seems to suggest that Óláfr cut out the tongue of one of these "kings" and the prose (p. 105) identifies him as Guðrøðr from Guðdalar, but this is still in the context of Óláfr's conquest.

When it comes to the waning of Óláfr's fortunes, the emphasis is on how King Knútr buys off the chieftains, not on any differences between Óláfr and the chieftains. A series of stanzas (107–8, 110–11), all by Sigvatr, dwell on the theme of treachery, and Hallvarðr Háreksblasi sums up Knútr's triumph in stanza 119. An interesting aspect of these stanzas is how well they accord with what we find in Theodoricus and *Ágrip* and how poorly they match what *Óláfs saga helga* tells us. Only one stanza (no. 120, p. 314) talks about conflict with a chieftain, and that stanza comes from a *flokkr* composed by Sigvatr on the death of Erlingr Skjálgsson. It describes the battle in which Erlingr fell. Stanza 135 (p. 334), by Bjarni Gullbrárskáld, is interpreted as being about the parting of Óláfr and Kálfr Árnason and Kálfr's seeking out of King Knútr, but that is only one possible reading.

Only in the actual Battle of Stiklarstaðir are Óláfr's most notorious antagonists among the Norwegian chieftains mentioned. In stanza 155 (pp. 383–84) Sigvatr alludes to Þórir's jacket made impenetrable by Lappish magic, and in the following stanza he recounts how Þórir wounded the king. Stanza 157 (p. 385) by Bjarni Gullbrárskáld is interpreted by the prose to be about the presence of Kálfr Árnason in the battle. Finally, stanza 160 (p. 391) by Þormóðr Bersason and 164 (p. 399) from Þórarinn loftunga's "Glælognskviða" are explicit about the fact that the battle is between the Danes and King Óláfr, not between the king and his chieftains. In other words, everything in the stanzas is perfectly reconcilable with Theodoricus's view that King Knútr bribed the Norwegian chieftains, raised troops, and defeated Óláfr at Stiklarstaðir. Nothing in the stanzas requires us to believe that there is a history of deep-seated animosity between Óláfr and the chieftains.

Should that suggest to us that Óláfr's political conflict with the magnates was an Icelandic hypothesis? If so, what inspired it? It may be oversimplified to suggest that Óláfr's acquisitiveness in Iceland and his differences with Hrœrekr and his Icelandic hostages spilled over into Icelandic tradition in such a way as to foster surmises about conflicts between Óláfr and his own chieftains, but some such dynamic may have contributed to the elaboration of history in Iceland. If the Icelanders had no great stake in Norwegian internal politics, they had every reason to reflect on the history of their own independence and the threat posed by the Norwegian king. Halvdan Koht thought that the historical conflict between king and magnates in Norway, as it was resurrected in *Óláfs saga helga*, was colored by the political clashes under King Sverrir, and Paasche agreed, but it seems rather more likely that this conflict owes something to the tensions between Iceland and Norway in the period 1215–1220. That these tensions could have literary consequences is amply documented by *Egils saga*, which, no less than *Óláfs saga helga*, tells not only of the conflict between Icelanders and kings but also between the king and such local magnates as Arinbjǫrn. Icelandic self-assertiveness could clearly work to raise the profile of Norwegian chieftains who also prized their independence. Whether *Óláfs saga helga* and *Egils saga* were, one or the other or both, written by Snorri Sturluson or not, they are products of Icelandic sensibilities and reveal analogous concerns.

We have still not addressed the question of whether the political thrust of *Óláfs saga helga* is calculated or involuntary. The question is connected with the much more general problem of whether the sagas lend themselves to overall interpretation, that is, an interpretation that isolates a particular argument throughout the text. The extreme difficulty of reaching an interpretive consensus on an obvious "problem text" such as *Hrafnkels saga* may well discourage us from pursuing such an inquiry. And yet the provincial bias and the anti-expansionist outlook in *Óláfs saga helga* seem rather insistent. How often must the author return to the theme of independence in order to convince the reader that he is advancing a general thesis? Here we have reviewed six relevant stories in the text, without even touching on the explicit plea for independence in the speech of the "Icelandic Demosthenes," Einarr Eyjólfsson.[23] These passages all work together and suggest resistance to the king. Despite this confluence of meaning, we may not be able to decide whether the passages in question add up to a *tendens* or merely a *syn*, but perhaps we can agree that there are definite authorial attitudes in *Óláfs saga helga*. These attitudes were no doubt foreshadowed in the oral sources, but they also went on to color the Icelanders' view of their own history, as we will see in Chapter 6.

Thus far it seems clear that oral tradition continued to penetrate the written kings' sagas down to the time of *Óláfs saga helga* in the second and third decades of the thirteenth century. Since that tradition was largely preserved and passed down by Icelanders, it would not be surprising if the narratives also carried with them certain Icelandic viewpoints and inflections, even to the point of suggesting questions about the Norwegian monarchy. The stories transmitted by oral tradition not only offer an account of the past but also color past events with what amounts to an implied commentary. **Hlaðajarla saga* seems to have entertained alternatives to strict monarchical control inside Norway and *Óláfs saga helga,* which was evolving at the same time, seems to have raised similar issues from the point of view of the Icelanders.

CHAPTER 5

Political Subtexts in *Morkinskinna*, *Heimskringla III*, and *Egils saga*

To extract an underlying political attitude from the *Óláfs saga helga* that forms the second part of *Heimskringla* is problematical because we do not have the original version from which the author worked. It is therefore not possible to extrapolate a point of view by comparison. When it comes to the third part of *Heimskringla*, however, we are in a much better position because we have the immediate source for most of the narrative after 1030 in the compilation known as *Morkinskinna*. Internal criteria suggest that *Morkinskinna* was written around 1220, and we may begin by reviewing the situation in Iceland at that time.[1]

The period 1215–1220 was in fact characterized by considerable hostility between Iceland and Norway, a degree of tension that amounted to not much less than a trade war.[2] In 1215 Sæmundr Jónsson at Oddi and Þorvaldr Gizurarson at Hruni had set prices on the goods of some Norwegian merchants. In 1216 Sæmundr's son Páll went to Bergen and was treated to such retaliatory abuse that he left Bergen and was drowned on the way to Trondheim. In 1217 Sæmundr gave vent to his wrath by exacting fines from Bergen and Greenland merchants. In 1218 the Greenland traders killed Sæmundr's brother Ormr in reprisal. In 1219 Norway appears to have imposed an embargo on shipping to Iceland, and in 1220 Jarl Skúli actually contemplated a naval expedition against Iceland.[3] These events have been seen in the context of the long-standing designs on Iceland by the Norwegian kings, a view that is, as we will see, borne out by the underlying suspicion of Norwegian motives in *Morkinskinna*.[4]

The trade war originated in southern Iceland, but there is evidence of a traditional opposition to foreign intrusion in northern Iceland as well, specifically in Eyjafjörður. A plan by King Haraldr Gormsson to attack Iceland was firmly resisted in a stanza by Eyjólfr Valgerðarson at Mǫðruvellir, and Eyjólfr's son Einarr þveræingr is alleged to have composed a like-minded stanza as well as being credited with a famous speech in *Óláfs saga helga* in opposition to Óláfr Haraldsson's request for the surrender of Grímsey in Eyjafjörður.[5] Political resistance therefore had strong precedents in Eyjafjörður, and this is precisely the area in which *Morkinskinna* seems most likely to have been written.[6] It is consequently understandable if we detect in *Morkinskinna* a deep-seated apprehension about Norwegian foreign policy.

It can be argued that *Morkinskinna* constructs its version of Norwegian history between 1030 and 1130 on two contrastive sets of kings, to whom I will refer as the "foreign adventurer" type and the "builder and lawmaker type."[7] These kings may be paired and contrasted as follows ("foreign adventurers" in the first column, "builders and lawmakers" in the second):

Haraldr harðráði	Magnús góði
Magnús berfœttr	Óláfr kyrri
Sigurðr Jórsalafari	Eysteinn Magnússon

The contrast emerges with special clarity in *Morkinskinna* because the careers of the first and last pairs are contemporary and intertwined. The characters of these kings are therefore constantly set off against each other. In *Heimskringla* some of the comparative effect is lost because the author works more in terms of single biographies and thus disentangles the careers of Haraldr harðráði and Magnús góði. He nonethess retains the two distinct types, which Sverre Bagge refers to as the "warrior hero" and the "peaceful ruler," or the "warrior, strong-willed and aggressive" and the "mild lover of peace."[8]

In *Morkinskinna* there is a clear preference for the kings dedicated to domestic welfare and a corresponding negative view of the foreign adventurers. The bias is so clear that it suggests a condemnation of Norwegian expansionism on the part of an Icelandic writer and a forceful recommendation that Norwegian kings should devote themselves to social progress within Norway. In political terms this outlook might well be construed as a reflection of the tensions between Iceland and Norway in the period 1215–1220. When we turn to *Heimskringla*, however, we find the bias considerably moderated. The author seems to have been at pains to remove the Icelandic perspective on Norwegian affairs and rebalance in some measure the contrast between warrior kings and commonweal kings. I will therefore argue that in the period 1030–1130 *Heimskringla* represents a royalist readjustment by comparison to its immediate source in *Morkinskinna*.

Haraldr harðráði and Magnús góði

The author of *Morkinskinna* takes a decidedly mixed view of Haraldr harðráði, who is described as being valiant and resourceful but also untrustworthy and deceitful.[9] His portrait is further complicated by a series of *Íslendinga þættir*, most of which show off the wit and wisdom of individual Icelanders somewhat to the detriment of King Haraldr. We can only remind ourselves of the gist here, but the general tendentiousness of the *þættir* hardly requires detailed demonstration.[10] The first, "Halldórs þáttr Snorrasonar," is perhaps the most indicative of all. In it the Icelander both confronts and confounds the king, concluding his dealings with the aging monarch with a dismissive "eldisk árgalinn nú" [the old cock is drooping now].[11] The well-known "Auðunar þáttr" is wittier, but also presents an Icelander who is stout enough to stand up to Haraldr and canny enough to subdue him with words and a superior display of tact.[12] In addition, "Auðunar þáttr" formulates a comparison between Haraldr and Sveinn Úlfsson that tends to favor the Danish king. In "Brands þáttr ǫrva" the Icelander manages to give the king a silent lesson in the rules of generosity. In "Þorvarðar þáttr krákunefs" another Icelander takes the king's gruff reception in stride and fares much better with his kinsman Eysteinn orri. "Sneglu-Halla þáttr" is characterized by a series of farcical episodes at the Norwegian court, in which the king plays the autocrat and Halli consistently has the best of it. In "Odds þáttr Ófeigsssonar" the Icelandic trader Oddr outwits an ill-disposed Haraldr with the aid of a Norwegian accomplice.

The focus of these *þættir* is a portrayal of Haraldr harðráði as the moral and intellectual loser in his dealings with Icelandic visitors. That depiction runs exactly counter to the drift of Haraldr's adventures in the Mediterranean and, for the most part, his fortunes in Norway and Denmark. In these latter contexts he emerges regularly as the superior intellect, though hardly a model of scrupulous conduct. It is as if his powers were more than adequate to deal with any race other than the Icelanders, a reading that would no doubt have been as gratifying to the author's countrymen as it would have been objectionable to loyal Norwegians. We can perhaps surmise that the suppression of the *þættir* in *Heimskringla* may have been intended in some part to remove the sting for a Norwegian readership.

Indeed, the author seems to have been intent on limiting the Icelandic presence in general, for example by eliminating a reference to Gizurr Ísleifsson, or the consecration of the Icelandic bishop Magnús Einarsson in Norway, or the mention of Sigurðr slembidjákn's stay with Þorgils Oddason at Saurbœr in Iceland.[13] We can observe that with the disappearance of an intrusive Icelandic presence in *Heimskringla* went the intrusive view of Norwegian kingship that we found in *Morkinskinna*. Icelanders are no longer admitted for political coloring but only for the sake of their stanzas.[14]

At one point the author even seems to offer an explanation for his suppression of the Icelandic *þættir*. He acknowledges that he knows more of King Haraldr than he has written (ÍF 28:118): "En þó er miklu fleira óritat hans frægðarverka. Kømr til þess ófrœði vár ok þat annat, at vér viljum eigi setja á bœkr vitnislausar sǫgur" [But still many of his famous deeds are not written down. The cause of that is our ignorance and, for another thing, that we do not want to record unattested stories]. The phrase "vitnislausar sǫgur" suggests a certain distaste, which could be inspired not only by the problem of attestation but also by the antimonarchism that lies just below the surface in the *þættir*. That impression can only be strengthened when the paragraph continues with a digression on Haraldr's special friendship for Iceland. The author seems to dedicate himself here to a normalization of relations between Iceland and Norway.

That tendency is carried one step further in the following paragraph, in which the author discredits Haraldr's greatest detractor, Halldórr Snorrason. There is no mention of Haraldr's provocations, duly noted in *Morkinskinna*. Instead, the author explains why Halldórr was an impossible presence at the Norwegian court (ÍF 28:120): "Halldórr var maðr fámæltr ok stirðorðr, bermæltr ok stríðlundaðr ok ómjúkr, en þat kom illa þá við konung, er hann hafði gnóga aðra með sér gǫfga menn ok þjónostufulla" [Halldórr was a taciturn man, laconic, direct and antagonistic and unrelenting, and that did not suit the king well since he had plenty of other distinguished and devoted men with him]. Far from being a hero of self-assertiveness, as in *Morkinskinna*, Halldórr simply becomes an unserviceable courtier in the reincarnation of *Heimskringla*.

The point is driven home by contrast in yet a third paragraph, which describes the ideal Icelandic courtier, Úlfr Óspaksson (ÍF 28:120): "Hann var inn vitrasti maðr, snjallr í máli, skǫrungr mikill, tryggr ok einfaldr" [He was a very wise man, ready with words, a very stalwart man, loyal, and straightforward]. When Úlfr stallari dies many pages later, King Haraldr stands over his grave and delivers a handsome eulogy (ÍF 28:175): "Þar liggr sá nú, er dyggvastr var ok dróttinhollastr" [Here lies a man who was most loyal and most faithful to his lord]. The eulogy is taken over from *Morkinskinna*, but not the deliberate juxtaposition of Halldórr Snorrason and Úlfr stallari.[15] That juxtaposition seems quite calculated; an Icelander who is not *þjónostufullr* stands next to another Icelander who is *dróttinhollastr*. Service to the crown was not on the *Morkinskinna* agenda, but it was clearly in the mind of the author of *Heimskringla*, who exposed the flaws of King Haraldr's antagonists and applauded his friends.

Another clue to the author's outlook lies in the use he made of *Hákonar saga Ívarssonar*. As Gustav Storm noted in 1873, this is the only saga in the whole corpus dedicated to a Norwegian chieftain unconnected to a royal house.[16] That in itself raises interesting questions about the genesis of such a text. Why would an Icelandic writer have turned to the career of such a marginal figure? The answer must lie not only in Hákon's heroic dimensions but also in the perception that he was an opposition figure in Norway and thus appealed to the Icelanders in a period of frictions with Norway. This is certainly the way he is portrayed by the author of *Morkinskinna*, who contrasts him to King Haraldr much as he sets up a series of Icelandic opposition figures.

Morkinskinna tells the story of how Hákon parts company with Finnr Árnason, who allies himself with the Danish king Sveinn Úlfsson while Hákon offers his service to King Haraldr in Norway. He then distinguishes himself in the Norwegian victory at the Battle of Niz, but also secretly secures the escape of King Haraldr's antagonist Sveinn Úlfsson. Hákon subsequently visits Haraldr at court, and the king offers him the hand of Magnús góði's daughter Ragnhildr. She hesitates to marry a man of lesser status, but the marriage takes place on the supposition that Haraldr will appoint Hákon as a jarl. Haraldr fails to do so, and Hákon avenges himself by killing a number of the king's men and destroying their property.[17] He then sails off on a viking expedition while Ragnhildr takes asylum in Denmark.

When Hákon reaches Denmark, Sveinn Úlfsson offers him the province of Halland in return for capturing his marauding kinsman Ásmundr Bjarnason. Instead, Hákon delivers Ásmundr's head. Though angered by the death of his kinsman, King Sveinn is as good as his word and grants Hákon his jarldom in Halland, where he settles with his wife Ragnhildr. The story concludes with a pitched battle between King Haraldr and Hákon in Sweden. Haraldr wins the battle, but Hákon boldly recaptures his banner and ambushes some of Haraldr's men, thus forcing the king to concede that their triumphs are equal.

This is the tale of a distinguished man who volunteers his assistance to King Haraldr and renders valuable service. Haraldr rewards him with a marriage, presumably in a bid to retain his service, but fails to observe the terms of the contract and obliges him to transfer his loyalty to his Danish rival Sveinn Úlfsson. Despite some provocation Sveinn is scrupulous in discharging his commitment to Hákon, and this contrasts favorably with King Haraldr. Hákon eventually loses the contest but wins the moral victory. That victory is reminiscent of what we find in the *þættir*, for example "Auðunar þáttr," which also pits Sveinn Úlfsson against Haraldr harðráði in a moral contest.

The story told in *Heimskringla* is quite different. In this version King Haraldr needs Hákon's help in coming to terms with the Þrœndir after the killing of Einarr þambarskelfir and his son Eindriði. It is no longer the king who offers Ragnhildr's hand in marriage, but Hákon who stipulates it. In contrast to *Morkinskinna*, Haraldr declines to grant the jarldom in advance and thus does not allow the marriage to go forward. Hákon then retaliates by taking service with Sveinn Úlfsson, but he kills the king's nephew Ásmundr and is banished. At this point Hákon returns to Norway makes peace with Haraldr, receives his jarldom, and marries Ragnhildr. He later distinguishes himself in the Battle of Niz but secretly helps Sveinn Úlfsson escape.

Apprised of the secret, Haraldr sets out to take revenge, but Hákon is able to escape to Sweden. Here the pitched battle is described as in *Morkinskinna*, but Haraldr's comment about equal triumphs and Hákon's reprisals are omitted.

This latter version of the story is clearly exculpatory with respect to Haraldr harðráði. The king no longer lures Hákon into an agreement that he fails to honor. Hákon makes his own terms, and Haraldr is candid about what he will and will not do. The marriage does not take place under false auspices. At the same time Sveinn Úlfsson is reduced in stature. Rather than rewarding Hákon, he banishes him. Back in Norway the marriage and jarldom are arranged without deception and precede the Battle of Niz, so that Hákon's betrayal in facilitating the escape of Sveinn Úlfsson is more palpable. Finally, Hákon's flamboyant moral victory in Sweden is somewhat curtailed. Perhaps most significant is the omission of the brilliant marriage portrait provided in *Morkinskinna*, in which the anguished tug of war between status considerations and personal affection engages the reader's special sympathy for Hákon and Ragnhildr. These alterations rebalance the scales in favor of King Haraldr just as the suppression of the *þættir* did. *Heimskringla* thus offers a more royalist reading than we can find in *Morkinskinna*. Because the remnants of *Hákonar saga* are so fragmentary, we cannot know how either version compares with the original, but a clear contrast between the biases in *Morkinskinna* and *Heimskringla* seems quite manifest.

It remains to ask whether the author of *Heimskringla* III reduces the contrast between King Haraldr and King Magnús in the same way he readjusts Haraldr's relations with such antagonists as Halldórr Snorrason and Hákon Ívarsson. A palpable difference is that *Morkinskinna* neglects Magnús's early reign and picks up the story only after Haraldr's return to Norway (ca. 1046). From the outset the focus in *Morkinskinna* is on Magnús's moral rather than his political stature. His clash with Haraldr over the royal mooring is calculated to demonstrate hereditary firmness of character. His visit with his steward Þorkell dyðrill illustrates how he insists on but also acknowledges faithful service. There follows an episode in which he rewards good advice given him before the Battle of Hlýrskógsheiðr, and another in which he rewards a certain Ormr with a jarldom even though Ormr spared the life of his enemy. That act draws the author's explicit approval because it shows that Magnús judges the quality of the man to be more important than a personal difference.[18]

The story line then turns once more to the direct relations between the coregents Magnús and Haraldr. In one encounter Magnús is able to help a relative of Kálfr Árnason's to escape Haraldr's clutches. In a second Haraldr proves to be grasping in his collection of taxes and provokes the opposition of Einarr þambarskelfir. At the Eyrarþing an old man rises to enunciate the view that the greater allegiance is owed to King Magnús.[19] In yet a third encounter Haraldr composes some offensive stanzas at the expense of Magnús's taciturn brother Þórir. Magnús retaliates by instructing Þórir to recite an even deadlier reply. All three passages suggest that Magnús is capable of defending his turf against his more aggressive uncle. The interaction culminates in a visit by Arnórr jarlaskáld, who recites poems in honor of both kings, but Haraldr comments that his *drápa* is ephemeral, while Magnús's will be recited "as long as the northern lands are peopled."[20]

Two other episodes are less obviously tendentious. In the first both Haraldr and Magnús try their hand at healing a boy who has lost the capacity to dream, but it is finally Haraldr who succeeds. In the second Saint Óláfr signals to Magnús that he should refrain from sleeping with a certain Margréta. That may of course suggest that Magnús is to be seen as Óláfr 's special charge and true heir, but the comparison of kings becomes even more explicit in the only *þáttr* attached specifically to Magnús, "Hreiðars þáttr heimska." The gist of the story is again that Magnús is able to defend his interests; in this case he takes the part of a man commended to his keeping against Haraldr.

All of the incidents thus far are designed to establish Magnús as a model of probity and competence, and to shed a correspondingly unfavorable light on Haraldr. No space is devoted to what might be considered Magnús's political career. Only at the very end of his saga does he go off to harry in Denmark with his uncle, but even this episode serves to illustrate his wisdom and farsightedness. Foreseeing his own death, Magnús contrives to have his mother free the Danish captive Þorgils, a kinsman of Sveinn Úlfsson's, so that she will be welcome to take refuge in Denmark when she is no longer under Magnús's protection. A final comparison between Magnús and Haraldr is attributed to Sveinn Úlfsson, who caracoles on horseback before the Norwegian host and comments that there is a significant difference between his Norwegian opponents—he himself was guilty of betraying Magnús, whereas Haraldr betrayed him. Sveinn thus adds his voice to the poetic voice of Arnórr jarlaskáld, whose panegyrics seem to imply a preference for Magnús, and to the legal voice of the old man at Eyrarþing. The comparisons are plentiful and invidious, and they clearly resonate in favor of Magnús. The political difference is summed up by Magnús himself on his deathbed: "It may be that some people will think that my kinsman King Haraldr's counsels are colder and darker than my own."[21]

Whereas the author of *Morkinskinna* is interested almost exclusively in Magnús the moral man, the author of *Heimskringla* is interested primarily in Magnús the political man. In this latter capacity Magnús is far from unblemished. He is moved to take reprisals against those who fought against his father at Stiklarstaðir, and he must be recalled to a more scrupulous observance of Hákon góði's laws, especially by Sigvatr's "Bersǫglisvísur." In the foreign arena Magnús pursues his goals aggressively. He secures the Danish succession, then loses it to Sveinn Úlfsson and regains it in three successive victories, though only after destroying the fortress of the Jomsvikings and subduing the Wends with the aid of Saint Óláfr. Finally he extends his ambition to England, but wisely refrains from pressing his good fortune.

In these chapters Magnús appears as a daring but prudent military leader, an image not hinted at in *Morkinskinna*. On the other hand, the author of *Heimskringla* III drops the morally paradigmatic incidents of *Morkinskinna* almost without exception. Of the implied comparisons between Haraldr and Magnús there remains only the contested mooring site. But, as in the case of Haraldr, this writer gives us to understand that he knows more than he writes. He knows that there were more disagreements, though he tries to dismiss them as the work of malicious men: "There were soon differences in the understanding of the kings, and there were many who were of sufficient ill will that there was dissension between them." And again: "In the face of such differences word soon spread among foolish men to the effect that there was disagreement between the kings. There were a number of issues causing the kings to have their own opinions, even if not much is written about it here."[22] It is as if the author does not want to hear of the dissension between the kings; he certainly does not want to use Magnús to cast a shadow on Haraldr.

To be sure, Magnús emerges as an extraordinarily popular king, but the invidious comparisons with Haraldr that operate so clearly in *Morkinskinna* are completely abandoned.[23] The judgments of Arnórr jarlaskáld, the old man at the Eyrarþing, and Sveinn Úlfsson on the battlefield are not repeated. On the contrary, *Heimskringla* shows every indication that Haraldr and Magnús cooperated in reasonable amity. That tendency emerges in such small matters as a revised treatment of the attempt on Sveinn Úlfsson's part to win Haraldr over for an alliance against Magnús. Haraldr's response in *Morkinskinna* is simply noncommittal, but in *Heimskringla* he responds angrily to the idea of betraying his kinsman (ÍF 28:96). It might even appear that the author of *Heimskringla* works against the idea of an implied contrast by comparing King Haraldr at the end of his saga not with Magnús but rather with Saint Óláfr. The comparison, though attributed to Halldórr Snorrason, is surely intended to favor Haraldr's memory. By further implication it counteracts the view promoted in *Morkinskinna* that Magnús is under Saint Óláfr's special protection.

In sum, *Morkinskinna* creates a sharp contrast between Magnús and Haraldr. Magnús is portrayed as in every way exemplary, much beloved by the people and almost saintly in his final days. Haraldr, on the other hand, is autocratic, ambitious, and unreliable. In *Heimskringla* there is a distinct effort to reduce the gap by retouching both portraits. Magnús is still popular but by no means saintly. He makes political mistakes at the beginning of his career, and though he has no adventures to match Haraldr's Varangian romance, he is much involved in military expeditions in the Baltic and Denmark. It is only at the end of his career that he sees the wisdom of withdrawing from foreign entanglements. Haraldr, on the other hand, is much softened. His dealings with Magnús are troubled to be sure, but they remain within the bounds dictated by kinship and treaty obligations. His penchant for trickery, especially in dealing with Halldórr Snorrason and Hákon Ívarsson, is greatly moderated, and reemerges only after Magnús's death in his machinations against Einarr þambarskelfir and Kálfr Árnason. The author of *Heimskringla* III goes a long way toward neutralizing the morality tale inherited from *Morkinskinna*.

Óláfr kyrri and Magnús berfœttr

The sagas of Magnús and Haraldr occupy half or more of the extant *Morkinskinna*, 120 of 237 pages in Unger's edition, including the supplements from *Flateyjarbók*, 285 of 462 pages in Finnur Jónsson's edition, and 325 of the 664 pages in the new ÍF edition by Ármann Jakobsson and Þórður Ingi Guðjónsson. By contrast the story of Óláfr kyrri is notoriously brief, seven pages in Unger's edition, eleven in Finnur Jónsson's edition, fourteen in the ÍF edition, and only seven in Bjarni Aðalbjarnarson's *Heimskringla*. We would hardly expect to find many clues to a political reading of so short a text, but there are nonetheless at least two instances of tendentiousness. *Morkinskinna* includes a very enthusiastic review of Óláfr explicitly at the expense of Haraldr harðráði. It reads in part: "King Óláfr was lenient in many matters that his father King Haraldr had promoted and maintained aggressively."[24]

This authorial comment is followed up by a speech in which Óláfr specifies the difference between his reign and Haraldr's: "I will be joyful now that I see both happiness and liberty in my people. . . . But in the days of my father these people were subject to great intimidation and fear, and most people hid their gold and precious objects, but now I see you wearing what is yours brightly. And your freedom is my joy."[25]

The comparison is not quite so glowing in *Heimskringla*. Here Óláfr is asked to explain why he has a larger retinue than the law prescribes when he makes his rounds in Norway, and he must reply a little defensively: "I cannot govern the realm better than my father, nor do I inspire more fear though I have twice as large a retinue as he had, but it does not represent any threat to you nor does it mean that I wish to oppress you."[26] In other words, the author of *Morkinskinna* continues to use Haraldr harðráði as the negative pole of royal authority, while the author of *Heimskringla* III depolarizes the two kings. He even converts Óláfr's words from the invidious original into an expression of modesty. Óláfr merely suggests that despite the increased size of his retinue he is neither as powerful nor as intimidating as his father.

The passages in *Morkinskinna* align the peaceable Óláfr against an aggressive Haraldr and keep the contrastive strategy in place. On the peaceful side of the balance Óláfr is in the company of Magnús góði. It was one of Magnús's characteristics that he put domestic security ahead of foreign conquest, with the result that he refrained from intervening in England and eventually judged it best to leave Denmark to Sveinn Úlfsson. Óláfr inherits his restraint. When he is urged by King Knútr of Denmark to join an expedition against England, he declines, citing the fate of his far more accomplished father at Stamford Bridge. He is therefore content to give Knútr sixty ships for his enterprise while he remains behind in Norway. Óláfr is thus, according to *Morkinskinna*, the polar opposite of Haraldr and the natural heir of Magnús, but the author of *Heimskringla* moderates the contrast to Haraldr and eliminates altogether Óláfr's refusal, in emulation of Magnús góði, to join the attack on England, despite the fact that these subtractions leave him with a mini-saga of no more than seven pages. In *Morkinskinna* Óláfr has paradigmatic value, in *Heimskringla* very little.

Magnús berfœttr clearly reverts to the behavioral model established by Haraldr harðráði, though again more overtly in *Morkinskinna* than in *Heimskringla*. Magnús's autocratic streak is illuminated by *Morkinskinna*'s account of his dealings with the east Norwegian chieftain Sveinki Steinarsson, who fails to submit. Magnús dispatches his officials to recall the chieftain to his duty, but they are treated first to ironical riddles and finally to an obscene dismissal.[27] Magnús follows up in person, but is headed off by the regional chieftains, who conduct exquisitely delicate negotiations leading to a minimal three-year exile for Sveinki. As it turns out, Magnús is obliged to recall him even before that term is up in order to contain the depredations of robbers and bandits. The whole episode is clearly seen as a credit to Sveinki and a humiliation for Magnús. Particularly telling is the need for Sveinki to deal with local banditry, traditionally a preeminent duty of kings. The whole episode is dropped in *Heimskringla*, perhaps to spare Magnús the embarrassment. According to this version Magnús alone suppresses the robbers and vikings. That leads to a direct comparison with his father Óláfr and his grandfather Haraldr: "He was a stalwart, warriorlike, and persistent man, in all respects more like his grandfather in disposition than like his father."[28] This comparison is not found in *Morkinskinna*, where it would clearly have had a negative valence.

In *Heimskringla* it is placed in the context of Magnús's achievements and has no negative connotations.

Although Magnús is not compared to Haraldr harðráði at this juncture in *Morkinskinna*, such a comparison is made later during his expedition to Ireland. Here Magnús harangues his men, urging the expedition "for the greater glory of Norway" and for the sake of plentiful booty.[29] But his men are not so certain, and their spokesman replies:[30]

> Lord, everyone is ready to strive for your honor, but we are doubtful about what can be done to achieve honor in this country. The country is populous and the people treacherous, and we harbor doubts about how well we can guard against it. It fell to the lot of your kinsman King Haraldr that initially everything was surrendered to him in England wherever he went. But at the end he himself died. It would seem far better to all your friends if you had stayed peacefully in your realm considering how well off you are.

Magnús is naturally not inclined to accept such advice and dies abroad in circumstances not unlike those that brought about the downfall of Haraldr harðráði. The advice pinpoints the issue of foolhardy foreign adventurism and prudent domestic policy once again. Significantly the author of *Heimskringla* eliminates the exchange of speeches and thus continues to blur the distinction between risky and safe foreign policy. His concluding summation on Magnús formulates a temporizing balance between Magnús's successes at home and his risk-taking abroad. Magnús is fully cognizant of the risks and relativizes them with the maxim "Til frægðar skal konung hafa, en ekki til langlífis" [A king is for the purpose of fame, not longevity].[31] The author of *Morkinskinna* took no such balanced view of Magnús's reign.

Sigurðr Jórsalafari and Eysteinn Magnússon

Turning to Magnús's sons, we find that *Morkinskinna* carries through the same contrastive pattern in the most explicit terms yet. Sigurðr Jórsalafari, like Haraldr harðráði before him, is famed for his adventures in the Mediterranean and Constantinople, while Eysteinn, even more obviously than Magnús góði, is a peaceful and constructive stay-at-home. The two kings ultimately work out the contrast in the words of their famous flyting. Their confrontation is by no means neutral because the author makes it abundantly clear that Sigurðr is a flawed personality. At the height of his trajectory in Constantinople a sage prophesies that his honor will be shaped like the lion, massive in the forequarters but tapering off further on.[32] That inauspicious prophecy is later confirmed by Eysteinn, who predicts that his brother will succumb to "some dire calamity."[33]

The calamity in question is a madness that haunts Sigurðr at unpredictable intervals through the last chapters of his saga. In the first episode he casts his most valuable book into the fire and slaps his queen. In another episode he almost drowns a certain Jón for no apparent reason. In yet a third he is barely restrained from a wanton consumption of meat on a Friday, and in a fourth he craves meat and a woman on Christmas. Finally, at an advanced age, he abandons his wife and takes a new one, who in turn abandons him before he dies. Several of these episodes turn into tests of retainers with enough courage to oppose his irrational behavior. There is no doubt in *Morkinskinna* that Sigurðr ends his days as a capricious madman.

The author of *Heimskringla*, on the other hand, curtails his symptoms drastically. In the first place, he eliminates the invidious prophecies voiced by the sage in Constantinople and by Eysteinn, but he also reduces the suggestion of madness. In the cameo chapter 22 he merely notes that Sigurðr was subject to uncontrollable fits of mirth, though in chapter 28 he does retain the episode in which Sigurðr nearly drowns a man (here an anonymous Icelander). All the other indications of madness disappear. Particularly telling is the deletion of the moments that run counter to Church prohibitions (fasting rules and divorce) in an apparent attempt to make Sigurðr a better Christian. That tendency is perhaps borne out by a new chapter (24) in which Sigurðr is credited with a crusade to Sweden.

The author of *Heimskringla* succeeds in closing the gap between Sigurðr and Eysteinn to such an extent that Sverre Bagge judged his kingship ideal to be a composite of both types.[34] I believe that there is enough residue from the bias in *Morkinskinna* to vindicate a preference for Eysteinn, but the contrast between the two kings is toned down greatly. This is surely a conscious operation because the author seems to be cognizant of the divergence in *Morkinskinna*. His comparison of Magnús berfœttr with Haraldr harðráði shows that he recognized this aspect of the continuity in *Morkinskinna*, but *Morkinskinna* also aligned Eysteinn with Magnús góði.[35] *Heimskringla* retains that comparison, but the parallelisms are otherwise so blurred that the overall contrast of types is no longer so obvious.

In *Morkinskinna* the contrast culminated in the flyting between Sigurðr and Eysteinn, which subsumes the two personality strains dating back to Magnús góði and Haraldr harðráði. In an interesting speculation on the appearance of Snorri Sturluson, who is more often than not assumed to be the author of *Heimskringla*, Helgi Þorláksson studied the flyting on the supposition that Snorri's changes in *Heimskringla* hint that he is recasting Eysteinn in his own image. In the course of his discussion Helgi arrives at the same general conclusions reached here, namely that Snorri favors Eysteinn and that he minimizes the opposition between the two brothers.[36] I do not propose another detailed analysis of the flyting, but I believe that there are several indications that the author of *Heimskringla* moderates the contrasts. Eysteinn is the manifest winner in *Morkinskinna*, and perhaps in *Heimskringla* as well, but in the latter the author makes a number of changes in order to balance the score.

On the evening in question *Morkinskinna* notes that Sigurðr is taciturn, a mood which, in the context of this saga, could be construed as a sign of his approaching madness. In *Heimskringla* the onus is removed by the statement that everyone, not just Sigurðr, was taciturn. In *Morkinskinna* the host of the feast appeals to Eysteinn because Sigurðr and his men are given to arrogant behavior. *Heimskringla* drops that charge. In *Morkinskinna* Eysteinn shows signs of being irritated by his brother's responses, so that he appears to be more challenging. In *Heimskringla* he merely tries to lighten the atmosphere in the hope of making the situation less charged and antagonistic. Finally, the author of *Heimskringla* reduces Eysteinn's concluding speech by about two thirds, from thirty-three lines in Unger's edition, forty-four lines in Finnur Jónsson's edition, or thirty-six lines in ÍF 24 to a mere nine lines in *Heimskringla*.[37] The effect in *Morkinskinna* is that Eysteinn delivers an overwhelming and crushing final statement that makes his case incontrovertible. In *Heimskringla* the debate spends itself in a more stichomythic and inconclusive exchange, in which the winner is not quite so predetermined.

A comparison such as the one presented here is contingent on the accuracy of the transmitted texts. In the case of *Heimskringla* we probably have something approximating the original text, though not in every detail.[38] In the case of *Morkinskinna* the latitude for doubt is considerable, and there are strong suspicions that the extant text is an interpolated version of the original, although the extent of the interpolations cannot be ascertained. Thus each individual comparison offered above is subject to doubt. On the other hand, the overall tendency is so consistent that the total comparison can hardly be disqualified on the basis of individual questions. It seems apparent that *Morkinskinna* gives a politicized version of the period 1030–1130, in which a set of peaceful monarchs dedicated to sound domestic policy is opposed to a set of warrior kings of more questionable character who engage themselves rashly in foreign exploits. It seems equally clear that in *Heimskringla* the author set about neutralizing the opposition between the peaceable kings and the foreign adventurers. We may suspect further that the politicized version in *Morkinskinna* is inspired by an Icelandic distrust of Norwegian foreign policy, and that the adjustments in *Heimskringla* may reflect a desire to remove the signs of Icelandic distrust in order to promote better relations with the mother country. To test that hypothesis we will look at a contemporary book that is specifically about Icelandic-Norwegian relations and may offer further hints about prevalent attitudes at the time.

The Politics of *Egils saga*

In 1985 Melissa Berman published a paper in which she classed *Jómsvíkinga saga*, *Orkneyinga saga*, and *Færeyinga saga* as "political sagas" because they center on the political dealings of provincial chieftains with the kings of Norway and Denmark.[39] At the conclusion of her paper she notes that they share their political features with *Egils saga*, in which the Mýramenn of Iceland clash with a series of Norwegian monarchs over a period of some seventy-five years. She points out that *Jómsvíkinga saga* is distinctly anti-royalist and that *Orkneyinga saga* is royalist, while *Færeyinga saga* mediates between these two extremes. Berman judges that *Egils saga* is closest to the mediating position.

There is no doubt that the tension between provincial chieftains, broadly construed to include Icelanders, and the Norwegian crown is thematic in *Egils saga*. The saga begins with the story of Haraldr hárfagri's suppression of the petty kings of Norway, a story told with obvious sympathy for the cause of the losers. Haraldr's policy is referred to (ÍF 2:8 and 12) as "enslavement" (*áþján*), and his crushing of the resistance is ruthless. It leads to extensive emigration and the settling of Iceland, which may thus be regarded as a product of royal aggression. The question posed in the early chapters is how local chieftains will respond to the new threat, and the more honorable alternative appears to be resistance. Sǫlvi klofi is politically clear-sighted, chooses to resist, is forced into exile, but continues to assail the king from abroad. Kveld-Úlfr is similarly perspicuous and has no difficulty in resisting King Haraldr's blandishments. When his son Þórólfr is swayed by the prospect of royal service, Kveld-Úlfr foresees the dire consequences for the family (ÍF 2:15).

Þórólfr's experience with Haraldr bears out his father's worst fears. Despite a predilection for high living, Þórólfr is a model retainer and serves the king faithfully. When he is slandered by his enemies, he cannot believe that the king will credit such malice (ÍF 2:37), but his confidence is misplaced, with the result that he is removed from his lucrative position and kept at court under the king's watchful eye. It is of course a major criticism of the king that he is unable to distinguish between faithful service and palpable malice. Kveld-Úlfr can only repeat his dire predictions and advise his son to take service with the English, Danish, or Swedish king, a recommendation that does not speak well for their Norwegian brother. Haraldr's wrongful suspicion goes so far that he has one of Þórólfr's ships seized, thus provoking retaliation and open hostility. Kveld-Úlfr harks back to his refrain, reminding Þórólfr once again of his advice that service with the king would bring him and his family no luck. Þórólfr remains principled to the end, and in the final confrontation he refuses to accept a forced settlement. He falls in a gallant last assault three feet from the king (ÍF 2:54).

The question of whether it is advisable to serve the king is now raised again, this time with reference to Kveld-Úlfr's other son Skalla-Grímr. Skalla-Grímr declines point-blank, noting that he is unlikely to have more luck than his more distinguished brother. Kveld-Úlfr approves and they take revenge for Þórólfr's death by killing the two royal agents who had seized his ship. The break between Kveld-Úlfr's family and King Haraldr is thus complete, and the author concludes this section of the saga by stating that after Kveld-Úlfr's emigration the king not only seizes all their property but nurses a special hatred against the whole clan and continues to retaliate. This intransigence is reminiscent of his earlier ruthlessness against the petty kings.

The tone and tenor of this story are clearly weighted in favor of Kveld-Úlfr's family. He and Skalla-Grímr form an intelligent and effective opposition to an expansionist king. The idyllic description of their newly settled home in Iceland (ÍF 2:77) is calculated not only as a favorable contrast to a Norway that has passed under the king's iron grip but also as a just reward for their political acumen. Þórólfr, for all his brilliance, does not share their wisdom and dies at the hands of a king who is morally blind. There can be no doubt that Kveld-Úlfr and his kin group hold the high ground in this confrontation.

The second stage in the conflict between the Mýramenn and the Norwegian monarchy is not only more drawn out but also more complex and difficult to interpret. It pits Skalla-Grímr's sons Þórólfr and Egill against King Haraldr's son Eiríkr blóðøx. Þórólfr courts the favor of Prince Eiríkr with some success, but King Haraldr, now advanced in years, warns his son that the Mýramenn are very arrogant and that Eiríkr will live to regret his new friendship (ÍF 2:93). Eiríkr persists nonetheless and sends an ax to Iceland as a gift for Skalla-Grímr, who receives it in meditative silence. When Þórólfr prepares to set sail once more, his father warns that he is not likely to return and sends the ax back with a dismissive stanza. Þórólfr conceals the hostile gesture by throwing the ax overboard and giving Eiríkr a sail, ostensibly as a reciprocal gift from Skalla-Grímr. This system of silence speaks louder than words about the deep rift between the two families.

As it turns out, Þórólfr does not fall victim to the feud, but succumbs in battle in the service of King Æthelstan of England. It is left to his younger brother Egill to take up the family cudgel. Egill responds to a magic attempt on his life by killing Eiríkr's steward Bárðr in a scene of drunken confusion (ÍF 2:106–11). Þórir Hróaldsson notes Egill's hereditary propensity to underestimate the king's wrath, and Eiríkr bursts out in a belated recognition of the truth in his father's words and the realization that the Mýramenn are not to be trusted. His wife Gunnhildr later specifies the threat by predicting that Skalla-Grímr's progeny will ultimately kill some of his close kin (ÍF 2:123).

It is at this juncture that the lead passes into the hands of Gunnhildr, who becomes the most implacable enemy of the Mýramenn. She instructs her brothers Eyvindr skreyja and Álfr askmaðr to waylay one or both of Skalla-Grímr's sons, but they succeed only in killing two of Þórólfr's men. In retaliation Egill seizes Eyvindr's ships, though Eyvindr himself is able to escape. At this point there is no hope of reconciliation. King Æthelstan suggests that it would be best for Egill to stay in England, and Arinbjǫrn warns him not to settle in Norway as long as Gunnhildr holds sway.

Prudence is not part of Egill's nature, and he exacerbates the quarrel by going to law with a certain Berg-Ǫnundr in order to recover an inheritance to which he feels entitled. Unabashed, he appeals to King Eiríkr to give him the benefit of the law, and surprisingly Eiríkr does so (ÍF 2:152). Egill cites the case to the Gulaþing, where Berg-Ǫnundr feels confident in the protection of king and queen, and where Gunnhildr in fact breaks up the court when it seems about to find in favor of Egill. With the peaceful remedies exhausted, Egill challenges Berg-Ǫnundr to a duel but is overborne by Eiríkr. Egill then departs with a thunderous denunciation of the legal breaches. Eiríkr is determined to kill him at the first opportunity, but Egill turns the tables and kills one of the king's men before escaping. The king must be content to outlaw Egill in the whole length of Norway.

That seems only to inspire Egill to greater outrages. He kills Berg-Ǫnundr in an ingeniously designed nocturnal ambush, then kills the king's foster son Fróði to boot. These killings are followed up by twelve more, which include the king's own son Rǫgnvaldr, and Egill concludes his campaign by planting a scorn pole to spite and curse Eiríkr and Gunnhildr. Ostensibly as a result they lose their foothold in Norway and go to York, where Gunnhildr exercises her magic in order to lure Egill from Iceland. He is now at the mercy of his archenemies, who, though it taxes the reader's credulity, allow him to return to Iceland.

The story of Egill and Eiríkr is balanced on a sword's edge. It is no longer possible to conclude simply that the Norwegian king has wronged an Icelander. At several junctures Eiríkr seems almost implausibly patient. At others Egill seems wantonly overreactive and litigious. There is always some reason for his action, but often no necessity. He does not *need* to kill the steward Bárðr. He does not *need* to prosecute Berg-Ǫnundr in the teeth of such obvious, and not unjustified, royal disfavor. He certainly does not need to kill the king's foster son and plant a scorn pole. At some point Egill simply goes too far and vindicates the royal opinion that his family is congenitally dangerous and not to be trusted.

On the other hand, Eiríkr is remarkably restrained in allowing Egill access to the courts, and spectacularly so in letting Egill out of his clutches in York. There are also signs of a conscious authorial strategy to shift royal aggressiveness from Eiríkr to his notorious wife Gunnhildr. To be sure, Haraldr hárfagri was also subjected to malicious advice in his dealing with Þórólfr Kveldúlfsson, but the reader feels that he should have penetrated the deception easily. In Eiríkr's case there appears to be no malice but rather a genuine instinct for leniency.

How, then, are we to understand the clash between Egill and Eiríkr? Who bears the primary responsibility? Surely it is Egill. We are left with the impression that a more moderate and circumspect Egill could have gotten most of what he wanted. It is only his uncompromising and unreflective nature that stands in the way of his wishes. But how does that recognition accord with the anti-royal rhetoric aimed at Haraldr hárfagri earlier in the saga? Is the author moderating his view of the Norwegian crown as he progresses, or is he illustrating the idea from *Morkinskinna* that some kings are good and others bad? Or is he perhaps serving notice that the circumstances of the original alienation of the nobles in the days of Haraldr hárfagri are not duplicated in every generation, and that the aggression can sometimes be laid at the doorstep of the provincials?

Perhaps we must conclude that the saga does no more than state that there has been (or once was) a long-standing feud between the Mýramenn and the house of Haraldr hárfagri. Perhaps the thrust is purely historical, and not political in the sense that it suggests an ongoing disaffection between Icelanders (represented by one clan) and the Norwegian throne (represented by Haraldr and his sons). The idea that history is variable and that circumstances change may be supported by Egill's experience with King Hákon Aðalsteinsfóstri. Egill brings his inheritance case before Hákon, who, though mindful of the injury done his kin, allows him access to the law, just as Eiríkr had done. Not content with that, Egill presses for another inheritance, which King Hákon has already seized. Arinbjǫrn once more intercedes for his friend, but Hákon's patience is exhausted and nothing comes of his efforts. Once more Egill seems to have pressed his claims beyond reason.

Egill's final contact with the Norwegian king comes about indirectly. Hákon decides to send a certain Þorsteinn Eiríksson to Värmland on a perilous mission to collect overdue taxes. Egill assumes the task on his behalf and carries it out with legendary prowess. Hákon is reconciled with Þorsteinn, and Egill returns to Iceland. The author makes the significant comment that there is no mention of further duels or slayings after Egill settled down in Iceland (ÍF 2:257). It is as if trouble is confined to the Norwegian scene and vanishes in a more orderly and less autocratic Icelandic environment.

There is, however, one final indication that autocracy is not restricted to Norway. In advanced old age Egill reappears one more time in all his chieftainly authority to settle a quarrel between his son Þorsteinn and a certain Steinarr Ǫnundarson. He settles it dictatorially, invoking historical privilege on the basis that all the land in the district was distributed in the form of gifts from his father Skalla-Grímr. In other words, the Mýramenn retain a kind of moral title to the land and the right to retract what they once bestowed. This is a final, highly questionable, example of Egill's propensity to give himself every possible benefit of the law in support of his own claims. His claim is comparable to the earlier ones in Norway, to the extent that both are historical in nature. Egill severs his ties with Norway but is not deterred from pursuing his interests there. He will forego no right because his rights are grounded in history. The Mýramenn are a historical entity, coeval with the centralized monarchy in Norway and therefore coentitled. In historical terms at least, the conflict between the Mýramenn and the Norwegian crown is a confrontation of equals.

It is difficult to determine which side the author favors in this conflict. Haraldr hárfagri is, at the very least, flawed in his judgment, but Eiríkr and Hákon are by no means portrayed negatively. It is therefore not possible to align *Egils saga* with *Jómsvíkinga saga* as anti-royalist, or with *Orkneyinga saga* as royalist. It must be sufficient to say that *Egils saga*, along with the other "political sagas," deals with the issue of relations between kings and provincial chieftains.

Conclusion

How does the thrust of *Egils saga* conform to the tone of the kings' sagas in the period 1220–1230? *Morkinskinna* distinguished dramatically between kings in pursuit of foreign glory (Haraldr harðráði, Magnús berfœttr, and Sigurðr Jórsalafari) and those devoted to domestic prosperity (Magnús góði, Óláfr kyrri, and Eysteinn Magnússon). At the same time the prototype of the foreign adventurer type, Haraldr harðráði, is burdened with a series of episodes in which he does not quite measure up to individual Icelanders. The Icelandic bias in *Morkinskinna* thus seems quite palpable. It patronizes with political advice and invidious comparisons. It suggests that good kings attend to the welfare of their countrymen and that bad kings covet foreign lands.

That message does not coincide with *Egils saga*, in which the Norwegian kings are not embroiled in foreign adventures. On the other hand, Haraldr hárfagri is critically portrayed, and Eiríkr is embarrassed by Egill to an even greater degree than Haraldr harðráði is embarrassed by his Icelandic visitors. The collision between royal authority and Icelandic assertiveness is about equally pronounced in both texts. *Heimskringla*, as we have seen, takes a different view of the Norwegian monarchy. Haraldr hárfagri is toned down in comparison with *Egils saga* and is no longer quite so inexorable in his campaign against the petty kings.[40] In those portions of *Heimskringla* dependent on *Morkinskinna* there is also a programmatic moderation of the aggressive qualities proper to the foreign adventurer type in *Morkinskinna*, as well as an elimination of the subversive *þættir* that were so calculatedly compromising for Haraldr harðráði in the earlier work. The practical question that confronts us here is whether *Egils saga* is more nearly associated with the stage of Icelandic literature represented by *Morkinskinna* around 1220 or with the stage that evolved a decade later in *Heimskringla*.[41]

Although the political sensibility in *Egils saga* by no means matches the contrastive paradigm in *Morkinskinna*, it nonetheless betrays the same preoccupation with heavily charged relations between Norwegian kings and notable Icelanders. The author of *Egils saga* has the same general perspective as the author of *Morkinskinna*, one that subsumes Norway and Iceland and is focused on the interaction between the two. *Heimskringla* simplifies that perspective and no longer implicates

Iceland in Norwegian affairs. It therefore seems more likely that *Egils saga* belongs to the earlier literary stage around 1220 rather than the later one around 1230.

This chronology remains no more than a plausibility among others. There is no reason why two somewhat contradictory books like *Egils saga* and *Heimskringla* could not have been written at the same time around 1230, even if they were written by the same author (for example, Snorri). One could have been written primarily for an Icelandic readership, the other primarily for a Norwegian readership. Nor is it impossible that the author could have abandoned the political neutrality of *Heimskringla* in order to write a more problematical book on the Icelandic experience of Norway some years later, perhaps as late as 1240. But the best guess might be that *Egils saga* was written in the heat generated by the Icelandic-Norwegian trade war of 1215–1220 and that it embodies a new sense of Icelandic identity and assertiveness engendered by recent history.

CHAPTER 6

Domestic Politics in Northern Iceland

The first biographies of Óláfr Tryggvason and Óláfr Haraldsson, both presumably written in Iceland, are largely celebratory and suggest some element of Norwegian patronage. It is only later, and a little tentatively, that a critical voice begins to be heard in the *Óláfs saga helga* incorporated into *Heimskringla*. For the most part *Heimskringla* seems to adhere to a certain diplomatic reticence in dealing with the Norwegian kings, and *Egils saga* shows considerable ambiguity. That the Icelanders had partisan views on royal policy in Norway is explicit only in *Morkinskinna*. But when the Icelanders began to write about their own history, they may have felt less constrained by diplomatic considerations and more inclined to express themselves openly about regional and family issues in Iceland. There are indications of this openness at the end of *Egils saga* and we will encounter an even more overt clash of interests in the present chapter. But before turning to our specific texts, we must say something in general about the emergence of saga literature in northern Iceland.

The Background

One of the key passages on saga writing is found in *Íslendinga saga* and recounts how, after a period of family hostilities, relations between Snorri Sturluson and his nephew Sturla Sighvatsson improved to the point that in 1230 Sturla spent considerable time with his uncle at Reykholt and was very assiduous in having the "saga books" compiled by Snorri copied down.[1] It is inviting to suppose that these "saga books" refer to Snorri's composition of *Heimskringla*, if he is the author. They could also include *Egils saga* if that text is early and if it too was written by Snorri, as so often hypothesized. The passage is usually evaluated in terms of Snorri's literary activity, but I propose to examine it with respect to his nephew Sturla's literary interests.

Sturla's copying of his uncle's books has sometimes been understood to suggest a transmission of saga writing from the west to Eyjafjörður in the north, where Sturla spent some early years.[2] Although Sturla was in western Iceland during his childhood, he did not necessarily acquire his literary tastes in the west. He was born in 1199 at Hjarðarholt and was fostered by Þorlákr Ketilsson to the south of Hjarðarholt at Hítardalr until 1214.[3]

He rejoined his father at the age of fifteen and presumably went with his family to Grund in Eyjafjörður in 1215.[4] We know in any event that he visited Miklagarðr just south of Grund in 1217.[5] Finally, we know that he had taken up residence at Sauðafell in the west in the spring of 1221 when he was twenty-two years of age.[6] The years from 1215 to 1220 at Grund must therefore have been the formative ones in Sturla's literary development. That period may also have been the crucial one for the development of saga writing in Eyjafjörður.

The most important manifestation of early literary activity in Eyjafjörður may be the first great compilation of kings' sagas in *Morkinskinna*. I have tried elsewhere to buttress the arguments advanced by Eivind Kválen in support of the view that *Morkinskinna* was composed in Eyjafjörður around 1220.[7] If those arguments hold, it is clear that saga writing in the north was not a secondary activity modeled on saga writing in Reykholt. On the contrary, when (and if) Snorri composed the third part of *Heimskringla*, he modeled it on *Morkinskinna* and may thus have been indebted to an initial impulse from Eyjafjörður. Sturla's interest in copying his uncle's books would therefore not have been an exercise in acquiring a new literary culture but merely an updating of his own literary culture.

Morkinskinna is not the only text that suggests saga writing in Eyjafjörður. *Víga-Glúms saga*, *Reykdœla saga*, and *Ljósvetninga saga* appear to belong to the same literary milieu and may well belong to the same period. The prominent Eyjafjörður chieftain Þorvarðr Þorgeirsson, who died in 1207, is mentioned in both *Reykdœla saga* and *Ljósvetninga saga*. Þorvarðr's father, Þorgeirr Hallason, was at Hvassafell in Eyjafjörður as early as the 1150s, and his brother Þórðr was a monk at the local monastery at Munkaþverá.[8] Þorgeirr Hallason retired to the monastery in 1168 and presumably died there in 1171.[9] It therefore appears that the association of Þorvarðr's family with the monastery goes back to the time of the first literary activity at Munkaþverá, the composition of Abbot Nikulás Bergsson's *Leiðarvísir* in the 1150s.

These circumstances do not necessarily suggest that Þorvarðr had literary interests, but there is a curious passage in *Prestssaga Guðmundar Arasonar* in which Þorvarðr, in his chieftainly and avuncular capacity, tries to browbeat Guðmundr Arason into accepting the episcopal rank.[10] Guðmundr replies with some pique that he has never received any favors from Þorvarðr other than being "beaten to the books," that is, presumably, being forced to acquire a clerical education whether he liked it or not. Þorvarðr's insistence on ecclesiastical training could betoken his own interest in the world of books, or it could suggest a wish to maintain a bookish tradition in the family such as may have been exemplified by his brother Þórðr at Munkaþverá. This learned tradition may not have been dissimilar from the one that blossomed in the Sturlung family after Snorri Sturluson's youth with Jón Loptsson at Oddi.

Þorvarðr's family was furthermore closely intertwined with the Sturlungs. We know, for example, that Þorvarðr and his brothers were with Hvamm-Sturla in 1157.[11] But if Þorvarðr was drawn to books, this was by no means a dominant preoccupation, any more than in the case of Snorri Sturluson or Sturla Sighvatsson. Þorvarðr was in fact destined to have an adventurous life. His first recorded adventure was an elopement with Yngvildr, the daughter of Þorgils Oddason.[12] Yngvildr was also connected with a tradition of learning; her brother Oddi Þorgilsson was fostered by Sæmundr Sigfússon at Oddi and would therefore have tapped into the same tradition that was later available to Snorri Sturluson. Literary traditions were thus alive in the households of Þorgils Oddason, Hvamm-Sturla, and Þorvarðr Þorgeirsson.

Þorvarðr remained a close ally of Hvamm-Sturla both politically and by marriage alliance.[13] His sister Ingibjǫrg was married to Hvamm-Sturla and he himself was married to Sturla's granddaughter Herdís

Sighvatsdóttir.[14] It might be imagined that the culture of the Sturlungs communicated itself to Ingibjǫrg's family, but if we bear in mind that Ingibjǫrg's family had ties with the monastery at Munkaþverá going back to the 1150s, we might rather suppose that the Eyjafjörður tradition interacted with the Sturlung tradition on an equal footing. The two traditions are likely to have been parallel rather than chronologically sequential.

The literary tradition in Eyjafjörður is, to be sure, a little shadowy and speculative. How much importance should we attach to the fact that Þorgeirr Hallason and his descendants lived in the vicinity of the monastery at Munkaþverá and that family members joined the order or retired there? Other families in the region presumably had similar connections, and a monastic link does not necessarily demonstrate a bookish streak. On the other hand, we may remind ourselves that another of Þorgeirr Hallason's sons, the priest Ingimundr Þorgeirsson, moved to Mǫðruvellir in Eyjafjörður in 1172.[15] Ingimundr's love of books is explicitly noted, "því at þar var yndi hans sem bækurnar voru" [for his delight was in books].[16] His delight is illustrated by the famous episode in which he loses a chest full of books in a shipwreck. A literary miracle fortunately causes the chest to fetch up on shore with one of the three clasps still intact so that the books can be salvaged. All of the other less precious chests are found broken apart when they wash ashore.[17]

After 1215 Sighvatr Sturluson was at Grund in Eyjafjörður, and we might ask whether he had some connection with the monastery at Munkaþverá, directly or indirectly. An indirect connection can be traced through Sighvatr's step father-in-law Sigurðr Ormsson.[18] We are told that Sigurðr gave his chieftainships to Sighvatr's son Tumi, with the result that they later passed into Sighvatr's hands.[19] Sighvatr thus in some sense becomes Sigurðr's heir.

Sigurðr was immediately involved in the affairs of Munkaþverá because, in 1204, Bishop Guðmundr Arason asked him to go to Munkaþverá to renovate the buildings, which had fallen into disrepair.[20] After a short time Guðmundr then established Sigurðr at Mǫðruvellir, where Ingimundr Þorgeirsson had been and where his love of books must have left some trace.[21] It was perhaps not coincidental that Bishop Guðmundr singled out Sigurðr to repair the fortunes at Munkaþverá because Sigurðr's father Ormr was the nephew of Bishop

Bjǫrn Gilsson, who had endowed the house at Munkaþverá in 1162.[22] Ormr also retired at Munkaþverá and died there in 1191.[23] Relations between Bishop Guðmundr and Sigurðr Ormsson later soured to the point that Sigurðr found himself excommunicated. Not content with this measure, the bishop went on to remove from Sigurðr's home at Mǫðruvellir a reliquary, relics, and some books, on the grounds that such things should not be in the hands of excommunicated men.[24] We thus learn that books were in the possession of Sigurðr Ormsson at Mǫðruvellir and that all or some of them were confiscated in 1208, a year after the death of Þorvarðr Þorgeirsson.

These chance indications gathered from *Sturlunga saga* suggest the existence of a literary network including the family of Þorgils Oddason in the west, the Sturlungs in the west and north, and the family of Þorvarðr Þorgeirsson in Eyjafjörður. These families are linked in various ways, and there is evidence of literary activity in all three. The network may in fact be taken to underlie the opening sagas in the Sturlung complex, *Þorgils saga ok Hafliða, Sturlu saga, Prestssaga Guðmundar Arasonar,* and the beginning of *Íslendinga saga.* In addition, a band of references reaching from Reykjanes in the west to Reykjadalr in the north suggests that *Morkinskinna* was at home in the same region, most likely in Eyjafjörður.[25]

There also emerged in this area a specific variety of regional saga. These sagas differ distinctly from the biographical sagas of the west, especially in Borgarfjörður (*Gunnlaugs saga*, *Bjarnar saga*, and *Egils saga*), because they focus on feuding in a limited region rather than on memorable individuals. They include *Víga-Glúms saga*, *Reykdœla saga*, and *Ljósvetninga saga*. All three have most often been dated near the middle of the century, that is to say, much later than *Morkinskinna*. On the other hand, Ólafur Halldórsson has suggested, albeit tentatively, that *Færeyinga saga*, which belongs to the same type of regional feud saga, may have been composed in Eyjafjörður in the period 1210–1215.[26] If this well-told saga is the work of such an early period, we may wonder why other regional sagas from the same area were so long delayed. It seems rather more likely that they should be assigned to the same chronological frame. We will begin with *Víga-Glúms saga* and *Reykdœla saga*, which have the peculiarity that they share a stretch of narrative and are therefore closely connected with each other. But the exact nature of this connection has proved to be a particularly recalcitrant problem that must be addressed before we can settle on a chronology.

Víga-Glúms saga and *Reykdœla saga*

The shared narrative describes an encounter between the chieftain Víga-Glúmr in Eyjafjörður and his son-in-law and antagonist Víga-Skúta at Mývatn to the east. The matching text is located largely in chapter 16 of *Víga-Glúms saga* and chapter 26 of *Reykdœla saga*. The hostility between the two chieftains comes to a head after a divorce is effected between Glúmr's daughter Þórlaug and Skúta, on Skúta's initiative according to *Víga-Glúms saga* and on Glúmr's initiative according to *Reykdœla saga*. Skúta hires a spy and agent provocateur to lure Glúmr to an isolated chalet, where Skúta ambushes him. Glúmr makes good his escape by leaping into a gulch where he knows there is a ledge to catch him. He then gathers forces, but Skúta disguises himself as a shepherd and successfully eludes the posse. Skúta in turn gathers forces, but the confrontation ends in a standoff.

Commentary on this overlap goes back as far as Theodor Möbius's monograph of 1852.[27] Möbius did not enter into details but assumed that the plus passages in *Reykdœla saga* were added to supplement *Víga-Glúms saga* and that in the two passages where the author points out alternate traditions, he is referring to *Víga-Glúms saga* specifically (p. 68). In the first edition of his literary history Finnur Jónsson took the view that the two versions of the episode were oral variants, despite the almost verbatim correspondence in wording.[28] It was not until a full fifty years after Möbius's publication that the problem became an independent object of study.

The new initiative came from an unlikely source, a young American from Knoxville, Tennessee, named Claude Lotspeich. He studied with Eugen Mogk in Leipzig and devoted his dissertation to the topic in 1903. He begins his discussion by quoting Möbius to the effect that the episode is isolated in *Víga-Glúms saga* and not connected with the main thread of the story, Glúmr's ongoing feud with the nearby Esphœlingar.[29] Lotspeich reinforces the idea of isolation by noting that only in this episode is the protagonist referred to as "Víga-Glúmr," whereas he figures elsewhere as "Glúmr" plain and simple.[30] This anomaly leads Lotspeich to agree with Finnur Jónsson's assessment that the episode was interpolated into *Víga-Glúms saga*, but, unlike Finnur, he does not believe in an oral source but rather in a written source, which he labels "X."[31] A written source indeed accounts better for the close match in wording in the two recordings of the story in *Víga-Glúms saga* and *Reykdœla saga*. Lotspeich argues that the two sagas made similar use of "X," but where the wording differs, he judged that the author of *Víga-Glúms saga* abbreviated "X."

Lotspeich's chief argument for the existence of a separate written text was stylistic; he pointed out that when the historical present is a possible option, it is used overall 28 percent of the time in *Reykdœla saga* and 26 percent of the time in *Víga-Glúms saga*.[32] In the interpolated episode, however, it appears 75 percent of the time in *Reykdœla saga* and 73 percent of the time in *Víga-Glúms saga*. The episode therefore has a special profile that sets it apart from the larger narratives. Although Lotspeich left open the possibility that the author of *Víga-Glúms saga* might have copied directly from *Reykdœla saga*, he did not come to grips with the purpose of a free-floating episode unattached to any larger context.

The episode has been viewed tacitly as a kind of *þáttr*, but the *þættir* are predominantly about young Icelanders in Norway.[33] Perhaps the written source "X" could be compared to the semi-independent *þættir* in *Ljósvetninga saga*, but in the case of this saga the *þættir* either belonged to the original redaction or they were interpolated as oral addenda. They probably had no separate written existence. Quite apart from the greater simplicity of assuming that *Reykdœla saga* copied from *Víga-Glúms saga* or vice versa, episodic narratives about Saga Age events in Iceland are hard to document before the advent of saga writing.

It is in fact surprising that Lotspeich's hypothesis carried as much weight as it did. When Knut Liestøl wrote an essay on *Reykdœla saga* in 1928, he did not refer to Lotspeich, but he may have been familiar with his conclusions through the second edition of Finnur Jónsson's literary history.[34] Liestøl focused on the mismatch between chapter 26 of *Reykdœla saga* and the saga as a whole; in the episode we find 41–42 percent direct discourse, whereas the saga from beginning to end shows about 6 percent.[35] Liestøl did not draw the perhaps obvious conclusion that the episode was lifted out of *Víga-Glúms saga*, which also shows about 40 percent direct discourse. He remains neutral on the relationship of *Reykdœla saga* and *Víga-Glúms saga,* saying only that it seemed quite certain that the episode in *Reykdœla saga* was an interpolation. On the origin of the interpolation he is agnostic: "Whether it was the author himself who added it in by using an unknown written source or a scribe who interpolated it (from an oral or written source), we have no way of deciding with certainty."[36] Nor does Liestøl clarify the problem in his subsequent book.[37] On the other hand, his reference to "an unknown written source" suggests that Lotspeich's hypothesis was still alive.

A few years later Gabriel Turville-Petre turned his attention to *Víga-Glúms saga.* In a paper from 1936 he was quite convinced that there had existed a written *þáttr* that was interpolated into both *Víga-Glúms saga* and *Reykdœla saga,* in compressed form in the *Mǫðruvallabók* version of the former and in fuller form in *Reykdœla saga.*[38] Though critical of Lotspeich's lack of clarity, Turville-Petre supports his conclusion. As verification of the distinctive, and hence interpolated, state of the episode he cites Lotspeich's observation that the name "Víga-Glúmr" occurs only here and that the historical present is used disproportionately. He also notes that the name form "Víga-Glúmr" occurs in *Reykdœla saga* for the first time in chapter 23 and believes that this occurrence reinforces the idea of a separate *þáttr.* He does not consider the possibility that the use of the name form "Víga-Glúmr" at this point could have been prompted by the fact that the author of *Reykdœla saga* was copying from *Víga-Glúms saga*, or that the rich use of the historical present could be explained in the same way.

But Turville-Petre may have had second thoughts because he was rather more circumspect when he published his comprehensive edition of *Víga-Glúms saga* four years later. Here he neither accepts nor rejects Lotspeich's view but, like Liestøl, leaves the question open, suggesting that "the *þáttr* must first have been copied into *VGl* [*Víga-Glúms saga*] either from a text which was also the source of Ch. xxvi of *R.* [*Reykdœla saga*], or else from a manuscript of *R.* itself."[39] That phrasing shows Lotspeich's persistent footprint. Unfortunately, Turville-Petre did not pursue the matter further; we therefore do not know whether he favored Lotspeich's separate text or a direct loan from *Reykdœla saga.*

Between Turville-Petre's first and second statements there appeared the posthumously printed lectures of Björn M. Ólsen from the years

1911 to 1917. Ólsen refers to the problem briefly but decisively.[40] He emphasizes the discrepancies between the accounts of Þórlaug's marriage in the two texts and the identifications of the weapon Fluga: "In both places where *Víga-Skútu saga* addresses the discrepancies it plainly refers to the narrative of *Glúma*. That makes it clear that *Skútu saga* made use of *Glúma* in this section and not the other way around." In the latter mention (p. 424) Ólsen adds that the author of *Reykdœla saga* made use of a redaction of *Glúma* closer to the *Vatnshyrna* fragment than the *Mǫðruvallabók* redaction.

If Turville-Petre became less certain of an independent *þáttr* underlying the two sagas, the same is not true of Björn Sigfússon, who brought out his edition of *Reykdœla saga* in the same year in which Turville-Petre's edition of *Víga-Glúms saga* appeared. Far from downplaying the hypothetical *þáttr*, he advocated fuller dimensions for it, theorizing that it included the narrative pertaining to Glúmr's daughter Þórlaug and her marriage to and divorce from Skúta. He therefore identified Þórlaug as the central character and named the *þáttr* "Þórlaugar þáttr" in her honor.[41] According to *Víga-Glúms saga* Skúta married Þórlaug but later repudiated her, giving rise to the subsequent enmity between Glúmr and Skúta. But *Reykdœla saga* offers a different account. Here Glúmr and his daughter connive to procure a better marriage, and she abandons Skúta. The author of *Reykdœla saga* knows the version in *Víga-Glúms saga* ("some people take the view that Skúta sent her home to Glúmr") but opts rather for the tale of trickery.

Björn Sigfússon does not understand the repudiation motif as a reference to *Víga-Glúms saga* and suggests instead that the author took the motif from "Þórlaugar þáttr" but changed it to improve Skúta's image. This is a complicated hypothesis that piles unknown on unknown; we do not know that there was a "Þórlaugar þáttr" or, if there was, what it contained, but Björn not only treats it as a given but goes on to speculate about the content, then speculates further that the author of *Reykdœla saga* rejected the content. Far simpler would be the assumption that the author of *Reykdœla saga* knew the repudiation motif directly from *Víga-Glúms saga* but also knew another version (perhaps a regional variant) more favorable to Skúta.

More compelling than Björn Sigfússon's hypothesis was Jónas Kristjánsson's analysis of the problem in his edition of *Víga-Glúms saga*.[42] His contribution was remarkable both for clarity and independence, especially with respect to the inherited assumption that a separate *þáttr* was interpolated into the saga. He begins by noting how out of keeping the style of the episode is with *Reykdœla saga* as a whole. In particular he calculates that, whereas chapter 26 of *Reykdœla saga* has 41–42 percent direct discourse, chapters 23–25 have only about 4.5 percent. He therefore considers it unlikely that these chapters all derive from a single source, Björn Sigfússon's "Þórlaugar þáttr." He argues that it is furthermore unlikely that the author of *Reykdœla saga* would have borrowed only one chapter from a long *þáttr* if such a text had really been at his disposal. That consideration makes him open to Björn M. Ólsen's idea that *Reykdœla saga* borrowed directly from *Víga-Glúms saga* and used other sources as a basis for chapters 23–25.

The chief objection to such a direct borrowing had been the widely held belief that the episode was an interpolated *þáttr* in *Víga-Glúms saga*. Jónas systematically reviews the reasons used to support that belief: the fact that the daughter Þórlaug is mentioned nowhere else in *Víga-Glúms saga*, not even in the listing of Glúmr's children in the following chapter; the sole occurrence of the name form "Víga-Glúmr" in chapter 16; Lotspeich's observation of a disproportionate use of the historical present in chapter 16. With respect to the historical present, Jónas expresses some doubt about the significance of Lotspeich's figures; his own calculation suggests a 63–64 percent use of the historical present rather than 73 percent, and he thinks that the sample may be too small to exclude coincidence.

Jónas attaches more weight to the author's apparent unfamiliarity with the terrain in chapter 16, whereas elsewhere he seems perfectly at home in the area. Another discrepancy is that the action of chapter 16 seems less realistic and more improbable than in the remainder of the saga. These factors conspire to isolate chapter 16 and suggest that it was not written by the author of the main saga, although Jónas finds it difficult to decide whether the episode was incorporated by the author himself or was a later interpolation. That the incident is well positioned in both manuscripts of the saga inclines him to believe that it belongs to the original composition rather than being an interpolation. In his later survey of medieval Icelandic literature Jónas settled on a compromise solution; he accepted that there was a separate "Skútu þáttr," but he considered that it was not absorbed independently into both sagas, only into *Víga-Glúms saga*, from which it was adopted by the author of *Reykdœla saga*.[43]

Jónas Kritjánsson's edition was not available to Walter Baetke when he published a paper that appeared two years later, but he arrived independently at similar conclusions.[44] Like Jónas, he criticizes Björn Sigfússon's hypothetical "Þórlaugar þáttr" and challenges Lotspeich's figures on the historical present. Echoing Jónas's doubts about such a small sample, he makes the interesting observation that other small samples also produce disproportionate percentages of the historical present. Thus chapter 13 of *Reykdœla saga* shows 64 percent and chapter 15 shows 71 percent.[45] Baetke also reemphasizes the fact that the high percentage of direct discourse isolates the episode in the context of *Reykdœla saga* but not in the context of *Víga-Glúms saga*.

In general Baetke favors the simpler option of deriving one saga from the other rather than introducing unknown quantities into the relationship. In addition he points out that Glúmr's character in the episode is in line with *Víga-Glúms saga*, whereas Víga-Skúta's personality is at odds with *Reykdœla saga* as a whole. That suggests that the episode is more naturally situated in *Víga-Glúms saga* than in *Reykdœla saga*. On the other hand, the mention of narrative variants in chapter 26 of *Reykdœla saga* is characteristic of that saga and makes it easy to believe that the author altered what he found in *Víga-Glúms saga*, especially since the most explicit deviations respond specifically to variants found in chapter 16 of *Víga-Glúms saga*.

Baetke notes a further echo of *Víga-Glúms saga* in *Reykdœla saga*. The latter characterizes a certain Þorvarðr Ǫrnólfsson in chapter 15 as "vitr maðr en miðlungi góðgjarn" [a wise man but not altogether well disposed]. The wording is close to a characterization of the same man in *Víga-Glúms saga* (ÍF 9:73): "Þorvarðr var vitr maðr ok var þá gamall, meðallagi góðgjarn" [Þorvarðr was a wise man, old at the time, and indifferently well disposed].[46] That the wording in *Reykdœla saga* is a draft on *Víga-Glúms saga* is made plausible by the fact that Þorvarðr has a role in *Víga-Glúms saga* but is mentioned only twice and is as good as invisible in *Reykdœla saga*. From his accumulation of evidence Baetke concludes that the author of *Reykdœla saga* lifted the encounter between Víga-Glúmr and Víga-Skúta directly from chapter 16 in *Víga-Glúms saga*.

One additional argument might be deduced from Baetke's material. He notes the old argument that the name form "Víga-Glúmr" occurs only in chapter 16 of *Víga-Glúms saga*, with the result that this chapter stands apart from the rest of the saga. He notes too that the name "Víga-Glúmr," alongside "Víga-Skúta," is used the first time Glúmr is mentioned in *Reykdœla saga* (chapter 23). This correspondence has more often than not been viewed as evidence that the name form derived from a separate *þáttr*, but it could also be construed to mean that when the author of *Reykdœla saga* set out to describe the encounter between the two warriors, he was looking at chapter 16 of *Víga-Glúms saga*, where, perhaps not coincidentally, the forms "Víga-Glúmr" and "Víga-Skúta" also appear more or less side by side.

With the publication of Jónas Kristjánsson's probing recapitulation and Walter Baetke's decisive assignment of the priority to *Víga-Glúms saga*, it looked as though there was a consensus in the making, but a third contribution appeared at about the same time (1956) and complicated the issues considerably.[47] Arie C. Bouman's monograph provided a veritable flood of stylistic statistics on such matters as direct and indirect discourse, sentence length, and tense. The statistics are so unsurveyable as to make the argument difficult to evaluate, but they led Bouman to the conclusion that chapters 13–16 in *Víga-Glúms saga* stand apart from the rest of the saga in terms of sentence brevity, parataxis in preference to hypotaxis, predominance of historical present, and abundance of direct discourse. This profile is particularly evident in the *Mǫðruvallabók (M)* redaction, which Bouman believed to be primary. The run of chapters 13 to 16 includes not only the encounter between Glúmr and Skúta but also the episode in which Glúmr kills Kálfr of Stokkahlaða and then incriminates a certain Ingólfr. Because Bouman found the two episodes to be stylistically uniform, he theorized that they were joined in a common written text "X," which was copied into the *M* version of *Víga-Glúms saga*. The *M* version then became the source of the *Vatnshyrna* version as well as chapter 26 of *Reykdœla saga*.

Bouman appears to embrace the idea of a separate *þáttr* incorporated independently into *Víga-Glúms saga* (chapter 16) and *Reykdœla saga* (chapter 26), but his *þáttr* is in fact quite different. It is about two disconnected episodes (the Kálfr episode and the encounter between Glúmr and Skúta), and it was not copied into *Reykdœla saga*; rather, it was copied from *Víga-Glúms saga (M)* into *Reykdœla saga*. In our assessment of the relationship between these two sagas the *þáttr* is not implicated. It is merely a source for *Víga-Glúms saga*, which in turn became a source for *Reykdœla saga*. From the limited perspective of the two sagas it can be said that Bouman agrees with Baetke's conclusion that *Víga-Glúms saga* is the direct source for *Reykdœla saga*. In effect Bouman's work strengthens the growing consensus favoring the priority of *Víga-Glúms saga*.

That consensus was upset again in 1972 when Dietrich Hofmann published a tightly argued paper reversing the priorities.[48] Hofmann found the idea of an episodic *þáttr* intrinsically implausible and therefore concentrated on the direct relationship between *Reykdœla saga* and *Víga-Glúms saga*. He asks in which saga the episode is better integrated and gives the decided preference to *Reykdœla saga*, taking note of Jónas Kristjánsson's observation that the author of the episode in *Víga-Glúms saga* betrays a lack of familiarity with the locale. He also enlists the isolated appearance of Þórlaug in the episode and emphasizes the poor motivation of the episode in *Víga-Glúms saga*, in which Skúta repudiates Glúmr's daughter and then adds injury to insult by launching an unexplained attack on his father-in-law. In *Reykdœla saga,* by contrast, the episode follows logically on the heels of other strained dealings between the two.

The most palpable problem for those favoring the priority of chapter 26 in *Reykdœla saga* is the great disproportion of direct discourse in relation to the rest of the saga, a feature that argues for a poor fit of chapter 26 in the narrative as a whole. Hofmann seeks to counter this anomaly by suggesting that the encounter between the two warriors may have spurred the author on to an uncharacteristically lively presentation, but the argument that there can always be an exception is not necessarily persuasive. Hofmann also argues that the use of spies and assassins is quite in the spirit of *Reykdœla saga*, but we might demur on the ground that subterfuge is an even more recurrent feature in *Víga-Glúms saga*.

One of the reasons sometimes marshaled against the view that *Víga-Glúms saga* is the borrower is the unlikelihood that the author would have taken over the episode in chapter 26 without making use of the narrative pertinent to Víga-Glúmr in chapters 23–25 of *Reykdœla saga*. Hofmann disallows this reasoning on the ground that the author, or more likely a later reviser, was under no compulsion to adopt everything available to him but was in a position to pick and choose. In a subsequent passage Hofmann goes on to argue that the borrowing of certain materials in chapter 23–25 would have involved the writer in awkward revisions. He also points out that the episodes in chapters 23–25 are largely located to the east of Eyjafjörður, where the focus of *Reykdœla saga* is centered. These episodes may therefore have been peripheral for the reviser of *Víga-Glúms saga*. Hofmann believes that Viga-Glúmr's somewhat isolated daughter Þórlaug may also have belonged to this eastern tradition and was therefore not well lodged in *Víga-Glúms saga*; the information given about her may well be spurious.

Hofmann turns then to the variant traditions recorded in *Reykdœla saga*, according to which the weapon Fluga could have been an ax or a sword. Hofmann finds it not surprising that the author (or reviser) of *Víga-Glúms saga* dropped the ax variant and settled on a sword, because he could deduce that Fluga was a thrusting weapon. When Skúta sees Glúmr's cloak floating in the water, the text says (ÍF 10:233): "Hann hleypr at ok leggr til kápunnar" [he runs up and thrusts at the cloak]. Quite apart from the fact that a sword is a hewing as well as a thrusting weapon, one could object that it is possible to use "leggja" with an ax if Skúta was poking at the cloak with the top of the ax shaft to ascertain whether it enveloped Glúmr's body. Finally, Hofmann disallows Baetke's argument that *Reykdœla saga* borrowed its characterization of Þorvarðr Ǫrnólfsson (ÍF 10:197) from *Víga-Glúms saga* (ÍF 9:73). He admits that the introduction of Þorvarðr is awkward in *Reykdœla saga* but sees no reason not to attribute the awkwardness to the writer, who can be observed retrieving missing information in other passages as well.

Apart from the not always convincing critique of those who have given *Víga-Glúms saga* the priority, it should be noted that Hofmann was pleading a special conviction. He was a strong proponent of the role of oral tradition in the sagas and he begins his paper by recalling the once widespread view that *Reykdœla saga* stands particularly close to that tradition, although skepticism had in the meantime overtaken the old consensus. From Hofmann's point of view, the new skepticism could only be abetted if it were judged that *Reykdœla saga* was written later than *Víga-Glúms saga*, which Jónas Kristjánsson assigned to the period 1220–1250 (ÍF 9:LIII). Indeed, Björn Sigfússon hesitated to date *Reykdœla saga* earlier than "close to the middle of the century" (ÍF 10: LXXXIX), that is, in the full flowering of saga writing. Hofmann, who believed in the saga's proximity to the transition from oral tradition, therefore had a specific motive for making it as early as possible, hence earlier than *Víga-Glúms saga*.

Despite Walter Baetke's clear prioritizing of *Víga-Glúms saga* and Dietrich Hofmann's clear reversal, subsequent comments have been tentative. There are brief references to the problem in John McKinnell's translation of *Víga-Glúms saga* and in the second volume of the collaborative Icelandic literary history from 1993.[49] The former assumes interpolation of the Ingólfr and Skúta episodes from different sources, and the latter presupposes Arie C. Bouman's hypothesis of an interpolated narrative including both the Ingólfr and Skúta episodes. That is to say, both revert to the idea that the correspondence should be explained from an interpolated *þáttr*; the author of *Víga-Glúms saga* interpolated a whole *þáttr* or more (covering both the anecdote concerning Ingólfr and Hlǫðu-Kálfr and Glúmr's encounter with Skúta), whereas the author of *Reykdœla saga* included only the encounter with Skúta because the story of Ingólfr and Hlǫðu-Kálfr had nothing to do with the action of his saga.

The idea of a separate *þáttr* suffers from the same implausibility that besets Lotspeich's thesis: what is the precedent for and the purpose of such a partial narrative? Why introduce the complication of an additional text when the relationship between *Reykdœla saga* and *Víga-Glúms saga* can be explained more simply by a loan from one saga to the other? It is furthermore evident that the author of *Reykdœla saga* knew the story of the encounter between Glúmr and Skúta from oral tradition because he refers to variant versions of the story and adds more information on the interaction between Glúmr and Skúta than could be found in *Víga-Glúms saga*. If we ask why he copied from the earlier saga rather than retelling the tradition, the answer may be that he found the episode so well told in *Víga-Glúms saga* that he elected to take a shortcut and avail himself of the ready-made version in front of him.

Jónas Kristjánsson began the discussion in his edition with a strong statement to the effect that the encounter between Glúmr and Skúta was lodged more naturally in *Víga-Glúms saga* than in *Reykdœla saga*, where it is stylistically anomalous (ÍF 9:XV): "It [chapter 26 of *Reykdœla saga*] is the main adornment of the saga and far exceeds anything else in it, like a new restoration on an old pot." This praise attaches particularly to the lively dialogue in chapter 26, which is quite in line with the dialogue that we find throughout *Víga-Glúms saga* but is absent from the rest of *Reykdœla saga*. The latter has in fact the lowest percentage of direct discourse in any saga.[50] Despite Dietrich Hofmann's representation that the author may have risen to a higher plane for an especially inspired incident, a sudden jump from 6 percent to 40 percent in a single chapter strains credulity. The average for *Víga-Glúms saga* is, however, precisely in the area of 40 percent and therefore seems to be the right context for the episode.

A minor point that must have been noticed but has not drawn comment is the presence of a half stanza in the encounter between Glúmr and Skúta. Skaldic verse is a regular feature of *Víga-Glúms saga*, but this is the only scrap of verse in *Reykdœla saga*. That too might suggest that the episode belongs originally to *Víga-Glúms saga*. A similar conclusion could be drawn from Walter Baetke's observation that the characterization in the episode accords well with the thrust of *Víga-Glúms saga*, in which Glúmr is consistently remarkable for his "foresight and presence of mind."[51] Skúta's trickery, on the other hand, is not in keeping with his characterization in *Reykdœla saga*.

Another indication that has been observed but not exploited occurs at the very beginning of the crucial chapter 16 in *Víga-Glúms saga*, where Þórlaug's marriages are accounted for (ÍF 9:50): "Síðan [after her divorce from Skúta] bað hennar Arnórr kerlingarnef ok átti hana. Frá þeim eru komnir gǫfgir menn" [Later Arnórr kerlingarnef asked for her hand and was married to her. Distinguished men are descended from them]. These words recur in chapter 24 of *Reykdœla saga* (ÍF 10:228): "Síðast átti hana Arnórr kerlingarnef, ok eru gǫfgir menn frá þeim komnir." The author of *Reykdœla saga* in fact mentions three husbands for Þórlaug, not just the two mentioned in *Víga-Glúms saga*. The easiest explanation is that the author of *Reykdœla saga* was already looking at chapter 16 of *Víga-Glúms saga* and borrowed the phrasing, but he also had additional information from oral sources and supplemented what he found in his written source. It is a little more difficult to believe that the author of *Víga-Glúms saga* borrowed from *Reykdœla saga* but dropped one of the husbands.

Much has been made of the fact that Glúmr is referred to as "Víga-Glúmr" only in chapter 16 of his saga, the implication being that this usage is not in line with the rest of the saga and could derive from a different source. But it should be pointed out that the author of *Grettis saga* names Barði Guðmundarson 32 times but calls him Víga-Barði only once (ÍF 7:116); the departure in name form in chapter 16 may therefore not be significant. On the other hand, it may provide another clue suggesting that the author of *Reykdœla saga* had *Víga-Glúms saga* in front of him.

As the author of *Reykdœla saga* begins the tale of Glúmr's encounter with Skúta in chapter 23, he identifies Skúta's aunt Þorbjǫrg (ÍF 10:221): "Hon var fǫðursystir Víga-Skútu" [she was Víga-Skúta's paternal aunt]. He also identifies Glúmr's sister Þorgerðr: "Hon var systir Víga-Glúms at Þverá ór Eyjafirði" [she was the sister of Víga-Glúmr at Þverá in Eyjafjörður]. Apart from the opening genealogy and the end of the saga (ÍF 10:240–41), this is the only time in *Reykdœla saga* that Skúta is referred to as "Víga-Skúta." It is also the only time that Glúmr is referred to as "Víga-Glúmr." It may be coincidence that the prefix "Víga-" in the body of the saga is restricted to this passage, but it might also be explained by the supposition that the author of *Reykdœla saga*, as he began to tell the story of the encounter, was looking at the beginning of chapter 16 in *Víga-Glúms saga*, which also uses the forms Víga-Skúta and Víga-Glúmr only here.

In calculating the probabilities, we may also observe that it has been a majority view that *Reykdœla saga* borrowed from *Víga-Glúms saga* rather than vice versa. This was the opinion expressed by Theodor Möbius and Björn M. Ólsen.[52] Lotspeich and Turville-Petre left latitude for the opposite view, but Bouman's more complicated scheme again suggested that *Víga-Glúms saga* had the original.[53] Jónas Kristjánsson could find no contrary evidence (ÍF 9:XVI): "Is it thinkable that chapter 26 of *Reykdœla saga* was taken directly from *Glúma*? That was the opinion of Björn M. Ólsen, and I have not noted anything that would speak categorically against it." Walter Baetke was an outspoken advocate for this option, and only Dietrich Hofmann formulated arguments for the opposite view. The position taken here in favor of a priority for *Víga-Glúms saga* is therefore well anchored in the previous literature.

Although the relative dating of these two sagas may be fairly secure, absolute dates are even more difficult to fix. The dating of *Reykdœla saga* turns on a small passage in chapter 12. The saga as a whole begins with the settlement of Reykjadalr by two Norwegian brothers and goes on to tell the story of their descendants. This story is one of hostile encounters, notably a protracted feud between Vémundr kǫgurr Fjǫrleifarson in Reykjadalr and Steingrímr Ǫrnólfsson to the west in Eyjafjörður. Vémundr is tirelessly aggressive, and despite the best efforts of his chieftain and uncle Áskell, the hostilities are never settled and result in Steingrímr's death.

At one point Vémundr persuades a somewhat imbecilic fellow named Þorgeirr to strike Steingrímr with a sheep's head attached to a pole during a heated horse match, an occasion always conducive to mischief. In exchange for this wanton misdeed Vémundr offers the malefactor a winter's lodging. Þorgeirr carries out the commission and is immediately killed, but he calls out to Vémundr for help so that it is clear who is behind the plot.

During the negotiation between troublemaker and henchman, Þorgeirr asks what his compensation will be, and Vémundr makes the following offer (ÍF 10:182):

> Vémundr kǫgurr svarar, at hann mun fá honum vetrvist, ef Þorgeirr vill þat vinna til, at ljósta Steingrím um daginn með sauðarhǫfðinu fyrir augum ǫllum mǫnnum.
>
> [Vémundr kǫgurr [coverlet] replies that he will give him a winter's lodging if he will agree to strike Steingrímr during the day with a sheep's head for all to see.]

The action itself is described in the following terms (ÍF 10:183):

> Ok í einhverri hvíld, þá er menn varði minnst, lýstr Þorgeirr Steingrím mikit hǫgg með sauðarhǫfðinu á hálsinn ok kallar nú á Vémund, at hann skyldi duga honum. En Steingrímr hleypr þegar eptir honum ok þeir mágar hans, Steinn ok Helgi, ok vá Steingrímr Þorgeir, fekk honum nú vetrvistina ok tók nú starf af Vémundi.
>
> [During an intermission, when people were least expecting it, Þorgeirr struck Steingrímr a great blow on the neck with a sheep's head and called out to Vémundr to help him. But Steingrímr immediately ran

after him, together with his kinsmen Steinn and Helgi, and Steingrímr killed Þorgeirr, giving him the winter's lodging and saving Vémundr the trouble.]

This is a quite minor incident in *Reykdœla saga*, but some of the wording recurs in the *Þórðarbók* redaction of *Landnámabók* (ÍF 1.2:257) in a passage that reviews Steingrímr's ancestry:

> Þeira synir váru þeir Þórðr ok Þorvarðr í Kristnesi ok Steingrímr at Kroppi, er Vémundr kǫgurr lét ljósta með sauðarhǫfði ok lézk mundu fá þeim vetrvist, er þat gerði, en sá hét Þorgeirr smjǫrkengr, en þat endisk, því at Steingrímr drap hann þegar, ok kvazk þess hǫggs skyldu hefna, meðan hann lifði.

> [Their sons were Þórðr and Þorvarðr at Kristnes and Steingrímr at Kroppr, whom Vémundr kǫgurr caused to be struck with a sheep's head; he said he would give the man who did it a winter's lodging, and his name was Þorgeirr smjǫrkengr, and that was carried out because Steingrímr killed him immediately and said that he would avenge that blow as long as he lived.]

In the footnote to his edition Jakob Benediktsson referred to several explanations of the correspondence between the saga and *Landnámabók*, all of them to the effect that the incident found its way into the saga from a redaction of *Landnámabók*. Dietrich Hofmann argued the reverse, that the lost redaction of *Landnámabók* compiled by Styrmir Kárason (died 1245) and known as *Styrmisbók* borrowed the episode from *Reykdœla saga* and that the composition of *Styrmisbók* therefore serves as a terminus ante quem for *Reykdœla saga*.[54]

The filiation of the various redactions of *Landnámabók* is a complicated puzzle. Jón Jóhannesson and, following him, Jakob Benediktsson (ÍF 1.1:CV), believed that *Styrmisbók* was the source for *Melabók*, from which the passage under discussion would have passed into *Þórðarbók*. They also believed that *Styrmisbók* was written ca. 1220 or a little later. If the passage in *Styrmisbók* is derivative from *Reykdœla saga*, that would locate the saga before 1220, but there are uncertainties. The evidence that *Styrmisbók* was written around 1220 includes among other things the *argumentum e silentio* that

Styrmisbók did not make use of *Egils saga*, but that is a slender reed. Subsequent to the publication of Dietrich Hofmann's paper Sveinbjörn Rafnsson also wrote a book in which he proved to be quite skeptical about the view that *Styrmisbók* was the source of *Melabók*.[55] It is therefore entirely possible that *Styrmisbók* is not as early as Hofmann thought and that it did not contain the sheep's head incident.

To these reservations should be added the consideration that Jón Jóhannesson's hypothesis is quite complex.[56] He thought the phrasing in *Þórðarbók* too archaic to be a recasting of the saga and traced it instead to *Melabók*, from which it migrated into *Styrmisbók*, *Reykdœla saga*, and ultimately into *Þórðarbók*. Sturla Þórðarson, he surmised, deleted the passage from his redaction of *Landnámabók* because he was familiar with the saga and knew that the story was told in greater detail there. This hypothesis is in line with Jón Jóhannesson's general thinking, which allowed for extensive borrowing from *Landnámabók* into the sagas and privileged literary derivation over oral derivation.[57]

Although Jón Jóhannesson thought that the source of the sheep's head incident was *Styrmisbók*, Sveinbjörn Rafnsson was doubtful about the proposition that *Melabók*, *Sturlubók*, and *Hauksbók* all made use of *Styrmisbók*; he was more inclined to believe that *Melabók* was entirely independent of the other redactions.[58] If he is right, *Þórðarbók* inherits the passage directly from *Melabók* and not through the mediation of *Styrmisbók*. In this case the dating of *Styrmisbók* is again irrelevant, and Hofmann's terminus ante quem evaporates. But what can we say about the dating of *Melabók*? Sveinbjörn Rafnsson suggests evidence that would make Snorri Markússon the author of *Melabók* sometime between 1275 and 1313. He also argues that Snorri Markússon's exemplar could have been composed in the time of his grandfather Snorri Magnússon, who died in 1226. The original of *Melabók* might therefore be from the same period as *Styrmisbók*, and if the sheep's head incident was taken over from *Reykdœla saga* into *Melabók* rather than *Styrmisbók*, the terminus ante quem would be roughly the same.

But even if we concede that the story originated in *Reykdœla saga*, as seems not unlikely, we must remain in doubt about how and when it entered the *Landnámabók* transmission. It may not have been in the original *Styrmisbók* or the original *Melabók* and could have been interpolated at some later date. Any use of *Landnámabók* to arrive at an absolute date for *Reykdœla saga* therefore seems quite precarious, and we are left with the general indications early in this chapter that there may well have been some saga writing in Eyjafjörður around 1220. All that we can say with any degree of certainty is that *Víga-Glúms saga* probably preceded *Reykdœla saga*. But before concluding the discussion, we may ask how the theme of partisanship plays out in these two sagas.

If we look back to our point of departure in Chapter 3, we may well allow that the early Icelandic biographies of Norwegian kings, notably Óláfr Tryggvason and Óláfr Haraldsson, are largely celebratory, with the hint of some acquiescent relationship between Icelandic author and Norwegian patronage. It is only gradually and rather tentatively that a critical voice begins to be heard in the *Óláfs saga helga* that forms the second part of *Heimskringla*. But for the most part *Heimskringla* seems to adhere to a certain diplomatic reticence with respect to the Norwegian kings. This cautious outlook seems also to have left traces, even contradictions, in *Egils saga*. That the Icelanders may have had definite opinions about royal policy in Norway becomes apparent, though not overtly so, only in *Morkinskinna*.

When the Icelanders began to write about their own history, however, they may have felt less trammeled by diplomatic considerations and more inclined to express themselves unguardedly about regional and family issues. There were indications of this openness at the end of *Egils saga*, and we will find an even more uncompromising clash of interests below. But before turning to *Ljósvetninga saga*, we must say a word about the covert contentions in our first two sagas.

We have seen that in the evolution of the kings' sagas there is an increasingly well developed dialogue on matters pertaining to personality and political outlook. When the narrative scene shifts to Iceland, these preoccupations appear in *Egils saga*, but somewhat more subtle antagonisms may be found in the northern sagas as well. It is evident that Víga-Glúmr is a special blend of personal opaqueness and political astuteness, a personality designed for conflict. He grows up as a male Cinderella, but his self-isolation is only a disguise adopted for the purpose of allowing him to bide his time until the right moment for action presents itself.

Although Norway is not much involved in the saga plot, both Glúmr's father Eyjólfr and Glúmr himself begin their careers there.

Eyjólfr makes a Norwegian friend and asks for passage to Norway, but, once arrived, his friend hesitates to extend hospitality. It turns out that he is apprehensive because he has a brother with a special dislike of Icelanders. The brother's sentiments get considerable coverage, but Eyjólfr, by dint of patience, is able to overcome them and establish himself by killing a bear, participating in viking expeditions, and defeating a berserk. Capitalizing on his new-found standing, he marries the daughter of a district chieftain and returns to Iceland.

Eyjólfr's son Glúmr follows in his father's footsteps and makes his way in Norway too. At first he gets a tepid reception from his maternal grandfather, but then asserts himself by driving out a berserk who has made it a habit to terrorize his grandfather's hall. Such Norwegian preludes become a regular feature of the Icelandic sagas, but the link with Norway is cut off decisively in *Víga-Glúms saga*; the remainder of the action is almost willfully Icelandic. It may be pressing a point, but it is as if Norway is mentioned only to be relegated, as if the author wishes to suggest that Norway has yielded the stage to Iceland. The literary initiative has passed from one country to another.

Glúmr is best known as a master of subterfuges. His career as chieftain in Eyjafjörður is to some extent a sequence of subterfuges and to some extent an alternation of subterfuges and determined actions. His trick to escape the clutches of Víga-Skúta is one illustration of his resourcefulness, but the more famous examples are the killing of a calf in a barn to inculpate another man for his own killing of an antagonist named Hlǫðu-Kálfr (barn calf) and an ingeniously worded ambiguous oath that serves to put his enemies off the scent for a time. Glúmr has his heroic moments, but he is not primarily a heroic figure, in the mold, for example, of Egill Skallagrímsson. He triumphs more often by deceit than by confrontation.

The appropriate comparison is perhaps with Þrándr í Gǫtu, who makes his way against the Norwegian crown and his fellow Faroe Islanders by dissembling. Like Víga-Glúmr he lives to a ripe old age, and ultimately dies of grief over the death of a nephew. Both *Víga-Glúms saga* and *Færeyinga saga* could have been written in Eyjafjörður around 1215. They share a certain sardonic view of what makes a chieftain successful. This image could have been fostered by Norwegian hegemony and an emerging view that the dominant state lives by the power of authority while the subordinate state lives by its wits. The triumph of wit over power is a recurrent, if not *the* recurrent theme in the *þættir*, in which resourceful Icelanders repeatedly hold their own against kings. *Víga-Glúms saga* may therefore be both about political separation from Norway and about a new paradigm for political success.

Reykdœla saga lends itself to generalization less readily than *Víga-Glúms saga*. If the latter is a tale of political sagacity, the former initially eludes any search for an overarching theme. It reads like a detailed but unfocused account of regional feuds and disputes extending over two generations, the first dominated by Áskell Eyvindarson and the second by his son Skúta now familiar from *Víga-Glúms saga*. We have devoted a considerable space to making the case that the author of *Reykdœla saga* knew and borrowed from the latter. He in fact concludes with an evaluation of Skúta Áskelsson that sounds like an echo of *Víga-Glúms saga* (ÍF 10:243):

> En þó er þat eina satt af honum at segja, at hann var vitr maðr ok inn mesti fullhugi, ok margir gengu ekki betr en til jafns við hann, þótt miklir þœttisk fyrir sér vera, en eigi þótti hann ǫllum jafnaðarmaðr vera.

> [But it can truly be told of him that he was a wise man and a great warrior, and many were no better than his equals though they thought themselves very eminent, but he did not impress everyone as being an equitable man.]

This phrasing recalls the judgment passed on Glúmr at the end of his saga (ÍF 9:98):

> Þat er ok [mál] manna, at Glúmr hafi verit tuttugu vetr mestr hǫfðingi í Eyjafirði, en aðra tuttugu vetr engi meiri en til jafns við hann.

> [People say that for twenty years Glúmr was the greatest chieftain in Eyjafjörður, and for another twenty no one was more than his equal.]

Reykdœla saga seems to be making the assertion that Skúta was one of those who, during Glúmr's last twenty years, was definitely his equal, whatever the exaggerated claims in *Víga-Glúms saga* might be.

"Skútu saga" could even be understood as a counterpoise to *Víga-Glúms saga* as a whole, in effect telling the other side of the story. Going a step further, we could surmise that *Reykdœla saga* is a counterthrust on the qualities that are appropriate for a chieftain. Whereas Víga-Glúmr is secretive and deceitful, Áskell is in every way the model chieftain, open, admired and trusted by everyone, and consistently just. He achieves no fewer than eight reconciliations in a persistent series of bloody disputes; even when mortally wounded, his only thought is to effect a peaceful settlement. The contrast to Víga-Glúmr could hardly be more explicit, and it could well be calculated. If so, *Reykdœla saga* might be considered as a polemical response to the political perspective that unfolds in *Víga-Glúms saga*.[59]

Ljósvetninga saga

We turn now to the third early saga from Eyjafjörður, *Ljósvetninga saga*. The study of this saga is beset by particularly difficult textual issues. It exists in two very different redactions known as A and C, and the dating and relationship of these redactions have been viewed very differently. The editor, Björn Sigfússon, considered the fragmentary A redaction to be original, but the translators, Andersson and Miller, considered the full C version to be original.[60] The dating is contingent on this choice as well as other matters. There are two clear literary borrowings, one from *Morkinskinna* (less likely *Heimskringla*) and one from *Þorgils saga ok Hafliða*. Such links often provide dating indices, but in this case there are too many uncertainties. If the author borrowed from *Morkinskinna*, the dating is likely to be early, but if the source is *Heimskringla*, which superseded *Morkinskinna*, it could be quite late. A study of the parallel columns from these texts printed by Björn Sigfússon (ÍF 10:XXXIV–XXXV) suggests to this reader that the order of composition was *Morkinskinna—Ljósvetninga saga—Heimskringla*, but such matters have often become mired in inconclusive debates.

A borrowing from *Þorgils saga ok Hafliða* seems equally certain, but dates for this saga have run the gamut from an unlikely 1160 to after 1237.[61] There is thus too much latitude for such a source to be useful. In addition, both literary borrowings are at the very end of *Ljósvetninga saga* and look like afterthoughts that could have been added late in the manuscript tradition. Given these uncertainties, the most likely dating indication may be the mention of Þorvarðr Þorgeirsson (died 1207). In chapter 23 a spy is sent to observe the doings at a farm named Veisa. He is roughly treated and prevented from entering so that he must return with nothing accomplished, though with a strong suspicion that there was a large group of armed men inside. The manhandling of the would-be spy became quasi-proverbial, and the saga states (ÍF 10:73): "Þorvarðr Þorgeirsson was subsequently in the habit of saying, whenever there was a ruckus, 'Let's try the Veisa grip'." This reference suggests that at the time of writing Þorvarðr was within living memory; it would seem strange to quote a trivial phrase spoken by a man who had already been dead for forty or fifty years.

Þorvarðr is also mentioned in *Reykdœla saga* (ÍF 10:213) from the same neighborhood, but the two sagas are remarkably different. Although there are compositional weaknesses and real questions about the narrative relevance in some passages, *Ljósvetninga saga* is endowed with a dramatic structure and a scenic vividness not to be found in *Reykdœla saga,* apart from the episode borrowed from *Víga-Glúms saga.* The dramatic line is particularly well managed in the first of the two generations described in *Ljósvetninga saga.* The story pits the great Eyjafjörður chieftain Guðmundr ríki against the family of the Ljósvetningar to the east. It is revealed that there is gossip in the region to the effect that Guðmundr is homosexual. This is the kind of rumor that cannot be confronted directly, but Guðmundr's revenge is narrated in brilliant and escalating detail, with a sequence of sharply focused scenes. Guðmundr holds the better cards and duly accomplishes his revenge, but the author works almost surreptitiously against the grain. Although Guðmundr succeeds, he gains no credit. Indeed, the author allows the charge against him to stand. The saga is thus a drama of cross-purposes. The political winner becomes the moral loser, and the two victims of his revenge emerge as the heroes of the story.

If the saga indeed dates from as early as the 1220s, we can observe that saga narrative has already achieved real complexity in psychological terms. More important than the actual events or the spoken words are the unarticulated thoughts and ponderings that motivate them. This art of insinuation is destined to become one of the hallmarks of the sagas in their full flower. It is not altogether new in *Ljósvetninga* *saga*; we have seen the operations of subterfuge in the remnants of **Hlaðajarla saga* as well as in *Víga-Glúms saga*, but the art is more fully and consistently evolved in *Ljósvetninga saga*. It leads the reader to reflect on what is really being said, and to imagine what is not being said. This fondness for a subnarrative with crucial intimations must have been anticipated in some way in the antecedent oral narrative art, but it becomes tangible only in the written versions.

Another prominent feature of *Ljósvetninga saga* is a peculiarly moralizing outlook. The sagas overall have often been credited with a special brand of authorial objectivity, but in the case of this saga such a generalization is particularly misplaced. We have seen that the author indirectly but quite explicitly undermines the greatest chieftain of the region, Guðmundr ríki, on moral grounds.[62] The critique does not stop with Guðmundr but persists into the next generation in the person of his son and successor Eyjólfr Guðmundarson. Eyjólfr embodies a number of flaws also peculiar to his father, notably a consuming sense of his own importance. He too becomes involved in a protracted and uncompromising feud, but whereas Guðmundr's antagonists were scattered and located both to the west and east, Eyjólfr's hostility is focused on a particular family to the east around Ljósavatn (hence "Ljósvetningar"). Eyjólfr's behavior is characterized chiefly by intransigence, but the Ljósvetningar, especially their chieftain Þorvarðr, display more admirable qualities, a degree of flexibility, loyalty to one another, and group solidarity. As in the first generation, Eyjólfr has all the material advantages and consequently gets the better of the feud, but, like his father, he gains only opprobrium.

The saga thus pits an eastern group, the Ljósvetningar, against the chieftains in Eyjafjörður. This confrontation suggests something about regional sympathies and perhaps about the author's location. Although the literary activity in northern Iceland in the early thirteenth century probably centered in the most prosperous area in Eyjafjörður, the home turf of Guðmundr and Eyjólfr, the author's sympathies are clearly aligned against these chieftains and favor the easterners. The author is likely to have been associated with the latter, and if the writing was done in Eyjafjörður, it was surely done by someone with eastern family connections or an eastern allegiance.

It is difficult to think of another saga that is quite so regionally colored as *Ljósvetninga saga*, and we may inquire where the idea of regional conflict originated. Perhaps the precedent may be found in the orbit of the kings' sagas. These sagas are replete with conflicts between Norway and Denmark or Norway and Sweden. We might also think of *Færeyinga saga*, tentatively dated around 1215, in which a major theme is the conflict between the Faroese chieftains and the Norwegian kings. This tension is no less characteristic of *Orkneyinga saga*, whatever the date and original form of that saga may have been.[63] These texts incorporate a sympathetic view of local resistance to monarchical overlordship, and that is, in an extended sense, the gist of *Ljósvetninga saga*. Regal instincts have been detected in Guðmundr ríki, and the Ljósvetningar might be considered the victims of oppression.[64]

Another form of regionalism may be hypothesized for **Hlaðajarla saga*. Since we do not have it, we cannot speculate on the degree to which it not only promotes the special status of Þrœndalǫg but also portrays tensions between that region and the central monarchy, but some such opposition seems likely. If my supposition that **Hlaðajarla saga* reached down to the middle of the eleventh century and included the contest between Haraldr harðráði and Einarr þambarskelfir is correct, that clash may have sown the literary seeds of regional conflict in Iceland as well. Furthermore, if **Hlaðajarla saga* underlies both *Fagrskinna* and *Morkinskinna*, it too must date from ca. 1215 and could have exercised an influence on *Ljósvetninga saga*.

Political antagonism is in any event a fundamental theme in the feud between Mǫðrvellingar and Ljósvetningar. The political dimension is reinforced by a sharp contrast in portraiture. Guðmundr and Eyjólfr are systematically disparaged and are not given the benefit of redeeming qualities, while the leading Ljósvetningar, notably Þorvarðr Hǫskuldsson, Ófeigr Járngerðarson, and Hallr Ótryggsson, are exalted, sometimes extravagantly. Personal qualities count for a great deal in the story, and contrastive personalities are also a prominent feature of the kings' sagas.

In **Hlaðajarla saga* the contrast between a supremely guileful Hákon jarl and an unsuspecting King Haraldr Gormsson guides the action. In this case the regional chieftain triumphs. If the saga included the contest between Einarr þambarskelfir and King Haraldr Sigurðarson, the contrast between guile and sturdy independence is central, but guile is condemned and all the sources prefer the regional chieftain. It seems not unlikely that the author of *Ljósvetninga saga* stood heir to these patterns of regional antipathy and personal craftiness that were well established in the sagas about Norwegian kings and their antagonists at home and abroad. Such oppositions became thematic especially in *Morkinskinna* with its persistent distinctions between peaceable and militant kings. In *Ljósvetninga saga* these large-scale conflicts were translated onto a more limited local scene, but with no loss of vigor.

CHAPTER 7

Warrior Poets in the Northwest

In the critical literature on the sagas there has been a certain prioritizing of the western sagas, notably *Egils saga*. To some extent this preference is a question of quality because *Egils saga* and *Laxdœla saga* have a particular claim to excellence, but there has been a tendency to give the western sagas pride of place in the chronology as well. It might therefore be logical to turn our attention to the Borgarfjörður group, *Bjarnar saga Hítdœlakappa*, *Egils saga*, and *Gunnlaugs saga ormstungu*. The first two have normally been considered early and *Gunnlaugs saga* late, but Bjarni Guðnason thought that *Bjarnar saga* was late, and I have suggested that *Gunnlaugs saga* was the earliest of the three.[1] It can be argued that the author of *Bjarnar saga* borrowed the motif of the procrastinating groom from *Gunnlaugs saga* to structure his plot and that the author of *Egils saga* borrowed material on Egill's son Þorsteinn and other ancestral lore from *Gunnlaugs saga*. If we posit that *Bjarnar saga* is after all early and that *Egils saga* was composed not too long after 1220, that would place *Gunnlaugs saga* and *Bjarnar saga* a few years earlier, at about the same time that saga writing may have begun in Eyjafjörður. On the other hand, although there could have been borrowing among the sagas of the Borgarfjörður region, I can find no evidence of the ideological debate that seems to have left traces in the northern sagas. I will therefore focus on two sagas from northwestern Iceland that perhaps lend themselves more readily to such analysis, *Fóstbrœðra saga* and *Gísla saga Súrssonar*.

I take the view that *Fóstbrœðra saga* was written at the beginning of the thirteenth century and *Gísla saga* closer to the middle of the century, but the dating of both sagas is open to doubt, and the dating of *Fóstbrœðra saga* in particular is an unresolved issue. A hundred years ago Sigurður Nordal argued for a date not much later than 1200. His view was generally accepted until 1972, when Jónas Kristjánsson published a detailed investigation in which he advocated a date toward the end of the thirteenth century.[2] The question turns to a large extent on the relationship of *Fóstbrœðra saga* to the various versions of *Óláfs saga helga*. Nordal argued that the finale of *Fóstbrœðra saga* (describing the role of Þormóðr Bersason in the Battle of Stiklarstaðir) and the *Oldest Saga of Saint Olaf* converged in a lost text that he named the *Middle Saga. In turn the *Middle Saga afforded the basis for the *Legendary Saga* and Styrmir Kárason's largely lost version of the work; this last in turn served as the source for the version of the saga included in *Heimskringla*. The reader will grasp immediately that we are confronted by too many lost sources. We have only six fragments of the *Oldest Saga*, none of the hypothetical *Middle Saga, and a few random sentences from Styrmir's version.

In such a partially documented transmission there is a good deal of latitude for alternative explanations, and Jónas Kristjánsson construed the material quite differently. He assumed that the *Oldest Saga* was the source of both the *Legendary Saga* and Styrmir's book, and that all three of these versions, the *Oldest Saga*, the *Legendary Saga*, and Styrmir's version, fed into the finale of *Fóstbrœðra saga*. I have dealt with the main objections to this construction elsewhere and will summarize them only very briefly here.[3]

Perhaps the greatest stumbling block is the derivation of Þormóðr's last stand in *Fóstbrœðra saga* from the *Legendary Saga* (or the equivalent passage in the *Oldest Saga*) despite the fact that there are virtually no verbal correspondences.[4] When one saga copies another, the match is generally very close and the act of copying is obvious. In this case there is no evidence of copying. It therefore seems most likely that the accounts of Þormóðr's last stand in the *Oldest Saga*/*Legendary Saga* and *Fóstbrœðra saga* are independent of each other and represent different recordings of the same story. If the source of the story is oral rather than textual, that is perhaps indicative of an early date.

A second problem in Jónas's construction of the evidence is the supposition that a saga author in the late thirteenth century would have based his account on the earliest versions of *Óláfs saga helga*. If *Fóstbrœðra saga* dates from the end of the century, these versions would have been sixty or seventy years old and would long since have been replaced by the fuller and much superior version in *Heimskringla*. It is surely *Heimskringla* that such a late author would have turned to.

A third difficulty is that the author of *Fóstbrœðra saga*, who made no obvious use of written sources, should, at the very end of his saga, have suddenly consulted no fewer than three different texts to cobble together his finale.[5] For these reasons I find Nordal's early dating more convincing. If it is in fact correct, *Fóstbrœðra saga* may have a claim to being the earliest of the sagas devoted to the lives of Saga Age Icelanders. The saga may not be quite as early as Nordal thought because he dated the *Oldest Saga* around 1180 rather than around 1200, as is now more commonly done, but a date close to 1210 for *Fóstbrœðra saga* would be entirely reasonable.

The action of *Fóstbrœðra saga* is straightforward and singularly unembellished. It might be divided into the following stages:

1. Þorgeirr Hávarsson and Þormóðr Bersason engage in a series of youthful adventures that culminate in the separation of the two close companions and Þorgeirr's outlawing for a killing, his exile, and his service with King Óláfr Haraldsson in Norway (ÍF 6:121–60).
2. Left to his own devices, Þormóðr pursues two amorous adventures, more out of boredom than affection (ÍF 6:161–77).
3. Þorgeirr returns to Iceland, where he avenges one of King Óláfr's retainers and kills a certain Gautr Sleituson (ÍF 6:177–201).
4. Þorgrímr Einarsson and Þórarinn ofsi Þorvaldsson avenge Gautr and kill Þorgeirr after a notable defense (ÍF 6:201–12).
5. Þormóðr takes service with King Óláfr in Norway, then experiences a series of extravagant adventures in Greenland in the course of avenging Þorgeirr against Þorgrímr Einarsson (ÍF 6:213–60).
6. Þormóðr participates in the Battle of Stiklarstaðir and falls (ÍF 6:261–76).

This rough outline is sufficient to show that the saga is a tale of unvarnished vengeance and bloodshed. The tone is set in the first section, as each adventure concludes with a killing. Both aggressors and victims seem equally endowed with sanguinary instincts. Indeed, this proclivity is established even for the previous generation, because Þorgeirr's father is no better disposed (ÍF 6:123): "Hávarr var kynjaðr sunnan af Akranesi ok hafði farit þaðan fyrir víga sakar, því at hann var mikill vígamaðr ok hávaðamaðr ok ódæll" [Hávarr was a native of Akranes to the south and had moved away because of killings, for he was a notable warrior [or killer] and an arrogant and quarrelsome fellow]. Þormóðr does not have the same family history, but he shares Þorgeirr's inherited disposition (ÍF 6:124):

> Snimmendis sagði þeim svá hugr um, sem síðar bar raun á, at þeir myndi vápnbitnir verða, því at þeir váru ráðnir til at láta sinn hlut hvergi eða undir leggja, við hverja menn sem þeir ætti málum at skipta. Meir hugðu þeir jafnan at fremð þessa heims lífs en at dýrð annars heims fagnaðar.
>
> [There was an early intimation, as was later confirmed, that they would succumb to weapons, for they were not inclined to defer or submit in any way, no matter who they were dealing with. They always thought more about promoting their welfare in this world than about [gaining] the glory of joy in the next.]

They become constant companions, but their activities in the district are sufficiently unedifying that they arouse universal disapproval (ÍF 6:125): "[F]ara þeir víða um heruð ok váru eigi vinsælir, tǫlðu margir þá ekki vera jafnaðarmenn" [they roamed far and wide in the districts and were not popular; many people thought they were not equitable men]. The chieftain and neighbors therefore confront their fathers, and Hávarr is obliged to move south to Borgarfjörður, although Þorgeirr's conduct does not improve. Such is the initial recommendation that the author provides for his protagonists.

Hávarr returns to the scene just long enough to lend a horse to a certain Jǫðurr. When the horse is not returned at the agreed time, Hávarr tries to seize it by force, and Jǫðurr promptly kills him. Þorgeirr does not react visibly on learning of his father's death, but the author provides some comments on his character (ÍF 6:128): he is not much interested in women, is not given to laughing, and is generally unpleasant to people. He also has a broad ax that procures death for quite a few people.[6] It is unclear whether that remark applies to killings we learn about in the narrative or to others we are not told about; in a later stanza (ÍF 6:210) Þorgeirr appears to be credited with a total of thirteen killings. On this occasion, despite his impassive reaction to the news of his father's death, Þorgeirr, at the age of fifteen, shows up at Jǫðurr's front door and runs him through with his spear, then reports the killing to his mother in demonstratively laconic terms. People in the district betoken admiration for such a feat at such an early age, though Þorgeirr and Þormóðr continue in their unpopular ways.

In the sequel they confront a father and son named Ingólfr and Þorbrandr, who are notorious evildoers in the district but are under the protection of the chieftain Vermundr. A woman named Sigrfljóð goads Þorgeirr and Þormóðr into action against these malefactors, and they duly kill them in a pitched combat. Sigrfljóð settles the matter with Vermundr, pointing out that the victims got no more than their just deserts. Thus, the matter seems to be passed off as justified in the interest of maintaining law and order.

Þorgeirr next faces a certain Butraldi, who seems to share some of his own characteristics (ÍF 6:142–43):

> Hann var einhleypingr, mikill maðr vexti, rammr at afli, ljótr í ásjónu, harðfengr í skaplyndi, vígamaðr mikill, nasbráðr ok heiptúðigr.
>
> [He was a loner, a big man, strong, ugly, of a tough disposition, a great warrior (or "killer"), unrestrained and aggressive.]

The two of them happen to share the same lodging, and their silent antagonism is vividly described. It culminates when Þorgeirr pitches down a snowy slope and dispatches Butraldi with spear and ax. No aftermath is reported, and there is no judgment against Þorgeirr.

Together Þorgeirr and Þormóðr become involved in a dispute over the ownership of a beached whale. This time their antagonist, a certain Þorgils Másson, is not described as a local predator; though big and tough, he is credited with being a worthy farmer. As a result, when Þorgeirr defeats and kills him, he suffers the consequences and is outlawed, though without comment on the author's part. More important is what follows. It is noted that, given their success, the companions had become very arrogant, and Þorgeirr wonders out loud who could possibly be their superiors, and who would emerge victorious if the two of them tested their strength against each other. That tacit challenge alienates Þormóðr, who now elects to go his own separate way.

Undeterred, Þorgeirr continues his aggressive behavior along the northeast coast of the Westfjords. He kills two more men over the borrowing of his horse and failure to return it on demand. Since he is already outlawed, there seems not to be much recourse. He now sets sail for Norway on a Norwegian ship. Aboard the same ship is a man named Gautr Sleituson, a kinsman of the Þorgils Másson Þorgeirr had killed in the dispute over a whale. The Norwegians think it best not to foster dissension on their ship and discharge Gautr. Once in Norway, Þorgeirr takes service with King Óláfr and is not slow to gain fame. He subsequently divides his time between Norway and Iceland, but there is no further comment on his outlawry.

What is remarkable about this sequence of adventures is not so much Þorgeirr's callousness as the author's silence. In the course of the action Þorgeirr kills six men without prompting a word of disapproval. The killing of Jǫðurr may be justified as revenge for a father, and the slaying of Þorbrandr may be viewed as good riddance of a ne'er-do-well, but Butraldi falls only because he is disagreeable and challenging, while Þorgils Másson succumbs in a quarrel in which he may be defending a just cause. The two men who fall in the last encounter, Bjarni and Skúfr, pay a high price in a trivial matter; Bjarni borrows a horse without leave and is provocative in not returning it promptly, but it is questionable whether two deaths in reprisal are really proportionate.

The judgment here and elsewhere is left up to the reader because the author makes no pronouncements and offers no hint of reproach in any of the cases, direct or indirect. Nor is anything said in defense of the victims, some of whom (Jǫðurr, Þorbrandr, and Butraldi) seem to be ruffians on the same level as Þorgeirr. It is as if we are witnessing an internecine feud among bandits. The author simply tabulates the killings and leaves it in the reader's purview to decide whether Þorgeirr is a serial killer or merely overzealous in asserting his claims. Although the sagas are famous for their dispassionate style, the neutrality in *Fóstbrœðra saga* may seem exaggerated, and we may wonder whether it is an oversight or intended for special effect.

A short interlude on Þormóðr's amours is relatively bloodless, though in an encounter with an attacker dispatched by an indignant mother Þormóðr does lose the use of his right arm. He proves to be an unreliable lover and switches his affections from one woman, Kolbrún, to another, Þorbjǫrg, at the same time recasting his verse in honor of the former in order to celebrate the latter. This poetic infidelity is punished by sorcery, and Þormóðr must publicly restore his verses to their original recipient. But these amorous misdemeanors seem tame in comparison to the earlier killing spree.

The story now reverts to Þorgeirr, who picks up where he left off. He rides by the farm of a certain Hœkils-Snorri, whose description is almost identical to the unflattering one bestowed on Butraldi earlier in the saga.[7] Þorgeirr's horses elect to graze on Snorri's inner yard, and Snorri, not unreasonably, tries to drive them off. Þorgeirr responds by attacking and eventually killing both Snorri and two of his farmhands, thus increasing the number of his known killings in Iceland to nine. He also takes aim at a certain Þórir, who had wounded one of King Óláfr's retainers, and eliminates him with the same dispassion that characterizes his earlier killings. The author once more withholds comment. In a curious reversal of his customary murderous role, Þorgeirr unaccountably takes the part of a thief named Veglágr, saves him from hanging, and transports him to Orkney. Veglágr ends up in Scotland, where he renews his thievery and is eventually killed.

In the harbor at Slétta Þorgeirr has a further encounter with Gautr Sleituson. Initially each provokes the other by using his spear and shield as firewood. Þorgeirr, exhibiting his usual bland indifference, enters Gautr's tent one night, awakens him, and delivers a fatal ax blow. Sometime later he sees a ship approaching, which turns out to be under the command of Þorgrímr Einarsson and Þórarinn ofsi Þorvaldsson. As the nickname "ofsi" [arrogance] suggests, these are tough characters in their own right. Þorgeirr negotiates a truce with them, withholding the news of Gautr's death, but it emerges that Þórarinn is a kinsman of Gautr's. When Þórarinn learns of the killing, he therefore conspires with Þorgrímr to take revenge. They manage to pick off some of Þorgeirr's men and gain a numerical advantage for a head-on assault. Þorgeirr mounts a memorable defense, kills two more men, but succumbs in the end. Þorgrímr and Þórarinn mistreat the corpse, then go their separate ways; Þórarinn is killed in a separate incident and Þorgrímr settles in Greenland.

The rest of the story is devoted to Þormóðr. Although it is the most entertaining, as well as extravagant, part of the saga, we need not recapitulate in detail. Þormóðr, like Þorgeirr before him, takes service with King Óláfr, then asks for permission to go to Greenland. Óláfr, surmising that it is for the purpose of avenging his retainer Þorgeirr, grants permission, and the killing recommences. When Þormóðr returns to King Óláfr, he modestly claims five victims in a stanza, but in reality there were four other victims.[8]

It would be pedantic to tally up the killings in individual sagas, and *Fóstbrœðra saga* may not have the greatest number, but the indifference with which they are treated is striking. The known killings add up to twenty-five (prior to the Battle of Stiklarstaðir), and they are uniformly unlamented. The one exception may be Þorgeirr himself, to whom Þormóðr, even after their parting, remains faithful. The proof is that he undertakes such disproportionate vengeance, although he never gives voice to his sense of loss. That Þormóðr is no stranger to sentiment is suggested not only by his short-lived love affairs but also by his great devotion to King Óláfr, which is conveyed both by his verse and by the words of the saga. But on the whole, even up to the day of his death, the saga is dominated by unrelenting reticence.

Although the sagas are famous for being emotionally undemonstrative, this reputation is not always or everywhere deserved. There are highly charged moments of love and grief in *Gunnlaugs saga*, *Bjarnar saga*, and *Egils saga*, and *Laxdœla saga* is saturated with repressed sentiment. The best contrast to *Fóstbrœðra saga* may, however, be *Gísla saga Súrssonar* because it comes from the same region, the West Fjords, and centers on another famous warrior-poet. If *Fóstbrœðra saga* is a tale of hard-bitten blood revenge, *Gísla saga* is a tale of competing sentiments, often disguised but always close to the surface.

A palpable difference between the two sagas is that one is quite devoid of family attachments whereas the other is organized precisely around family interactions. Þorgeirr's father enters the story briefly, then dies. Þormóðr's parents are barely mentioned and have no part in the action. Neither of the companions seems to have brothers or sisters. Neither of them marries, and there is no mention that either has children. They are close friends for a time, but as far as the reader can tell, it is a wordless friendship. On the other hand, *Gísla saga* traces Gísli's family back to the previous generation in Norway and has much to say about all the family members in both generations. The story of the first generation and the beginning of the second generation is transmitted in two manuscript versions so that, as in the case of *Ljósvetninga saga*, there are questions about which version has priority, at least down to the time of the family's settlement in Iceland.[9] Fortunately, the story of family tensions does not begin in earnest until this point. We can therefore dispense with the disputed prelude in Norway to a large extent.

The central characters in the saga are Gísli, his brother Þorkell, and his sister Þórdís. Whereas in *Fóstbrœðra saga*, no one has an intense relationship with anybody else until the very end, in *Gísla saga* all the main characters have one or more intense relationships. Gísli marries a woman named Auðr, and that marriage becomes the greatest love match anywhere in the sagas. At the same time Gísli forms a particularly tight friendship with Auðr's brother Vésteinn.

Gísli's brother Þorkell marries a certain Ásgerðr, but this marriage turns out to be more problematical. A little later Þórdís is wooed by the chieftain Þorgrímr Þorsteinsson, who moves into the vicinity of Gísli and Þorkell so that they all become friends and neighbors. The first sign of trouble is a prediction at a local thingmeeting that they will not always be so close. Gísli proposes to solidify their bonds by inducing them to swear oaths of blood brotherhood, but Þorgrímr, whether from instinctive apprehension or some prior knowledge of what is afoot, withdraws at the last moment and declines to swear oaths that would bind him not only to his in-laws but also to his in-laws' in-law (Vésteinn).

The actual rift in the family becomes apparent when it is revealed that Þorkell's wife Ásgerðr is amorously involved with Vésteinn. This revelation puts Þorkell at odds with his brother Gísli because Vésteinn is Gísli's close friend and sworn brother. As a consequence, Þorkell, who up until now has shared a farm with Gísli, moves away and takes up residence with Þorgrímr, although he is a somewhat irresolute fellow and cannot bring himself to abandon his marriage with Ásgerðr. The tightly knit family of four is thus split down the middle with the brothers-in-law Þorkell and Þorgrímr on one side and Gísli and Vésteinn on the other.

Gísli does his best to keep Vésteinn out of harm's way, but Vésteinn ignores his warning and takes up residence in his house. One stormy night when almost everyone is outside trying to salvage the hay, an unidentified assassin enters the house and kills Vésteinn. There has been an interesting "whodunit" debate on the identity of the killer, but it is probably Þorgrímr.[10] Gísli and Þorkell, who are after all brothers and have a close though frayed relationship, try to stay on good terms, but there is growing hostility between Gísli and Þorgrímr. It culminates when Gísli takes revenge for his sworn brother Vésteinn, enters Þorgrímr's house secretly, and kills him in the dead of night. This famous passage is fraught with emotional overtones because Þorgrímr, as he is killed in bed, is of course sleeping next to his wife, Gísli's sister Þórdís. The situation is one in which Gísli must, of necessity, alienate his sister at the same time he is avenging his sworn brother.

It is not known at first who Þorgrímr's murderer is, but Gísli, the irrepressible poet, composes a stanza acknowledging that he is the killer. He intends to recite the stanza under his breath, but Þórdís overhears it. The faultlines in the family are now multiplied; they run between Gísli and Þorkell, Þorgrímr's good friend, and between Gísli and his sister Þórdís, Þorgrímr's wife. The family that began as a model of concord is now riddled with resentments, spoken and unspoken. Gísli's secret is kept for a time, but we can imagine Þórdís's state of mind once she knows the truth. In the long run she cannot remain silent; in a memorable scene she stops in her tracks, literally puts her foot down, and reveals the secret to her brother-in-law Bǫrkr. That brings about Gísli's outlawry.

From this point on and for the duration of Gísli's outlawry the story is about the inner lives of the various characters. After Vésteinn's murder his sister Auðr is deeply affected. Gísli composes three stanzas, one in memory of Vésteinn (5), one about Auðr's hidden tears (6), and one about her flow of tears (7). We never see Gísli reflecting on Vésteinn, and we never see Auðr actually weeping, but the stanzas amply visualize their grief. The last two are in response to Þorkell's repeated inquiries into whether Auðr is shedding tears (ÍF 6:46–47). On the one hand, these stanzas are about Auðr's state of mind and her grief for her brother. On the other, they offer a tantalizing glimpse into Þorkell's state of mind. Why is he so persistently interested in his sister-in-law's feelings? Is it sympathy? Is his anger over the adultery so great that he wants Auðr to suffer the consequences along with her brother? Or is he apprehensive that Auðr in her grief will foment revenge? We cannot know. The most plausible answer might be that he experiences each of these feelings in turn or in a jumble. In any event the author opens the door to the reader's imagination, even though the affected siblings never exchange words with each other, at least not in the reader's hearing. We therefore have no inkling of how they would formulate the feelings that the author is so careful to let us know that they have but are so chary in communicating.

There is one little chink in the wall of silence. When Gísli learns that Þórdís has betrayed his secret to her brother-in-law Bǫrkr, he composes a stanza in which he reproaches her for not resembling the Guðrún Gjúkadóttir of heroic poetry, who sided with her brothers against her husband. The reproachful tone is picked up in the following prose, which is more explicit on blame than one expects in the sagas (ÍF 6:62):

> Ok þóttumk ek eigi þess verðr frá henni, því at ek þykkjumk þat lýst hafa nǫkkurum sinnum, at mér hefir eigi hennar óvirðing betri þótt en sjálfs mín; hefi ek stundum lagt líf mitt í háska fyrir hennar sakar, en hon hefir nú gefit mér dauðaráð.

> [It has not seemed to me that I deserved this of her, for I think I have shown more than once that I have thought her dishonor no less important than my own; I have on occasion risked my life for her sake, but now she has conspired in my death.]

Gísli's allusion to his sister's dishonor pertains to two episodes in the Norwegian prelude in which Gísli intervenes to kill her ostensibly unwanted suitors in order to protect her reputation.[11] The problem is that, although we can be certain that her father does not want the suitors, we cannot be sure, in one case at least, that Þórdís is of the same mind. She may have felt that, far from clearing her name, Gísli has interfered with her love life. From her point of view, therefore, his killing of Þorgrímr does not necessarily hark back to moments of fraternal solicitude but merely exacerbates an earlier tension. This tension may be of many years' standing and run deep. We know in fact that Þorkell was befriended with one of the "unwanted" suitors and expressed displeasure at his killing in the longer version of the Norwegian prelude.[12]

Gísli consequently has an emotional prehistory with his brother as well as his sister.[13] When Þorkell informs him of his sister's betrayal and Gísli has expressed his disappointment, he turns to Þorkell to ask what he may expect of him; it is as if, having lost the support of his sister, he now wonders whether he will lose the support of his brother too (ÍF 6:62). In fact, Þorkell's response is quite half-hearted; he promises to give Gísli warning of any attempt on his life but not shelter, which would make him liable to prosecution for harboring an outlaw. Þórdís marries her brother-in-law Bǫrkr and disappears from the action until the very end of the saga, but Þorkell's half-measures to help his brother become an intermittent refrain throughout the saga. The meetings of the brothers are colored with Þorkell's self-preoccupation and Gísli's sadness at the failure of brotherly affection. After their first meeting, the author comments (ÍF 6:75): "Gísla þykkir fyrir, er þeir skiljask" [Gísli is distressed at their parting]. Given the severity of saga understatement, this is an unusually overt expression of emotion.

Gísla saga has much to say about alienation, but no less to say about closeness. Once outlawed, Gísli spends a winter with a certain Þorgerðr, who provides a temporary hideout, but he soon returns to his wife, who is now resident in Geirþjófsfjörður to the south of their previous residence. The reason for this potentially dangerous reunion is not strategic but sentimental (ÍF 6:75):

> Þegar er várar, ferr Gísli aptr í Geirþjófsfjǫrð ok má þá eigi lengr vera í brott frá Auði, konu sinni; svá unnask þau mikit.
>
> [In early spring Gísli returns to Geirþjófsfjörður and cannot bear to be away from his wife Auðr any longer, so greatly do they love each other.]

The sagas are not greatly preoccupied with married love, but *Gísla saga* is a notable exception. The inability of the couple to stay apart for very long becomes thematic, and Auðr's devotion culminates, as we will see below, in an episode in which she humiliates Gísli's pursuers beyond reprieve.

Gísli's bonds are, however, not exclusively with his family. His thirteen years of outlawry can be read as an exciting drama of narrow escapes with the help of others, but they can also be read as a record of intercessions on his behalf by devoted friends and admirers. The first of his guardian angels is the woman Þorgerðr who hides him for a winter. The author comments as follows on the quality of her reception (ÍF 6:75): ". . . ok hefir hvergi verit jafnvel gǫrt við hann í sekðinni sem þar" [nowhere was he treated so well as there during his outlawry]. Such words echo later in the saga.

Gísli now acquires a boat from his, as always reluctant, brother, capsizes it so as to make it appear that he has drowned, and takes refuge with a certain Ingjaldr on the island of Hergilsey. He is ultimately tracked down by his enemies, and Ingjaldr is willing to give up his life in defense of the fugitive. But Gísli is ready with a handsome rejoinder (ÍF 6:81):

> "Nú fór sem mik varði," sagði Gísli, "at þú myndir hitta þat ráðit, at þú mættir drengrinn af verða sem beztr; en verri laun sel ek þér þá fyrir liðveizluna en ek hafða ætlat, ef þú skalt fyrir mínar sakar lífit láta."
>
> ["Now it has come about as I suspected," said Gísli, "namely that you would choose the option of being the most outstanding man, but I would give you a worse reward for your help than I intended if you are to lose your life for my sake."]

Accordingly Ingjaldr gets the same authorial praise that Þorgerðr got before him (ÍF 6:84): "Ok þat hafa menn mælt, at Ingjaldr hafi Gísla mest veitt ok þat at mestu gagni orðit" [and people said that Ingjaldr had given Gísli the greatest help and afforded him the greatest benefit]. Rather than risking Ingjaldr's life, Gísli conceives a trick to allow his escape.

Once on land and seriously wounded, Gísli takes shelter with a certain Refr and his notorious harridan of a wife, Álfdís. It is unclear whether Refr even knows Gísli, but he is instantly ready to help and devises the remedy of hiding Gísli in his wife's bedclothes while she sits atop him. The pursuers arrive and ransack the house, but Álfdís treats them to such a barrage of ridicule and abuse that they do not search as carefully as they might otherwise have done. This sequence of rescues suggests that Gísli makes immediate friends wherever he goes, whereas his enemies harvest nothing but contempt.

The disparagement of the opposition reaches its climax in a scene that gathers together several emotional threads. The leader of the trackers, Eyjólfr Þórðarson, who has been paid by Bǫrkr to locate and kill Gísli, approaches Auðr and attempts to bribe her to betray Gísli (ÍF 6:99–100). She pretends to agree and actually starts to count up the money. Her foster daughter, Guðríðr, bursts into tears and runs out of the house to inform Gísli, who is in hiding nearby, that he is about to be surrendered. Gísli is completely unmoved and replies calmly (ÍF 6:99): "Ger þú þér gott í hug, því at eigi mun mér þat at fjǫrlesti verða, at Auðr blekki mik" [cheer up because the cause of my death will not be that Auðr betrays me]. To this he adds a stanza in which he says that he knows that Auðr (scil. in her heart of hearts) is weeping. What she in fact does is to put the proffered silver in a pouch, with which she bloodies Eyjólfr's nose, denouncing his gullibility and telling him to bear in mind that he has been beaten by a woman. This moment combines the lowpoint in the fortunes of Gísli's enemies with the highpoint of marital trust. At one extreme there is a complete incomprehension of emotional bonds and Eyjólfr's belief that Auðr is as venal as he is himself; at the other extreme is the security of perfect certitude.

Much of the remaining saga is given over to the alternating apparitions of a good and a bad dream woman who haunt Gísli's dwindling days. The authenticity of the stanzas inspired by these visions has been challenged on the ground that they are too Christian for a tenth-century poet.[14] But, aside from the fact that the early sagas do not seem to be given to the fabrication of stanzas, the gentle tonality is quite in line with the spirit of the prose. We might easily imagine that the tone of the stanzas contributed to the emotional preoccupations of the narrative as a whole.

After Gísli, vastly outnumbered, falls in an onslaught by Eyjólfr and his followers, the news is brought to Bǫrkr, who, as we may remember, is now married to Gísli's sister Þórdís. Bǫrkr is well pleased with the long deferred revenge for his brother and bids Þórdís make the avengers welcome. Þórdís has at this point been silent for fifty-five pages, but she responds with a famous retort (ÍF 6:116), also quoted in *Eyrbyggja saga* (ÍF 4:24): "Gráta mun ek Gísla, bróður minn . . . en mun eigi vel fagnat Gíslabana, ef grautr er gǫrr ok gefinn?" ["I will weep for my brother Gísli . . . but will it not be sufficient welcome for Gísli's killer if gruel is made and served?"]. Once again the tears are more metaphorical than real, but Þórdís is not content with mere words. As she serves Eyjólfr, she tries to plunge a sword through him under the table, but the hilt catches on the edge of the table, the thrust is deflected, and she inflicts only a serious leg wound. Eyjólfr is once more bested by a woman.

The present chapter is about poets and warriors; Þorgeirr, Þormóðr, and Gísli are all famous outlaws and great warriors. Þormóðr kills nine during his mission of vengeance for Þorgeirr, and Gísli kills eight attackers in his epic last stand. But we may ask whether it is of any importance in Gísli's saga that he is a great warrior. The answer must be that it adds to his legendary status but that it is clearly not the focus of the saga. The focus is on his unique relationship with his wife and his profoundly troubled relationship with his brother and sister. The stories about Saga Age Icelanders are often referred to as family sagas, but *Gísla saga* is perhaps the first in which family is the true subject. There were intimations of family dynamics in *Ljósvetninga saga*, especially between the brothers Guðmundr and Einarr, but family dynamics efface all other concerns in *Gísla saga*. The emotional life of the individuals claims the reader's attention, and the actions, however well told, are important only to the extent that they shed light on the characters.

Fóstbrœðra saga, on the other hand, is most assuredly a tale of action, and the action does not share the stage with family or social concerns. Þorgeirr and Þormóðr appear to have no family or personal connections, apart from Þormóðr's fleeting love affairs, inspired by boredom, and his last-minute attachment to King Óláfr. We have posed the question whether it is important that Gísli is a warrior, but we may also ask whether it is important that Þormóðr is a poet. In *Gísla saga* the stanzas are important because they are mood pieces and tell us something about Gísli's experience and inner life. In *Fóstbrœðra saga* they are more archival; they serve as a record of Þorgeirr's exploits and Þormóðr's service with King Óláfr. The author could have altered the tone substantially by setting down the love stanzas, but he chose not to. As a consequence there is no delineation of Þormóðr's personality or state of mind.

By refocusing on the individuals, *Gísla saga* marks a real revolution in saga writing. Individuals and personalities were conspicuously not central in the kings' sagas, in which neither Óláfr really comes to life. The breakthrough came with the cantankerous protagonist of *Egils saga*, and here too the poetry must have been a crucial factor in the development of character study. There were surely traditions about the kings, but there was not much of the personal verse that gave life to the poets who figure in the purely Icelandic sagas.

I have suggested in earlier chapters that there may have been a kind of chain reaction in the succession of sagas, with each saga responding to previous sagas in confirmation or rebuttal. *Egils saga* could be a response to *Morkinskinna*, *Reykdœla saga* to *Víga-Glúms saga*, and *Ljósvetninga saga* to all three of these. In the western group a case can be made that *Gunnlaugs saga* influenced both *Bjarnar saga* and *Egils saga*. The question in this chapter is whether there is any interplay between our two northwestern sagas. In the light of deep differences in outlook and the absence of any telltale echoes, it is difficult to make such a case. On the other hand, if *Fóstbrœðra saga* was composed around 1210 and *Gísla saga* at a best guess between 1230 and 1250, it seems unlikely that the author of the latter would not have known about his predecessor in the same region.[15] If there was saga writing in Eyjafjörður in the 1220s, it seems equally unlikely that he did not know about this tradition. But if he was aware of one or more of these texts, it must have been a deliberate choice to reject what may have appeared to him to be mere killing chronicles in favor of a more ambitious form.

The author of *Gísla saga* in effect redefined what a saga was. He abandoned the epic of armed confrontation and substituted a study of psychological conflict. In part his project is taken over from the tradition of heroic poetry, as Gísli's unfavorable comparison of Þórdís to Guðrún Gjúkadóttir suggests. Immutable love, silent grief, and repressed tears were also the gist of this tradition, but the author of *Gísla saga* makes the family relationships more complex. The contradictions in Gísli's relationship to both his sister and brother are unresolved; the principals are bound to each other by equally demanding accesses of love and disaffection.

With this problematizing of emotions, the author contrives a new narrative style designed to probe the inner workings of his characters. His experiment opened the way in particular for *Laxdœla saga*, which drew even more explicitly on heroic legend, and later for *Njáls saga*, both stories of dark interiors. The action tales lost ground and were replaced by psychological dramas in the latter part of the thirteenth century. *Gísla saga* was the turning point and set the scene for a significant intensification of the saga form.

Epilogue

The preceding pages attempt to trace and correlate some of the important moments in the earliest development of Icelandic prose literature. Since much of the scholarly debate over the last hundred years has focused on the question of what oral tradition may have paved the way for the sagas, the discussion does not begin with the first written records but with two chapters on the oral antecedents. These antecedents were minimized during much of the twentieth century, but three books by Gísli Sigurðsson and Tommy Danielsson in 2002 reemphasized the probability that there was a substantial storytelling tradition underlying the sagas. Chapter 1 supports this view and tries to adduce some evidence that the stories were not only plentiful but could also be long and detailed. It is of some importance to know from what materials the saga writers worked because the nature of these materials sheds light on the writing procedures that must have been employed. It will further our understanding of the sagas if we can establish whether the authors were creating imaginative fictions or were composing in imitation of familiar traditions. At this moment in history there seems to be widespread agreement that native traditions were the chief inspiration.

Whereas a good deal of labor has been devoted to defining what form these traditions may have taken in the case of the native sagas, no corresponding labor has been invested in the antecedents of the kings' sagas. Yet the wealth of information about the Norwegian kings found in a variety of Icelandic sagas suggests that they too must have left a considerable mark on the evolving narratives in Iceland. Accordingly a short second chapter tries to generalize about what the Icelanders would have known and what they would have transmitted about earlier kings in the preliterary period. Though abundant, this information would have been more remote than the native Icelandic stories and would have conveyed less personalized and dramatic images of the kings than of the Saga Age chieftains in Iceland. The information clearly also passed through a self-consciously Icelandic filter that detracted not a little from the stature of the kings and enhanced the stature of the Icelanders who interacted with them. This tendency is particularly apparent in the so-called *þættir*, which sometimes pit Icelanders against Norwegian kings in tests of character. This less than impartial perspective carries over to the written tradition in the course of time.

Nonetheless, the writing of kings' sagas begins in a panegyric vein with biographies of King Óláfr Tryggvason and King Óláfr Haraldsson, who are the subject of the third chapter. The initial problem is to establish the chronology of these texts, a somewhat vexed undertaking since neither survives in its original form. The saga of Óláfr Tryggvason is extant only in three redactions of an Icelandic translation from the Latin original by a Benedictine monk named Oddr Snorrason in the northern Icelandic monastery of Þingeyrar. The earliest saga of Óláfr Haraldsson survives only in six fragments and later redactions. The two texts nevertheless have a number of motifs and passages in common, and a close comparison suggests that the author of Óláfr Haraldsson's saga made use of Oddr's biography. We can therefore establish with some probability that the writing of the kings' sagas began in Þingeyrar.

Although the original purpose of these sagas seems to have been the praise of kings, this purpose was subject to a counterbalancing interest in the Norwegian colonial areas in the Orkney and Faroe Islands, and most particularly in what appears to have been a sharp provincial counterthrust in the lost **Hlaðajarla saga*. This text can be tentatively reconstructed from the later compilations in *Morkinskinna* and *Fagrskinna*, and it apparently promoted the cause of the jarls of Þrœndalǫg in opposition to the southern dynasty of Norwegian kings dating from the days of Haraldr hárfagri. The sagas thus seem to have incorporated something resembling a political dialogue dating from at least the second decade of the thirteenth century.

A particularly instructive commingling of Norwegian history with native Icelandic attitudes is evident in the version of Óláfr Haraldsson's saga that forms the centerpiece of *Heimskringla*. This text continues to draw heavily on Icelandic traditions that must have circulated orally. A number of *þáttr*-like stories record the interaction of various Icelandic visitors, and it is often possible to make informed guesses about the conduits that transmitted these stories to Iceland and how they were passed down over the generations. As in the other *þættir*, the Icelanders loom disproportionately large and sometimes raise questions about the conduct of the king. There is also a certain amount of overt political discussion about the relationship of the people to their kings, albeit located at the diplomatically safe distance of the Swedish royal court. Sometimes the authorial sympathies seem to lie with the Norwegian provincial chieftains, as if there were some association between Icelandic colonials and Norwegian provincials. This association is emphasized by the marked discrepancy between the saga prose and the contemporary stanzas recorded in it with respect to the tension between king and chieftains. These tensions are cast as an important factor in the downfall of King Óláfr, but they are scarcely alluded to in the stanzas. That suggests that resistance to the monarchy may have been more significant in the Icelandic transmission than in the Norwegian perception.

The *Heimskringla* version of King Óláfr Haraldsson's saga is conventionally dated in the third decade of the thirteenth century, but it is a work in progress and could have been in the making a little earlier. If there is an anti-monarchical bias, it is quite muted and must be read from between the lines. A clearer Icelandic perspective on kingship becomes explicit in another important compilation of kings' sagas known as *Morkinskinna* and written around 1220. This work covers the period 1035 to 1157 and appears to classify the kings in this period in two easily distinguishable groups, three kings who were notable for aggressive foreign policy and three others who promoted peace and prosperity on the domestic front. There seems to be no doubt that the author favors the latter group and is critical of the former. This structure is explored in chapter 5.

Although *Morkinskinna* can be read as a set of recommendations on Norwegian foreign policy, it did not bequeath this viewpoint to Part III of *Heimskringla*, for which it was the chief source. On the contrary, the author of *Heimskringla* III seems to have modified the political contrasts in his source systematically, with the result that the royal portraits are more uniformly positive in his version. Whether this revision represents a difference in opinion, a diplomatic accommodation, or a calculated adjustment for a Norwegian readership is hard to know without more evidence, but *Heimskringla* provides a distinctive reading of history. Most difficult to fathom is the political outlook in *Egils saga*, which may be contemporary with *Morkinskinna* and *Heimskringla*. Egill is an almost caricaturally larger-than-life figure in whose presence everyone else, including two Norwegian kings, skrinks by comparison. Whether he is to be understood as a serious representation of the individual Icelander at his most exalted or a comically exaggerated and over-assertive Icelandic bully is an open question. If we choose the first option, Egill serves to relativize the domination of the Norwegian crown, which is taken for granted in earlier sagas. But if we adopt the second option, the saga becomes a critique of Icelandic self-promotion. The choice is left to the reader, but either way, there is a political edge to the narrative.

Egils saga illustrates that the political preoccupations of the kings' sagas can echo quite distinctly in the native sagas. Chapter 6 pursues this line of inquiry with respect to three sagas from Eyjafjörður. Once more the problem is complicated by the need to resolve chronological issues that have been debated for more than a hundred years. The position taken here is that *Víga-Glúms saga* is the earliest text in this group and may date from ca. 1215–1220. *Reykdœla saga* made direct use of *Víga-Glúms saga* and must therefore be a little later. *Ljósvetninga saga* is the most advanced of the three, but there are reasons for believing that it too is quite early and was most probably written in the 1220s.

All three are concerned with regional hostilities, perhaps a local reflex of the larger national hostilities in the kings' sagas. All three resolutely dispense with the historical hegemony of Norway and the backdrop of emigration from Norway, as if to make the point that the action has now moved definitively to Iceland. Both Glúmr and his father Eyjólfr do, however, make their way in Norway, Eyjólfr to the extent of marrying a chieftain's daughter. Legitimation in Norway seems to be a matter of establishing credentials and will persist in that function in the Icelandic sagas throughout the century. Eyjólfr's success is particularly conspicuous because it is achieved in the teeth of anti-Icelandic sentiment.

The preponderant evidence suggests that the author of *Reykdœla saga* borrowed an episode describing a dramatic confrontation between Víga-Glúmr and Víga-Skúta from *Víga-Glúms saga.* Not only does it appear that he borrowed an episode, but a case can also be made that he built a total response to the earlier saga around the borrowed episode. Glúmr is one of the most notorious tricksters in saga literature and triumphs more often by guile than by force of arms. By contrast, Áskell Eyvindarson, who dominates the action in the first part of *Reykdœla saga,* is established as the most clear-browed and scrupulous chieftain to be found anywhere in the sagas, the antithesis of and antidote to Glúmr. In addition, the conclusion of *Reykdœla saga* seems to echo the conclusion of *Víga-Glúms saga* in order to controvert it, in effect to qualify Glúmr's preeminence by suggesting that Áskell's son Skúta was every bit Glúmr's equal. What we have before us then is a comparison of chieftains not unlike the comparison of kings in *Morkinskinna.* The author of *Reykdœla saga* is bent on contesting the version of history presented in *Víga-Glúms saga;* like the writers of kings' sagas he shapes the narrative as a political debate.

The most accomplished of the Eyjafjörður sagas is *Ljósvetninga saga.* It too is a story of regional conflict, pitting the all-powerful chieftain at Mǫðruvellir, Guðmundr ríki, against a considerably less well established group, the Ljósvetningar, a little to the east. Power prevails both in Guðmundr's generation and that of his successor Eyjólfr, but there is a novel twist. The author undermines Guðmundr at every turn, demonstrating that success is one thing but good character quite another. Guðmundr has a good deal in common with the overreaching kings of *Morkinskinna,* and his saga, far from being a celebration of his triumph, is an unsparing critique of his conduct. Although the feud framework familiar from *Víga-Glúms saga* and *Reykdœla saga* remains in place for the purpose of plot, action is no longer of capital importance and the panegyric mode has been abandoned. *Ljósvetninga saga* renders personal and moral judgments and opens up quite new perspectives in saga writing.

These new perspectives are pursued in greater depth in Chapter 7, in which a very early saga, *Fóstbrœðra saga* (1200–1210?), is compared with a later saga from the same region, *Gísla saga* (1230–1250?). This is not so much a comparison of individual texts as it is a comparison of an old style with a new style. The old style records a chronicle of hostile actions without much attention to the lives of those involved and without much comment; the action is rigorously externalized. The new style is just as rigorously internalized and probes the experience and relationships of the characters in considerable detail. The burden of the narrative in *Gísla saga* is shifted away from the actual occurrences, although these are exceptionally well told, and is refocused on the effect these occurrences produce in the characters. The clarification of character is indeed one of the larger trajectories in the development of the sagas and reaches a level of complexity in *Gísla saga* only to be matched in *Laxdœla saga* and *Njáls saga*. The study of personalities is quite limited in the kings' sagas and the early native sagas; in *Egils saga* it is overblown and not calculated to engage the reader in ordinary human terms. But beginning with *Gísla saga*, it becomes one of the great distinctions of saga literature.

What appears in this volume as a sequence of Chapters 1–5 originated as separate studies of particular texts or groups of texts. In their present reincarnation, only slightly revised, they retain the marks of their separate origin, but they have in common that they focus on the earliest sagas and how these texts relate to one another in terms of outlook. Chapters 6–7 are added to extend the idea of interlocking attitudes a little farther into the thirteenth century. The general thesis is that the sagas under study react to one another politically and literarily in such a way as to suggest an ongoing debate, never formulated in so many words but always implied in fairly tangible ways. Thus **Hlaðajarla saga* appears to be a Þrœndalǫg response to the exclusive claims of the central monarchy, and *Morkinskinna* can be read as an analysis of royal policy. *Heimskringla* in turn can be understood as a neutralizing and diplomatic counter to *Morkinskinna*, and *Egils saga* conceals its political outlook in ambiguity. The first sagas from

Eyjafjörður, perhaps in the spirit of **Hlaðajarla saga*, suggest a dismissal of the focus on kings and a countervailing assertion of Icelandic prerogatives. But even within this new regional context, *Reykdœla saga* can be interpreted as a rebuttal of *Víga-Glúms saga*, and *Ljósvetninga saga* as a commentary on chieftainship analogous to the discussion of kingship in *Morkinskinna*. Finally, in a purely literary sphere, *Gísla saga* looks like a firm rejection of the feud saga as it was practiced in Eyjafjörður and in *Fóstbrœðra saga*. Thus all of these sagas seem interconnected in an ongoing discussion about the political and literary issues of the day.

Notes

Chapter 1 — The Oral Prelude to Saga Writing

1. Milman Parry's studies are collected in *The Making of Homeric Verse* (1971; reprinted 1987); F. P. Magoun Jr., "The Oral-Formulaic Character of Anglo-Saxon Narrative Poetry" (1953) and "Bede's Story of Cædman: The Case History of an Anglo-Saxon Oral Singer" (1955); Ramón Menéndez Pidal, *La Chanson de Roland y el neotradicionalismo* (1959); trans. as *La Chanson de Roland et la tradition épique des Francs* (1960).
2. Larry D. Benson, "The Literary Character of Anglo-Saxon Formulaic Poetry" (1966; rpt. 1995).
3. Klaus von See, "Was ist Heldendichtung?" (1978), 17–18: "Magouns Entdeckung initiierte nun eine wahre Flut von Aufsätzen, die auf mechanische, rein quantitative Weise—durch Abdruck ausgewählter Textpartieen und Unterstreichung der auch andernorts vorkommenden Verse—die Formelhaftigkeit und damit die Mündlichkeit der altenglischen Epik nachzuweisen versuchten."
4. See in particular John Foley's annotated bibliography, *Oral-Formulaic Theory and Research* (1985). Four of his more recent studies are *Traditional Oral Epic* (1990), *Immanent Art: From Structure to Meaning in Traditional Oral Epic* (1991), *The Singer of Tales in Performance* (1995), and *Homer's Traditional Art* (1999).
5. The analysis of the verse stands, for example, at the center of Foley's *Traditional Oral Epic* (1990). For a brief survey of the situation in Homeric studies see E. J. Bakker, "Homer and Oral Poetry Research" (1999), 1: 163–83.
6. Robert Kellogg, "A Concordance of the Elder Edda," Ph.D. diss., Harvard University, 1958; later published as *A Concordance of Eddic Poetry* (1988). See also Kellogg's essay "The Prehistory of Eddic Poetry" (1990), 189–99, and Gísli Sigurðsson's essay "On the Classification of Eddic Heroic Poetry in View of the Oral Theory" (1999), 245–55. Joseph Harris provides a good overview of the early work in this area in "Eddic Poetry,"

in *Old Norse-Icelandic Literature: A Critical Guide* (1985; rpt. 2005), 111–26 (especially 111–15). See also Gísli Sigurðsson in his edition of Eddic poetry: "Munnleg geymd og aldur eddukvæða" in *Eddukvæði* (1998), xv-xxiii.

7. See for example Gerd Sieg, "Die Zweikämpfe der Isländersagas" (1966); Fredrik J. Heinemann, "*Hrafnkels saga freysgoða* and Type-Scene Analysis" (1974); Lars Lönnroth, *Njáls saga: A Critical Introduction* (1976a), 42–103.
8. *The Problem of Icelandic Saga Origins* (1964). A few years earlier the same ground was covered by Marco Scovazzi, *La saga di Hrafnkell e il problema delle saghe islandesi* (1960). These surveys were supplemented by Else Mundal, *Sagadebatt* (1977). See also her summation in "Den norrøne episke tradisjonen" (1990).
9. Andreas Heusler, "Die Anfänge" (1913; rpt. 1969). Björn M. Ólsen's most important contributions appeared in a series of specialized articles on the relationship between various sagas and *Landnámabók* published in *Aarbøger for nordisk oldkyndighed* in 1904, 1905, 1908, 1910, and 1920. In each case he argued for some degree of literary dependence on *Landnámabók*. Sigurður Nordal forged a general theory of literary evolution in the sagas beginning with his book *Snorri Sturluson* (1920), 103–31.
10. *The Icelandic Family Saga* (1967).
11. I remember being influenced by Eberhard Lämmert, *Bauformen des Erzählens* (1955) and Wayne C. Booth, *The Rhetoric of Fiction* (1961).
12. "The Textual Evidence of an Oral Family Saga" (1966). My paper was reviewed and supplemented by W. Manhire, "The Narrative Functions of Source-References in the Sagas of Icelanders" (1975–76). Cf. Klaus von See, "Altnordische Literaturgeschichte als Textgeschichte" (1981), 533.
13. See Robert Scholes and Robert Kellogg, *The Nature of Narrative* (1966), 309.
14. *Early Epic Scenery* (1976), especially 145–59; "The Epic Source of *Niflunga saga* and the *Nibelungenlied*" (1973).
15. "Hjálmar's Death-Song and the Delivery of Eddic Poetry" (1971); the chapter entitled "The Language of Tradition" in *Njáls Saga: A Critical Introduction* (1976a), 42–103; *Den dubbla scenen. Muntlig diktning från Eddan til Abba* (1978), 29–52; "Iǫrð fannz æva né upphiminn: A Formula Analysis" (1981); rpt. in his *The Academy of Odin* (2011), 219–41.
16. *Uppruni og þema Hrafnkels sögu* (1976); an abbreviated version was translated from the Norwegian in John Tucker's anthology *Sagas of the Icelanders: A Book of Essays* (1989), 257–71.
17. *Hrafnkatla* (1940); trans. R. George Thomas, *Hrafnkels saga freysgoða* (1958).
18. "Another Audience—Another Saga: How Can We Best Explain Different Accounts in *Vatnsdœla saga* and *Finnboga saga ramma* of the Same Events?" (1994); "Aðrir áheyrandur—önnur saga?: Um ólíkar frásagnir Vatnsdælu og Finnboga sögu af sömu atburðum" (1994); "Methodologies for the Study of the Oral in Medieval Iceland" (1997). Gísli's studies

culminated in the imposing book *Túlkun Íslendingasagna í ljósi munnlegrar hefðar* (2002) and were reconfirmed in Tommy Danielsson's two books *Hrafnkels saga eller Fallet med den undflyende traditionen* and *Sagorna om Norges kungar* (2002). I reviewed their work in "Five Saga Books for a New Century" (2004).

19. "The Long Prose Form" (1986).
20. "The Long Prose Form"(1986:36). John Foley made use of Clover's concept in *Immanent Art* (1991), 12. See also Gísli Sigurðsson, "Methodologies" (1997), 187–90.
21. Bååth, *Studier öfver kompositionen i några isländska ättsagor* (1885); Heusler, "Die Anfänge," (1913:74–80; reprinted 1969:449–54).
22. *Oral Tradition and Saga Writing* (1999).
23. On the dating see Finnur Jónsson, *OOLH* (1923), 2:550–51 and 557; Magnús Jónsson, *Guðmundar saga dýra* (1940), 60–61; Peter Foote, "Sturlusaga and Its Background" (1951; reprinted 1984, especially 29); Jacqueline Simpson, "Advocacy and Art in *Guðmundar saga dýra*" (1957–61), especially 334–35; Guðrún Nordal, Sverrir Tómasson, Vésteinn Ólason, *Íslensk bókmenntasaga* (1992), 1:316 (estimate of 1200–1220). In his study "Frásagnaraðferð Sturlu sögu" (1994), 2:803–17, Viðar Hreinsson considers this saga to be the oldest in *Sturlunga saga*. He provides a careful analysis of the authorial strategies that set Sturla off from his antagonists and allow him to emerge gradually as a properly endowed chieftain. My discussion below, which emphasizes the narrative and structural complications of the text, should not be understood to preclude the sort of controlling perspective that Viðar proposes. On the structuring of *Sturlu saga* and *Guðmundar saga* see most recently the balanced assessment of Úlfar Bragason, *Ætt og saga* (2010), 94–98 and 128–40.
24. Peter Erasmus Müller, *Sagabibliothek*, 3 vols. (1817–20). The genre boundaries are retained in two recent books on the sagas: Ármann Jakobsson, *Í leit að konungi* (1997) and Vésteinn Ólason, *Dialogues with the Viking Age* (1998).
25. Textual references are to *Sturlunga saga*, ed. Jón Jóhannesson, Magnús Finnbogason, and Kristján Eldjárn, 2 vols. (1946), here 1:68; or to *Sturlunga saga*, ed. Örnólfur Thorsson, 2 vols. (1988), here 1:56.
26. On occurrences in *Sturlunga saga* see Guðrún Nordal, *Ethics and Action in Thirteenth-Century Iceland* (1998), 161–63. In *Egils saga* Egill engages in an extended contest to recover the inheritance of his wife Ásgerðr, but his opponents are Norwegians. In *Laxdœla saga* (chapter 18) there is an episode that is more about legal trickery than about a dramatic confrontation. In *Vápnfirðinga saga* Brodd-Helgi Þorgilsson and Geitir Lýtingsson quarrel over the dowry of Halla, Brodd-Helgi's divorced wife and Geitir's sister (ÍF 11:36–38).
27. I proposed a date around 1220 for *Ljósvetninga saga* in Andersson and Miller, *Law and Literature* (1989), 78–84, and in "Guðbrandur Vigfússon's Saga Chronology" (1989). In *Íslensk bókmenntasaga,* 2:107, Vésteinn Ólason remained neutral on the question of dating *Ljósvetninga saga* around 1220 or later in the century. Jónas Kristjánsson, "Íslendinga

sögur og Sturlunga" (1988), 105, was inclined to believe that *Ljósvetninga saga* was among the earliest of the sagas about early Icelanders, but he did not hazard a date.

28. In her edition of *Þorgils saga ok Hafliða* (1952), x-xxix, Ursula Brown reviews the dating criteria in some detail and finds "no strong grounds for supposing that *Þorgils saga* was written much earlier than 1237, the latest date it contains" (xxix). In *Íslensk bókmenntasaga*, 1:321, Guðrún Nordal retains a date around 1240. I weigh an earlier date in Andersson and Miller, *Law and Literature* (1989), 80–82.
29. Knut Liestøl, *The Origin of the Icelandic Family Sagas* (1930), 55–100; Andreas Heusler, *Die altgermanische Dichtung* (1941; rpt. 1957), 210–13.
30. John D. Niles, *Beowulf: The Poem and Its Tradition* (1983), 152–62; Bernard Fenik, *Homer and the Nibelungenlied* (1986), 97–110.
31. ÍF 6:231 (from *Hauksbók*). The passage is referred to as an instance of oral performance by, for example, W. A. Craigie, *The Icelandic Sagas* (1913), 14–15; Knut Liestøl, *The Origin of the Icelandic Family Sagas* (1930), 57; Marco Scovazzi, *La saga di Hrafnkell* (1960), 272–74. Rolf Heller, "Zur Entstehung der Grönlandsszenen der Fóstbrœðra saga" (1977), 1:326–34, argued that the Greenland scenes are a literary fiction with little or no recourse to oral tradition.

Chapter 2 — The Prehistory of the Kings' Sagas

1. I have summarized Heusler's work in "Heusler's Saga Studies" (2005). For a survey of the field as a whole see Carol J. Clover, "Icelandic Family Sagas (*Íslendingasögur*)," in *Old Norse-Icelandic Literature: A Critical Guide* (1985; reprinted 2005), 239–315.
2. Knut Liestøl, *The Origin of the Icelandic Family Sagas* (1930).
3. T. M. Andersson, *The Problem of Icelandic Saga Origins* (1964).
4. These studies were summarized in Lönnroth's *European Sources of Icelandic Saga-Writing* (1965). An abbreviated version may be found in his *The Academy of Odin: Selected Papers on Old Norse Literature* (2011), 13–23.
5. *Sagan om kärleken: Erotik, känslor och berättarkonst i norrön litteratur* (2007).
6. *Uppruni og þema Hrafnkels sögu* (1976).
7. Sigurður Nordal, *Hrafnkels saga freysgoða,* trans. R. George Thomas (1958).
8. Else Mundal, *Sagadebatt* (1977); Carol J. Clover (as in note 1).
9. Carol J. Clover, "The Long Prose Form" (1986).
10. "The Long Prose Form in Medieval Iceland" (2002); revised as chapter 1 above.
11. Gísli Sigurðsson, *Túlkun Íslendingasagna í ljósi munnlegrar hefðar* (2002); trans. by Nicholas Jones as *The Medieval Icelandic Saga and Oral Tradition* (2004); Tommy Danielsson, *Hrafnkels saga eller Fallet med den undflyende traditionen* and *Sagorna om Norges kungar* (2002).

I have discussed these books in "Five Saga Books for a New Century" (2004).

12. Siegfried Beyschlag, *Konungasögur* (1950).
13. Ármann Jakobsson, *Staður í nýjum heimi* (2002), 78–86, has argued with good reason that the *þættir* were part of the original composition. See also ÍF 23:XLIV. I have tried to isolate the *þáttr*-like oral components in *Óláfs saga helga* in *Heimskringla* in chapter 4 below.
14. See Bjarni Guðnason, "Theodoricus og íslenskir sagnaritarar" (1977); T. M. Andersson, "Ari's *konunga ævi* and the Earliest Accounts of Hákon jarl's Death" (1979); Gudrun Lange, *Die Anfänge der isländisch-norwegischen Geschichtsschreibung* (1989), 166–71, 177–78.
15. See T. M. Andersson, *The Growth of the Medieval Icelandic Sagas* (2006), 21–59.
16. I have argued the dating of *Víga-Glúms saga* in "*Víga-Glúms saga* and the Birth of Saga Writing" (2006), the dating of *Fóstbrœðra saga* in "Redating *Fóstbrœðra saga*" (forthcoming), and the dating of *Gunnlaugs saga* in "The Native Romance of Gunnlaugr and Helga the Fair" (2008).
17. The most clear-cut examples are "Hreiðars þáttr," "Halldórs þáttr Snorrasonar," "Auðunar þáttr vestfirzka," "Brands þáttr ǫrva," "Sneglu-Halla þáttr," "Stúfs þáttr Kattarsonar," "Odds þáttr Ófeigssonar," and "Þáttr af Gullásu-Þórði."
18. On the conversion of five lands see MHN, 116, and *Ágrip af Nóregskonungasǫgum*, ed. M. J. Driscoll (1995; reprinted 2008), 30.
19. See *Heimskringla*, ÍF 27:214–18, 240.
20. *Morkinskinna*, ed. Finnur Jónsson (1932), 170; ÍF 23:205.
21. Adam of Bremen, *Gesta Hammaburgensis Ecclesiae Pontificum*, ed. Bernhard Schmeidler (1917; reprinted 1977), 159, 267.
22. Perhaps the most striking expression of the Icelandic claim to genealogical equality with the Norwegians may be found in "Halldórs þáttr Snorrasonar" in *Morkinskinna*, ed. Finnur Jónsson (1928–32), 149–55; ÍF 23:180–87.
23. The morphology was analyzed by Joseph Harris, "Theme and Genre in Some *Íslendinga þættir*" (1976; reprinted 2008).
24. *Morkinskinna*, ed. Finnur Jónsson, 199–200; ÍF 23:235–37.
25. Preben Meulengracht Sørensen, *Fortælling og ære* (1993), 78; Vésteinn Ólason, "The Icelandic Saga as a Kind of Literature with Special Reference to Its Representation of Reality" (2007), 34.

Chapter 3 — The First Written Sagas of Kings and Chieftains

1. Bjarni Guðnason, *Fyrsta sagan* (1978).
2. This still unresolved puzzle is reviewed by Lárus H. Blöndal, *Um uppruna Sverrissögu* (1982). Blöndal himself is open to the idea that Karl Jónsson composed the whole saga, which would therefore have been completed before his death in 1213.

3. Gustav Storm, *Otte brudstykker* (1893), 23; Sigurður Nordal, *Om Olaf den helliges saga* (1914), 54.
4. See Bjarni Aðalbjarnarson, *Om de norske kongers sagaer* (1937), 59.
5. I argue for this looser dating in *Oddr Snorrason's Saga of Olaf Tryggvason* (2003), 3–5.
6. See Jonna Louis-Jensen, "'Syvende og ottende brudstykke'" (1970) and Jónas Kristjánsson, "The Legendary Saga" (1976), 282.
7. *Saga Óláfs Tryggvasonar af Oddr Snorrason munk*, ed Finnur Jónsson (1932), 156; ÍF 25:272.
8. Bjarni Aðalbjarnarson, *Om de norske kongers sagaer* (1937), 63.
9. Konrad Maurer, *Ueber die Ausdrücke* (1867), 566–80 (esp. 576–79).
10. Nordal, *Om Olaf den helliges saga* (1914), 123.
11. Finnur Jónsson, *OOLH*, 2nd ed. (1920–24), 2:605–11.
12. Ibid., 608.
13. Ibid., 385.
14. Bjarni Aðalbjarnarson, *Om de norske kongers sagaer* (1937), 79.
15. Lars Lönnroth, "Studier i Olaf Tryggvasons saga" (1963): 60–64.
16. *Olafs saga hins helga*, ed. Oscar Albert Johnsen (1922), 19, or *Olafs saga hins helga,* ed. and trans. Anne Heinrichs et al. (1982), 66; Theodoricus monachus, *Historia de Antiquitate* in MHN (1880; reprinted 1973), 26, and *Historia de Antiquitate*, trans. David and Ian McDougall (1998), 20; *Ágrip af Nóregs konungasǫgum*, ed. and trans. M. J. Driscoll (1995; reprinted 2008), 36; *Saga Óláfs Tryggvasonar*, ed. Finnur Jónsson (1932), 94. See also Ólafur Halldórsson, "Mostur og Sæla" (1984).
17. See Bjarni Aðalbjarnarson in *Heimskringla* III (ÍF 28:XXXV).
18. Lars Lönnroth, "The Baptist and the Saint" (2000), 259.
19. Ibid., 263.
20. Jónas Kristjánsson, *Um Fóstbræðrasögu* (1972), 162.
21. Jónas Kristjánsson, "The Legendary Saga" (1976), 282.
22. Nordal, *Om Olaf den helliges saga* (1914), 31–37.
23. Jónas Kristjánsson, "The Legendary Saga" (1976), 290–91.
24. Ibid., 282.
25. *Konunga sögur*, ed. Guðni Jónsson, vol. 1 (1957).
26. Carol Clover, "The Politics of Scarcity" (1988): 154.
27. See Dietrich Hofmann, "Die *Yngvars saga víðfǫrla* und Oddr munkr inn fróði" (1981; reprinted 1988). The passage is cited from *Fornaldar sögur norðurlanda*, ed. Guðni Jónsson (1954), 2:425. See also *Yngvars saga víðfǫrla jämte ett bihang om Ingvarsinskrifterna*, ed. Emil Olson (1912), 1.
28. Lönnroth, "The Baptist and the Saint" (2000), 263.
29. See Maurer, *Ueber die Ausdrücke* (1867), 578; Nordal, *Om Olaf den helliges saga* (1914), 13; Bjarni Aðalbjarnarson, *Om de norske kongers sagaer* (1937), 79. In Peter Andreas Munch's edition *Saga Olafs konungs Tryggvasonar* (1853), 72, Munch suggested that there could have been a misunderstanding of Latin *suus* in Oddr's text.
30. See *Óláfs saga Tryggvasonar*, ed. Guðni Jónsson (1957), 60: "Leitt er mér um at hitta þess kyns menn eða þeira traust at sœkja."
31. *Ágrip*, ed. M. J. Driscoll (1995; rpt. 2008), 28–30.

32. See Andersson, *Oddr Snorrason's Saga of Olaf Tryggvason* (2003), 6–14.
33. MHN, 14; *Historia de Antiquitate*, trans. McDougall (1998), 10.
34. It has often been argued that Oddr made use of Theodoricus's text, but I have opposed this view in *Oddr Snorrason's Saga of Olaf Tryggvason* (2003), 6–7. It should be added that very recently Sverre Bagge, "Warrior, King, and Saint" (2010): 289, has expressed skepticism about the idea that the prophetic passages reviewed here can shed light on the chronology of the texts.
35. Lönnroth, "Studier i Olaf Trygggvasons saga" (1963): 63. Sverre Bagge, "Warrior, King, and Saint" (2010): 295n58, also believes that the motif is more likely to have originated at Nesjar than at Svǫlðr.
36. On this passage see Nordal, *Om Olaf den helliges saga* (1914), 33–34.
37. Maurer, *Ueber die Audrücke* (1867), 576.
38. See MHN, 76–82, or *A History of Norway*, trans. Devra Kunin (2001), 2–5.
39. See G. Turville-Petre, *Origins of Icelandic Literature* (1953; rpt. 1967), 137 and references.
40. Theological precedent can be found for or against "forced service." See the ambiguous discussion by Thomas Aquinas in the *Summa Theologica*, trans. Fathers of the English Dominican Province (1947), 2:1218–19. Aquinas begins by quoting John Chrysostom: "Our Lord says this so as to forbid the slaying of men. For it is not right to slay heretics, because if you do you will necessarily slay many innocent persons." Aquinas concludes: "Therefore it seems for the same reason unbelievers ought not to be compelled to the faith." He then quotes Augustine to the effect that "it is possible for a man to do other things against his will, but he cannot believe unless he is willing." In response to Luke 14:23 he writes: "I answer that, among unbelievers there are some who have never received the faith, such as the heathens and the Jews: and these are by no means to be compelled to the faith, in order that they may believe, because to believe depends on the will [*credere voluntatis est*]." The rest of the discussion is, however, more equivocal.
41. The material on Saint Óláfr is now conveniently assembled by Devra Kunin and Carl Phelpstead in *A History of Norway* (2001).
42. See *Sturlunga saga*, ed. Örnólfur Thorsson (1988), 1:117; Lárus H. Blöndal, *Um uppruna Sverrissögu* (1982), 169–70.
43. Finnur Jónsson suggested that the reference to a statement by King Sverrir in Oddr's *Óláfs saga Tryggvasonar* (1932; chapter 73, p. 226; ÍF 25:342) could have derived from Karl Jónsson's contact with the king after his return from Norway. See the "Indledning" to his edition, ii–iii.
44. See Lars Lönnroth, "Studier i Olaf Tryggvasons saga" (1963): 67, and Jan de Vries, *Altnordische Literaturgeschichte* (1967), 2:242. But cf. Lárus Blöndal, *Um uppruna* (1982), 170–71.
45. See Else Mundal, "The Dating of the Oldest Sagas of Early Icelanders" (forthcoming), and *Færeyinga saga*, ed. Ólafur Halldórsson (1987), ccxxii–ccxxxix, ccxlviii.

46. See his *OOLH,* 1st ed. (1901), 2:639–40; 2nd ed. (1920–24), 2:633–34.
47. *Fagrskinna* (1917).
48. *Fra sagn til saga* (1923), 183–217.
49. *Saga og oldfunn* (1927).
50. *Om de norske kongers sagaer* (1937).
51. Ibid., 186.
52. The following abbreviations are used: *Fagrskinna* (ÍF 29) = *Fsk; Heimskringla* I (ÍF 26) = *Hkr*; *Morkinskinna* (ÍF 23–24) = *Msk.*
53. Gustav Indrebø, *Fagrskinna* (1917), 269, observed that *Fsk* 65, in contrast to *Hkr*, only takes note of Haraldr hárfagri's helpers from Þrœndalǫg: "Fgsk. talar i det heile liksom kong Harald skulde ha havt hovustødet sitt i Trøndelag, og liksom riksens samling skulde ha gaatt ut derifraa." This version is almost too tendentious not to have originated in the regional bias of **Hlaðajarla saga.* If that is the case, then we must imagine that the author of **Hlaðajarla saga* rejected the vulgate version of events as we find them presented in *Hkr* 97–100 in favor of a hypothesis that both Haraldr's unification and Magnús's reunification proceeded from Þrœndalǫg. See also Bjarni Aðalbjarnarson, *Om de norske kongers sagaer* (1937), 218.
54. *Morkinskinna*, ed. Finnur Jónsson, xxxvi. But see also Gustav Indrebø, "Nokre merknader" (1938–39), 72–76.
55. *Orkneyinga saga*, ed. Finnbogi Guðmundsson, ÍF 34 (1965), 65–70; *Morkinskinna*, ed. Ármann Jakobsson and Þórður Ingi Guðjónsson, ÍF 23 (2011), XXXVII.
56. Indrebø, *Fagrskinna* (1917), 104–7, argued that *Fagrskinna* made no use of *Orkneyinga saga*, and in an unpublished review of the problem Kari Ellen Gade concludes that the link between *Morkinskinna* and *Orkneyinga saga* could be purely oral.
57. *Fagrskinna* (1917), 147–49.
58. See the genealogy in *Sturlunga saga* (1988), 3:100 (genealogy 51).
59. For the text of "Nóregs konunga tal" see Finnur Jónsson, ed. *Den norsk-islandske skjaldedigtning* B (rettet tekst), 1:575–90.
60. See G. Turville-Petre, *Origins of Icelandic Literature* (1953), 211; Guðrún Nordal, Sverrir Tómasson, Vésteinn Ólason, *Íslensk bókmenntasaga* (1992), 1:348.

Chapter 4 — Sources and Attitudes in *Óláfs saga helga* in *Heimskringla*

1. Elias Wessén, "Om Snorres Prologus" (1928–29) concluded that *Óláfs saga helga* was written initially without a prologue. It was then expanded into *Heimskringla* with a prologue added. Finally the *Heimskringla* prologue was refashioned to serve as a prologue for the *Separate Saga of Saint Olaf*. Even with the doubts about whether *Óláfs saga helga* originally was a part of *Heimskringla*, this sequence remains possible.

See most recently Jonna Louis-Jensen, "Dating the Archetype: *Eyrbyggja saga* and *Egils saga Skallagrímssonar*" (forthcoming).

2. It will be noted that I take into account the cautions formulated by Jonna Louis-Jensen, "Heimskringla—Et værk av Snorri Sturluson?" (1997), Jo Rune Ugulen, "AM 39 fol., *Óláfs saga helga* og *Heimskringla*" (2002), and Patricia Pires Boulhosa, *Icelanders and the Kings of Norway* (2005), 6–21, and refrain from attributing *Óláfs saga helga* to Snorri Sturluson.
3. On the author's responsibility for the oratory see Oscar Albert Johnsen, "Friðgerðar-saga" (1916): 515–16, 519, 537; Sigurður Nordal, *Snorri Sturluson* (1920), 206; Curt Weibull, *Sverige och dess nordiska grannmakter* (1921), 139; Hallvard Lie, *Studier i Heimskringlas stil* (1937), 90–105.
4. Oscar Albert Johnsen, "Friðgerðar-saga" (1916); Birger Nerman, "Torgny lagman" (1916); Otto von Friesen, "Fredsförhandlingarna mellan Olov skötkonung och Olav Haraldsson" (1942). See also Natanael Beckman, "Torgny lagman" (1918), "Sverige i isländsk tradition" (1922), "Ytterligare om Sigvats Austrfararvísur" (1934) and Jón Jónsson, "Athugasemd um Þorgný lögmann" (1918).
5. See Curt Weibull, *Sverige och dess nordiska grannmakter* (1921), 116–48, and Ove Moberg, *Olav Haraldsson, Knut den Store och Sverige* (1941), 88–147.
6. See also Bjarni Aðalbjarnarson in ÍF 27:XXXVI and XXXIX. More recently Sverre Bagge, *Society and Politics* (1991), acknowledges oral sources (pp. 239–40) but also believes that some of the stories are Snorri's invention (pp. 108, 279n34).
7. On the drama of the passage see Hallvard Lie, *Studier i Heimskringlas stil* (1937), 11.
8. In contrast to the popular reading suggested here, Lars Lönnroth offered a royalist reading in "The Ideology of *Heimskringla*" (1976b); rpt. in *The Academy of Odin* (2011), 141–62.
9. Þórleifur Jónsson included in his *Fjörutíu Íslendinga-þættir* (1904) the story of Steinn Skaptason (pp. 311–22) and a composite version of "Þórarins þáttr Nefjólfssonar" (pp. 344–63) but none of the others. Some of the texts he would have excluded because they are not "Íslendinga þættir," but it is not clear why he excluded the tale of Þóroddr Snorrason. None of the *þættir* discussed here was included in *The Complete Sagas of Icelanders* (1997), perhaps from a reluctance to dismember the unity of *Óláfs saga helga*.
10. *Studier i Heimskringlas stil* (1937), 36–52.
11. See Sigurður Nordal, "Om Orkneyinga saga" (1913): 36–49, especially 40–41.
12. I have reviewed this problem in "Lore and Literature" (1988).
13. See Sverre Bagge, *Society and Politics* (1991), 41.
14. See Michael J. Stitt, *Beowulf of the Bear's Son* (1992), 197.
15. Bjarni Aðalbjarnarson (ÍF 27:LI) expressed the view that Þóroddr himself transmitted the story, but he did not specify how much of it.
16. Nordal, *Om Olaf den helliges saga* (1914).
17. Toralf Berntsen, *Fra sagn til saga* (1923), tried to identify a Norwegian

"Háreks saga" and "Tore Hunds saga" (pp. 135, 144), but conceded that most of the stories in the saga come from Icelandic sources (pp. 104–6).

18. Halvdan Koht, "Sagaenes opfattelse av vår gamle historie" (1914); Fredrik Paasche, "Tendens og syn i kongesagaen" (1922).
19. *Society and Politics* (1991), 65 and 201.
20. Johann Schreiner, *Tradisjon og saga om Olav den hellige* (1926), 104. See also Hallvard Lie's discussion of these terms in *Studier i Heimskringlas stil* (1934), 20–21.
21. Gudmund Sandvik, *Hovding og konge i Heimskringla* (1955), delivered an explicit corrective to this viewpoint. See especially his concluding remarks (pp. 98–99). See also Sverre Bagge, *Society and Politics* (1991), 199, 204, 237–38 and "Warrior, King, and Saint" (2010), especially 314–15.
22. For Theodoricus see MHN (1880), 5–42 (esp. 29–30); *Ágrip*, ed. Bjarni Einarsson (ÍF29:25–30 [especially 27]).
23. The alias is Hallvard Lie's in *Studier i Heimskringlas stil* (1937), 103.

Chapter 5 — Political Subtexts in *Morkinskinna, Heimskringla* III, and *Egils* saga

1. The dating criteria are reviewed in *Morkinskinna*, trans. Andersson and Gade (2000), 66–67.
2. See Diana Whaley, *Heimskringla: An Introduction* (1991), 28 and 33.
3. These events can be traced in *Sturlunga saga*, ed. Örnólfur Thorsson et al. (1988), 1:254–62, and the various editions of *Hákonar saga Hákonarsonar*, ed. Gudbrand Vigfusson (1887), 37–38, 49–52; ed. Guðni Jónsson in *Konunga sögur* (1957), 3:52, 67, 69–71; ed. Marina Mundt, *Hákonar saga Hákonarsonar* (1977), 27, 35–36. See also *Islandske annaler*, ed. Gustav Storm (1888), 23, 63, 125, 183, 255, 326.
4. Bogi Th. Melsteð provided a full recapitulation of the events in "Útanstefnur og erendisrekar útlendra þjóðhöfðingja" (1899): 122–30. See also Jón Jóhannesson, *A History of the Old Icelandic Commonwealth* (1974), pp. 239–40.
5. Haraldr Gormsson's planned attack is reported in the *Heimskringla* version of *Óláfs saga Tryggvasonar* (ÍF 26:315–17). On this passage see Bo Almqvist, *Norrön niddiktning* (1965),1:119–85. The Grímsey incident is related in the *Heimskringla* version of *Óláfs saga helga* (ÍF 27:215–17). On the background of the Grímsey episode see Bjarni Aðalbjarnarson's introduction to *Óláfs saga helga* (ÍF 27:XLVII-L).
6. On the location of *Morkinskinna*, see Eivind Kválen, *Den eldste norske kongesoga* (1925), 46–53. I have supported his location in *Morkinskinna*, trans. Andersson and Gade (2000), 67–72.
7. I offered this suggestion in Andersson, "Snorri Sturluson and the Saga School at Munkaþverá" (1993), especially 16–17. The idea has not persuaded Ármann Jakobsson (see the studies listed in the Bibliography). Ármann offers a particularly well-balanced response and alternative in

"The Individual and the Ideal" (2000a:esp. 80–84). He believes that episodes in *Morkinskinna* and *Heimskringla* should not be read as positive or negative assessments of kings but as exempla on human qualities in general.

8. Sverre Bagge, *Society and Politics in Snorri Sturluson's Heimskringla* (1991), 139 and 156.
9. Gustav Indrebø contributed an interesting article on this contradiction in "Harald hardraade i Morkinskinna," *Festskrift til Finnur Jónsson* (1928), 173–80. He believed that the core story was based on skaldic authority and was positive with respect to Haraldr, while the *þættir* (and the final comparison with Magnús góði) were negative and secondary additions.
10. For a survey of the *þættir* see Heinrich Gimmler, *Die Thættir der Morkinskinna* (1976). It has long been suspected that many of the *þættir* in *Morkinskinna* are interpolations. Gimmler thought that six of the eight *þættir* he discussed were not in the original redaction. On the other hand, Jonna Louis-Jensen, *Kongesagastudier* (1977), 69 and 77–78, thought that a number of them may well have been in the original redaction. More recently Ármann Jakobsson, *Staður í nýjum heimi* (2002), preferred to consider the *þættir* in *Morkinskinna* as part of a general medieval esthetic rather than as interpolations or foreign bodies. See also ÍF 23:XL-L. Since many of the *þættir* are inspired by the same anti-royalist tendency that we find in *Morkinskinna* as a whole, I see no reason to disallow them as part of the original composition. They may not be the original creations of the *Morkinskinna* author, but he could well have refashioned them for his special project.
11. *Morkinskinna* ed. C. R. Unger (1867), 51 (hereafter "Unger"); *Morkinskinna*, ed. Finnur Jónsson (1932), 155 (hereafter "FJ"); *Morkinskinna*, ed. Ármann Jakobsson and Þórður Ingi Guðjónsson, 1:187 (hereafter ÍF 23–24); *Morkinskinna*, trans. Andersson and Gade, 194 and 435n12 (hereafter Andersson/Gade).
12. On this gem of a narrative see William Ian Miller's brilliant reading in *Audun and the Polar Bear* (2008).
13. Unger, 200–201; FJ, 409; ÍF 24:173; Andersson/Gade, 369.
14. A good example of such retention is the mention of Þorleikr fagri in *Heimskringla* III (ÍF 28:113).
15. Unger, 111–12; FJ, 265; ÍF 23:303; Andersson/Gade, 263.
16. Gustav Storm, *Snorre Sturlassöns historieskrivning* (1873), 49. The fragments of *Hákonar saga Ívarssonar* were published by Storm (pp. 236–59) and by Jón Helgason and Jakob Benediktsson, *Hákonarsaga Ívarssonar* (1952). For more recent discussions see Bjarne Fidjestøl, *Det norrøne fyrstediktet* (1982), 15–17, and Russell G. Poole, *Viking Poems on War and Peace* (1991), 66–68. See also Andersson/Gade, 512–15.
17. Unger, 85; FJ, 221; ÍF 23:258; Andersson/Gade, 236.
18. Unger, 24; FJ, 103; ÍF 23:133–34; Andersson/Gade, 159.
19. Unger, 27; FJ, 108; ÍF 23:137–38; Andersson/Gade, 162.
20. Unger, 32; FJ, 118; ÍF 23:146; Andersson/Gade, 167.
21. FJ, 143 [from *Flateyjarbók*]; Andersson/Gade, 183.

22. ÍF 28:102: "Brátt gerðusk greinir í um samþykki konunganna, ok váru margir svá illgjarnir, at þeira gengu svá illa í milli." ÍF 28:104: "Við slíkar greinir gerðisk brátt umrœða óvitra manna til þess, at konungum varð sundrþykki at. Mart fannsk þá til þess, er konungum þótti sinn veg hvárum, þótt hér sé fátt ritat."
23. ÍF 28:105: "Síðan andaðisk Magnús konungr góði, ok var hann allmjǫk harmdauði allri alþýðu." ÍF 28:107: "Allra konunga var hann vinsælstr, bæði lofuðu hann vinir ok óvinir."
24. Unger, 127.1–12; FJ, 291.13–28; ÍF 24:10; Andersson/Gade, 281: "Ok skipaði Óláfr konungr þeim mǫrgum hlutum til vægðar, er Haraldr konungr, faðir hans, hafði reist með freku ok haldit svá."
25. "Nú skal ek kátr vera, er ek sé bæði á lýð mínum glæði ok frelsi. . . . En á dǫgum fǫður míns var lýðr þessi undir aga miklum ok ótta, ok fálu þá flestir menn gull sitt ok gersimar, en nú sé ek á hverjum yðrum skína þat, er á. Ok er yðvart frelsi mín glæði."
26. ÍF 28:207: "Eigi fæ ek betr stýrt ríkinu ok eigi er meiri ógn af mér en af fǫður mínum, þótt ek hafa hálfa fleira lið en hann hafði, en engi pynding gengr mér til þessa við yðr eða þat, at ek vilja þyngja kostum yðrum."
27. Unger, 137; FJ, 308; ÍF 24:31–33; Andersson/Gade, 293–94.
28. ÍF 28:218: "Hann var maðr rǫskr ok herskár ok starfsamr ok líkari í ǫllu Haraldi fǫðurfǫður sínum, í skaplyndi heldr en feðr sínum."
29. Unger, 153.12, conjectured "*enn til sœmðar* váru ríki Nóregi." Finnur Jónsson (p. 332.19–20) omitted the conjecture. The ÍF edition 24:65 retains it in brackets.
30. Unger, 153; FJ, 333; ÍF 24:65; Andersson/Gade, 310: "Herra, allir mundu þess búnir at vinna yðr til sœmðar, en hræddir eru vér um nǫkkut í þessu landi, hvat til sœmðar vill gerask. Er land þetta fjǫlmennt en fólkit svikalt, ok er oss uggr á, hvé til verðr geymt. Fór svá um frænda yðvarn Harald konung, at fyrst var honum allt upp gefit í Englandi, þar sem hann kom við. En þó lauk svá, at hann lézk þar sjálfr. Myndi vinum þínum þykkja allra bezt, at þú hefðir kyrr setit í þínu ríki, svá gott sem þú átt um at véla."
31. ÍF 28:237.
32. Unger, 165.20–23; FJ, 351.25–29; ÍF 24:99; Andersson/Gade, 325.
33. Unger, 170.29–30; FJ, 359.20; ÍF 24:108; Andersson/Gade, 330.
34. Sverre Bagge, *Society and Politics in Snorri Sturluson's Heimskringla* (1991), 156.
35. ÍF 28:218, 263; Unger, 189.30–32; FJ, 388.3–6; ÍF 24:138; Andersson/Gade, 350.
36. "Hvernig var Snorri í sjón?" (1979), especially 174–80; here p. 175. On the flyting see also Marianne E. Kalinke, "*Sigurðar saga Jórsalafara*" (1984), especially 162–65. Kalinke, like Bagge, sees the ideals represented by the two kings as being equally balanced. Diana Whaley, *Heimskringla* (1991), 101, takes a view closer to the one advanced here.
37. Unger, 187.7–40; FJ, 384.1–385.10; ÍF 24:133–34; Andersson/Gade, 346–47; ÍF 28:261.
38. On the textual situation see Whaley, *Heimskringla* (1991), 41–62.
39. Melissa A. Berman, "The Political Sagas" (1985). Subsequently Preben

Meulengracht Sørensen provided a much fuller account of the political implications in *Egils saga* and the tension between the Icelandic ideals of individual freedom and the centralized authority of the Norwegian crown. See his *Fortælling og ære* (1993), 127–47. Meulengracht Sørensen warns that the political theme may not reflect current events as much as the underlying social ideal.

40. Compare Sǫlvi klofi's powerful speech against Haraldr hárfagri in *Egils saga* (ÍF 2:8) with the trimmed version in *Heimskringla* (ÍF 26:105). Haraldr's suppression of resistance in *Egils saga* (ÍF 2:11–12) has no counterpart in *Heimskringla* (ÍF 26:117–18).
41. Jónas Kristjánsson suggested a date as late as 1240 in "Egils saga og konungasögur" (1977), but in a later paper "Var Snorri Sturluson upphafsmaður Íslendingasagna?" (1990) he settled on a date around 1230. Torfi H. Tulinius, *Skáldið í skriftinni* (2004), especially 206, returned to a late date around 1240, but Jonna Louis-Jensen, "Dating the Archetype: Eyrbyggja saga and Egils saga Skallagrímssonar" (forthcoming) urges an early date before the composition of *Heimskringla* I and III.

Chapter 6 — Domestic Politics in Northern Iceland

1. *Sturlunga saga*, ed. Örnólfur Thorsson (1988), 1:329.
2. Sigurður Nordal, "Snorri Sturluson: Nokkurar hugleiðingar" (1941): 29–30; *Sagalitteraturen* (1952), 245.
3. *Sturlunga saga*, ed. Örnólfur Thorsson (1988), 1:252; 3:181 (map 18).
4. *Sturlunga saga* (1988), 1:245, 252.
5. *Sturlunga saga* (1988), 1:246.
6. *Sturlunga saga* (1988), 1:269; 3:181 (map 18).
7. *Den eldste norske kongesaga* (1925), 46–53; Andersson and Gade, *Morkinskinna* (2000), 67–69.
8. *Sturlunga saga* (1988), 1:100–01; 3:169 (map 9).
9. *Sturlunga saga* (1988), 1:107–8.
10. *Sturlunga saga* (1988), 1:201; 3:93–95 (genealogies 40 and 42).
11. *Sturlunga saga* (1988), 1:60.
12. *Sturlunga saga* (1988), 1:101.
13. *Sturlunga saga* (1988), e.g., 1:74.
14. *Sturlunga saga* (1988), 1:101; 3:93 (genealogy 40).
15. *Sturlunga saga* (1988), 1:108; 3:93 (genealogy 40).
16. *Sturlunga saga* (1988), 1:112.
17. *Sturlunga saga* (1988), 1:113.
18. *Sturlunga saga* (1988), 3:102 (genealogy 54).
19. *Sturlunga saga* (1988), 1:213.
20. *Sturlunga saga* (1988), 1:210.
21. *Sturlunga saga* (1988), 1:214.
22. *Sturlunga saga* (1988), 1:106.
23. *Sturlunga saga* (1988), 1:210.
24. *Sturlunga saga* (1988), 1:217.

25. Andersson, "The Literary Prehistory" (1994), 1:22–25; Andersson and Gade, *Morkinskinna* (2000), 67–68.
26. *Færeyinga saga*, ed. Ólafur Halldórsson (1987), ccxxxii–ix.
27. *Über die ältere isländische Saga* (1852).
28. Finnur Jónsson, *OOLH* (1894–1901), 2:218–19. The texts are reprinted in adjacent columns in Andersson, "*Víga-Glúms saga* and the Birth of Saga Writing" (2006): 26–33. They show the wording to be far too close to allow for the possibility of oral variation.
29. Lotspeich, *Zur Víga-Glúms- und Reykdœla saga* (1903), 63.
30. In "The Composition of the Icelandic Family Sagas" (1909): 220, he extended this comment to apply to Víga-Skúta as well as Víga-Glúmr.
31. Lotspeich (1903), 34.
32. Lotspeich (1903), 38.
33. In "The Composition of the Icelandic Family Sagas" (1909): 217, Lotspeich generalizes: "It is the purpose of this present study to show that the saga writers in some cases probably used, in connection with the oral tradition, small written sources in the composition of their works." He does not, however, adduce any parallel examples of "small written sources."
34. Knut Liestøl, "Reykdœla saga: Tradisjon og forfattar" (1928). Finnur Jónsson, *OOLH* (1920–24), 2:223 and 501.
35. Liestøl (1928), 40.
36. Ibid.
37. Liestøl, *The Origin of the Icelandic Family Saga* (1930), 53.
38. Turville-Petre, "The Traditions of *Víga-Glúms Saga*" (1936): 64.
39. Turville-Petre, ed., *Víga-Glúms saga* (1940), xxix.
40. Björn M. Ólsen, *Um Íslendingasögur* (1937–39), 356 and 424.
41. Björn Sigfússon, ed., *Ljósvetninga saga*, etc. (1940), LXIV-LXIX.
42. Jónas Kristjánsson, ed., *Eyfirðinga sǫgur* (1956), XV-XXI.
43. *Eddas and Sagas* (1988), 244.
44. Walter Baetke, "Die Víga-Glúms-saga-Episode" (1958).
45. Baetke (1958), 20.
46. Baetke credited the parallel to Björn Sigfússon (ÍF 10:LXVIII), and Björn Sigfússon in turn traced it to Björn M. Ólsen, *Um Íslendingasögur* (1937–39), 422.
47. Arie C. Bouman, *Observations on Syntax* (1956).
48. Dietrich Hofmann, "Reykdœla saga und mündliche Überlieferung" (1972).
49. John McKinnell, trans., *Viga-Glums Saga* (1987), 9–10; Böðvar Guðmundsson, Sverrir Tómasson, Torfi H. Tulinius, and Vésteinn Ólason, *Íslensk bókmenntasaga*, (1993), 2:104.
50. See Irmgard Netter, *Die indirekte Rede in den Isländersagas* (1935), 17–18.
51. Baetke (1958), 11.
52. Möbius, *Über die ältere isländische Saga* (1852), p. 68; Ólsen, "Um Íslendingasögur" (1937–39), 355–56.
53. Lotspeich (1903), 32; Turville-Petre (1940), xxix; Bouman (1956), 69.
54. Hofmann (1972), 14–18.

55. Sveinbjörn Rafnsson, *Studier i Landnámabók* (1974).
56. Jón Jóhannesson, *Gerðir Landnámabókar* (1941), 113–15.
57. See the critique by Gísli Sigurðsson, *Túlkun Íslendingasagna* (2002), 136–86.
58. Sveinbjörn Rafnsson, *Studier* (1974), 63 and 66.
59. I suggested this in *The Growth of the Medieval Icelandic Sagas* (2006), 66–67. The grouping and relative dating of the saga cluster in Eyjafjörður have now been more fully discussed by Sten Kindlundh in "Om Reykdœla saga ok Víga-Skútu" (2009).
60. T. M. Andersson and William Ian Miller, trans., *Law and Literature in Medieval Iceland* (1989), 64–74.
61. Andersson and Miller (1989), 80–82.
62. On the value system in general see Andersson and Miller (1989), 55–62 and 98–118.
63. On the dating of *Orkneyinga saga* see Else Mundal, "The Dating of the Oldest Sagas of Early Icelanders" (forthcoming).
64. See Björn Sigfússon, "Veldi Guðmundar ríka" (1934), 195.

Chapter 7 — Warrior Poets in the Northwest

1. Bjarni Guðnason, "Aldur og einkenni *Bjarnarsögu Hítdœlakappa*" (1994); T. M. Andersson, "The Native Romance of Gunnlaugr and Helga the Fair" (2008).
2. Sigurður Nordal, *Om Olaf den helliges saga* (1914); Jónas Kristjánsson, *Um Fóstbrœðrasögu* (1972).
3. "Redating *Fóstbrœðra saga*" (forthcoming).
4. Jónas Kristjánsson, *Um Fóstbrœðrasögu*, 201–8.
5. See the discussion by Björn K. Þórólfsson and Guðni Jónsson in ÍF 6:XII-XXI. Jónas Kristjánsson, *Um Fóstbrœðrasögu*, 226–35, tried to identify other echoes, but some are doubtful and some are dependent on Jónas's late dating of the saga.
6. On the locution used here see ÍF 6:128n3.
7. Compare the passage in ÍF 6:178 with the wording in ÍF 6:142–43.
8. See stanza 29 in ÍF 6:258–59; the other four killings are described in ÍF 6:257.
9. Guðni Kolbeinsson and Jónas Kristjánsson argued for the priority of the longer version in "Gerðir Gíslasögu" (1979).
10. The inquiry was initiated by Anne Holtsmark, "Studies in the Gísla saga" (1951), who identified Þorkell as the killer. I argued for Þorgrímr in "Some Ambiguities in *Gísla saga*" (1968): 28–39. The debate has continued especially in Icelandic journals. See for example Birgitte Spur Ólafsson, "Hver myrti Véstein?" in *Mímir* 19 (1980), 60–67, who also settles on Þorgrímr.
11. The killings of Bárðr and Skeggi are related in the short version in ÍF 6:7–8, 10–11; the long version has only the killing of Kolbeinn (as he is named here) because Skeggi is missing in a lacuna (ÍF 6:25).

12. See ÍF 6:25; the friendship, though not the displeasure, is also alluded to in the shorter version in ÍF 6:7.
13. In 1968 (note 10) I argued that Gísli has an ambiguous relationship with both brother and sister dating back to the Norwegian prelude and that he is himself a somewhat ambiguous figure, but Vésteinn Ólason, "Gísli Súrsson—a Flawless or Flawed Hero?" (1999), 163–75, takes a different view.
14. On the stanzas see Björn K. Þórólfsson and Guðni Jónsson in ÍF 6:V-XII and especially Peter Foote in *The Saga of Gisli*, trans. George Johnston (1963), 112–23.
15. Emily Lethbridge has provided a thorough review of the dating problem in "Dating the Sagas and *Gísla saga Súrssonar*" (forthcoming).

Sources for the Present Volume

The first five chapters are drawn from the following previously published papers:

Chapter 1: "The Long Prose Form in Medieval Iceland." *JEGP* 101 (2002): 380–411.

Chapter 2: "The Formation of the Kings' Sagas." *Scripta Islandica* 60 (2009): 77–87.

Chapter 3: "The First Icelandic King's Saga: Oddr Snorrason's *Óláfs saga Tryggvasonar* or *The Oldest Saga of Saint Olaf?*" *JEGP* 103 (2004): 139–55;

"The Continuation of *Hlaðajarla saga." *JEGP* 97 (1998): 155–67.

Chapter 4: "The Oral Sources of *Óláfs saga helga* in *Heimskringla*." *Saga-Book* 32 (2008): 5–38.

Chapter 5: "The Politics of Snorri Sturluson." *JEGP* 93 (1994): 55–78.

In addition, chapter 6 draws partially on "The Literary Prehistory of Eyjafjörður," in *Samtíðarsögur: Níunda alþjódlega fornsagnaþingið: forprent = The Contemporary Sagas: the Ninth International Saga Conference: Preprints: Akureyri 31.7.—6.8. 1994*, vol. 1 *(forprent)* (Akureyri, 1994) and "Víga-Glúms saga and the Birth of Saga Writing," *Scripta Islandica* 57 (2006): 5–39.

Bibliography

Texts and Translations

Adam of Bremen. *Gesta Hammaburgensis Ecclesiae Pontificum = Hamburgische Kirchengeschichte*. Ed. Bernhard Schmeidler. 3rd ed. Scriptores Rerum Germanicarum in Usum Scholarum. Hannover and Leipzig: Hahn, 1917; reprinted 1977.

Ágrip af Nóregskonungasǫgum: A Twelfth-Century Synoptic History of the Kings of Norway. Ed. and trans. M. [Matthew] J. Driscoll. Viking Society for Northern Research Text Series 10. London: Viking Society for Northern Research, 1995; reprinted 2008.

The Complete Sagas of Icelanders Including 49 Tales. Ed. Viðar Hreinsson. 5 vols. Reykjavík: Leifur Eiríksson Publishing, 1997.

Fagrskinna. Ed. Finnur Jónsson. SUGNL 30. Copenhagen: S. L. Møller, 1902–1903.

Fjörutíu Íslendinga-þættir. Ed. Þórleifur Jónsson. Reykjavík: Kostnaðarmaður Sigurður Kristjánsson, 1904.

Fornaldarsögur norðurlanda. Ed. Guðni Jónsson. 4 vols. [Reykjavík]: Íslendingasagnaútgáfan, 1954.

Færeyinga saga. Ed. Ólafur Halldórsson. Reykjavík: Stofnun Árna Magnússonar, 1987.

Hákonar saga Hákonarsonar. Ed. Gudbrand Vigfusson. Rolls Series 88. London: Her Majesty's Stationery Office, 1887.

Hákonar saga Hákonarsonar etter Sth. 8 fol., AM 325 VIII, 4° og AM 304, 4°. Ed. Marina Mundt. Norrøne Tekster 2. Oslo: I kommisjon hos Forlagssentralen, 1977.

Hákonar saga Ívarssonar. Ed. Jón Helgason and Jakob Benediktsson. SUGNL 62. Copenhagen: J. Jörgensen, 1952.

Islandske annaler indtil 1578. Ed. Gustav Storm. Christiania: Grøndahl & Søns Bogtrykkeri, 1888.

Konunga sögur. Vol. 1: *Óláfs saga Tryggvasonar eftir Odd munk; Helgisaga*

Óláfs Haraldssonar; Brot úr elztu sögu Óláfs helga. Ed. Guðni Jónsson. [Reykjavík]: Íslendingasagnaútgáfan, 1957.

Morkinskinna: Pergamentsbog fra første halvdel af det trettende aarhundrede. Ed. C. R. Unger. Christiania: Bentzens Bogtrykkeri, 1867.

Morkinskinna. Ed. Finnur Jónsson. SUGNL 53. Copenhagen: J. Jørgensen, 1932.

Morkinskinna: The Earliest Icelandic Chronicle of the Norwegian Kings (1030–1157). Trans. Theodore M. Andersson and Kari Ellen Gade. Islandica 51. Ithaca: Cornell University Press, 2000.

Olafs saga hins helga efter pergamenthaandskrift i Uppsala Universitetsbibliotek, Delagardieske samling nr. 8^{II}. Ed. Oscar Albert Johnsen. Kristiania: Jacob Dybwad, 1922.

Olafs saga hins helga: Die "Legendarische Saga" über Olaf den Heiligen (Hs. Delagard. Saml. nr. 8^{II}). Ed. and trans. Anne Heinrichs, Doris Janshen, Elke Radicke, and Hartmut Röhn. Heidelberg: Carl Winter, 1982.

Saga Olafs konungs Tryggvasonar. Ed. Peter Andreas Munch. Christiania: Brøgger & Christies Bogtrykkeri, 1853.

Saga Óláfs Tryggvasonar af Oddr Snorrason munk. Ed. Finnur Jónsson. Copenhagen: Gad, 1932.

Sturlunga saga. Ed. Jón Jóhannesson, Magnús Finnbogason, and Kristján Eldjárn. 2 vols. Reykjavík: Sturlungaútgáfan, 1946.

Sturlunga saga. Ed. Örnólfur Thorsson. 3 vols. Reykjavík: Svart á hvítu, 1988.

Theodoricus monachus. *Historia de Antiquitate Regum Norwagiensium*. Ed. Gustav Storm. MHN. Kristiania: A. W. Brøgger, 1880; reprinted 1973, 1–68.

Yngvars saga víðfǫrla jämte ett bihang om Ingvarsinskrifterna. Ed. Emil Olson. SUGNL 39. Copenhagen: S. L. Møller, 1912.

Critical Studies

Almqvist, Bo. 1965. *Norrön niddiktning: Traditionshistoriska studier i versmagi*. Vol. 1: *Nid mot furstar*. Stockholm: Almqvist & Wiksell.

Andersson, Theodore M. 1964. *The Problem of Icelandic Saga Origins: A Historical Survey*. New Haven, CT: Yale University Press.

———. 1966. "The Textual Evidence of an Oral Family Saga." *ANF* 81: 1–23.

———. 1967. *The Icelandic Family Saga: An Analytic Reading*. Cambridge, MA: Harvard University Press.

———. 1968. "Some Ambiguities in *Gísla saga*: A Balance Sheet." *Bibliography of Old Norse-Icelandic Studies 6*: 7–42.

———. 1973. "The Epic Source of *Niflunga saga* and the *Nibelungenlied*." *ANF* 88: 1–54.

———. 1976. *Early Epic Scenery: Homer, Virgil, and the Medieval Legacy*. Ithaca and London: Cornell University Press.

———. 1979. "Ari's *konunga ævi* and the Earliest Accounts of Hákon jarl's Death." In *Opuscula* 6. BA 33. Copenhagen: Reitzel, 1–17.

———. 1988. "Lore and Literature in a Scandinavian Conversion Episode." In *Idee—Gestalt—Geschichte: Festschrift Klaus von See: Studien zur europäischen Tradition*. Ed. Gerd Wolfgang Weber, 261–84. Odense: Odense University Press.

———. 1989. "Guðbrandur Vigfússon's Saga Chronology: The Case of *Ljósvetninga saga*." In *Úr Dölum til Dala: Guðbrandur Vigfússon Centenary Essays*. Ed. Rory McTurk and Andrew Wawn, 1–10. Leeds Texts and Monographs 11. Leeds: University Printing Service.

———. 1993. "Snorri Sturluson and the Saga School at Munkaþverá." In *Snorri Sturluson: Kolloquium anlässlich der 750. Wiederkehr seines Todestages*. ScriptOralia 51. Ed. Alois Wolf, 9–25. Tübingen: Gunter Narr Verlag.

———. 2003. Trans. *The Saga of Olaf Tryggvason by Oddr Snorrason* Islandica 52. Ithaca: Cornell University Press.

———. 2004. "Five Saga Books for a New Century." *JEGP* 103: 505–27.

———. 2005. "Heusler's Saga Studies." In *Germanentum im Fin de Siècle: Wissenschaftsgeschichtliche Studien zum Werk Andreas Heuslers*. Ed. Jürg Glauser and Julia Zernack, 194–209. Basel: Schwabe Verlag.

———. 2006a. *The Growth of the Medieval Icelandic Sagas (1180–1280)*. Ithaca: Cornell University Press.

———. 2006b. "*Víga-Glúms saga* and the Birth of Icelandic Saga Writing." *SI* 57: 5–39.

———. 2008. "The Native Romance of Gunnlaugr and Helga the Fair." In *Romance and Love in Late Medieval and Early Modern Iceland: Essays in Honor of Marianne Kalinke*. Ed. Kirsten Wolf and Johanna Denzin, 33–63. Islandica 54. Ithaca: Cornell University Press.

———. "Redating *Fóstbrœðra saga*" (forthcoming).

——— and William Ian Miller, trans. 1989. *Law and Literature in Medieval Iceland: Ljósvetninga saga and Valla-Ljóts saga*. Stanford: Stanford University Press.

Ármann Jakobsson. 1997. *Í leit að konungi: Konungsmynd íslenskra konungasagna*. Reykjavík: Háskólaútgáfan.

———. 1998. "King and Subject in *Morkinskinna*." *Skandinavistik* 28: 101–17.

———. 1999. "Rundt om kongen: En genvurdering af Morkinskinna." *Maal og minne* 1999, 1: 71–90.

———. 2000a. "Um uppruna Morkinskinnu: Drög að rannsóknarsögu." *Gripla* 11: 221–45.

———. 2000b. "The Individual and the Ideal: The Representation of Royalty in *Morkinskinna*." *JEGP* 99: 71–86.

———. 2001. "The Amplified Saga: Structural Disunity in *Morkinskinna*." *Medium Ævum* 70: 29–46.

———. 2002a. "Our Norwegian Friend: The Role of Kings in the Family Sagas." *ANF* 117: 145–60.

———. 2002b. *Staður í nýjum heimi: Konungasagan Morkinskinna*. Reykjavík: Háskólaútgáfan.

———. 2003. "Den kluntede afskriver: Finnur Jónsson og Morkinskinna." In

Opuscula 11. Ed. Britta Olrik Frederiksen. BA 42. Copenhagen: Munksgaard, 289–306.

———. 2007. "Textreferenzen in der *Morkinskinna*: Geschichten über Dichtung und Geschichten: Zwei Biographien." *Skandinavistik* 37: 18–30.

———. 2008. "En plats i en ny värld: Bilden av riddarsamhället i Morkinskinna." *SI* 59: 27–46.

Bååth, A. U. 1885. *Studier öfver kompositionen i några isländska ättsagor*. Lund: Gleerup.

Baetke, Walter. 1958. "Die Víga-Glúms-saga-Episode in der Reykdœla saga." In *Beiträge zur deutschen und nordischen Literatur: Festgabe für Leopold Magon zum 70. Geburtstag 3. April 1957*. Ed. Hans Werner Seiffert, 5–21. Berlin: Akademie-Verlag.

Bagge, Sverre. 1991. *Society and Politics in Snorri Sturluson's Heimskringla*. Berkeley: University of California Press.

__________. 2010. "Warrior, King, and Saint: The Medieval Histories about St. Óláfr Haraldsson." *JEGP* 109: 281–321.

Bakker, E. J. 1999. "Homer and Oral Poetry Research." In *Homer: Critical Assessments*. Ed. F. J. de Jong, 1:163–83. 4 vols. London and New York: Routledge.

Beckman, Natanael. 1918. "Torgny lagman: Ett bidrag till karakteristiken av Snorres författarskap." *Edda* 9: 278–86.

———. 1922. "Sverige i isländsk tradition." [Svensk] *Historisk tidskrift* 42: 152–67.

———. 1934. "Ytterligare om Sigvats Austrfararvísur." *ANF* 50: 197–217.

Benson, Larry D. 1966. "The Literary Character of Anglo-Saxon Formulaic Poetry." *PMLA* 81:334–41; reprinted in his *Contradictions: From Beowulf to Chaucer*. Ed. Theodore M. Andersson and Stephen A. Barney, 1–14. Aldershot: Scolar Press.

Berman, Melissa A. 1985. "The Political Sagas." *SS* 57: 113–29.

Berntsen, Toralf. 1923. *Fra sagn til saga: Studier i kongesagaen*. Kristiania: Gyldendalske Bokhandel.

Beyschlag, Siegfried. 1950. *Konungasögur: Untersuchungen zur Königssaga bis Snorri: Die älteren Übersichtswerke samt Ynglingasaga*. BA 8. Copenhagen: Munksgaard.

Bjarni Aðalbjarnarson. 1937. *Om de norske kongers sagaer*. NVAOS 2, hist.-filos. kl. 1936, 4. Oslo: Jacob Dybwad.

Bjarni Guðnason. 1977. "Theodoricus og íslenskir sagnaritarar." In *Sjötíu ritgerðir*. Ed. Einar G. Pétursson and Jónas Kristjánsson, 1: 107–20. 2 vols. Reykjavík: Stofnun Árna Magnússonar.

———. 1978. *Fyrsta sagan*. Studia Islandica 37. Reykjavík: Bókaútgáfa Menningarsjóðs.

———. 1994. "Aldur og einkenni *Bjarnarsögu Hítdœlakappa*." In *Sagnaþing helgað Jónasi Kristjánssyni sjötugum 10. apríl 1994*. Ed. Gísli Sigurðsson, Guðrún Kvaran, and Sigurgeir Steingrímsson, 1: 69–85. 2 vols. Reykjavík: Hið íslenzka bókmenntafélag.

Björn Sigfússon. 1934. "Veldi Guðmundar ríka." *Skírnir* 108: 191–98.

Blöndal, Lárus H. 1982. *Um uppruna Sverrissögu*. Reykjavík: Stofnun Árna Magnússonar.

Booth, Wayne C. 1961. *The Rhetoric of Fiction*. Chicago: University of Chicago Press.

Boulhosa, Patricia Pires. 2005. *Icelanders and the Kings of Norway: Medieval Sagas and Legal Texts*. Leiden and Boston: Brill.

Bouman, Arie C. 1956. *Observations on Syntax and Style of Some Icelandic Sagas, with Special Reference to the Relation between* Víga-Glúms saga *and* Reykdæla saga. Studia Islandica 15. Reykjavík: H. F. Leiftur.

Brown, Ursula, ed. 1952. *Þorgils saga ok Hafliða*. London: Oxford University Press.

Böðvar Guðmundsson, Sverrir Tómasson, Torfi H. Tulinius, and Vésteinn Ólason. 1993. *Íslensk bókmenntasaga*, vol. 2. Reykjavík: Mál og menning.

Clover, Carol J. 1985. "Icelandic Family Sagas (Íslendingasögur)." In *Old Norse-Icelandic Literature: A Critical Guide*, ed. Carol J. Clover and John Lindow, 239–315. Islandica 45. Ithaca: Cornell University Press; reprinted Toronto: Toronto University Press, 2005.

———. 1986. "The Long Prose Form." *ANF* 101: 10–39.

———. 1988. "The Politics of Scarcity: Notes on the Sex Ratio in Early Scandinavia." *SS* 60: 147–88.

Craigie, William Alexander. 1913. *The Icelandic Sagas*. Cambridge: Cambridge University Press.

Danielsson, Tommy. 2002a. *Hrafnkels saga eller Fallet med den undflyende traditionen*. Hedemora: Gidlunds förlag.

———. 2002b. *Sagorna om Norges kungar: Från Magnús góði till Magnús Erlingsson*. Hedemora: Gidlunds förlag.

Fenik, Bernard. 1986. *Homer and the Nibelungenlied: Comparative Studies in Epic Style*. Cambridge, MA: Harvard University Press.

Fidjestøl, Bjarne. 1982. *Det norrøne fyrstediktet*. Øvre Ervik: Alvheim & Eide.

Finnur Jónsson. 1894–1902. *Den oldnorske og oldislandske litteraturs historie*. 3 vols. Copenhagen: Gad; revised ed. 1920–24. 3 vols. Copenhagen: Gad.

Foley, John Miles. 1985. *Oral-Formulaic Theory and Research: An Introduction and Annotated Bibliography*. New York: Garland.

———. 1990. *Traditional Oral Epic: The Odyssey, Beowulf, and the Serbo-Croatian Return Song*. Berkeley: University of California Press.

———. 1991. *Immanent Art: From Structure to Meaning in Traditional Oral Epic*. Bloomington: Indiana University Press.

———. 1995. *The Singer of Tales in Performance*. Bloomington: Indiana University Press.

———. 1999. *Homer's Traditional Art*. University Park: Pennsylvania State University Press.

Foote, Peter. 1951. "Sturlu saga and Its Background." *Saga-Book* 13:207–37; reprinted in his *Aurvandilstá: Norse Studies*, 9–30. Odense: Odense University Press.

———. 1963. "An Essay on the Saga of Gisli and Its Icelandic Background." In *The Saga of Gisli*, trans. George Johnston, 93–134. Toronto: Toronto University Press.

Friesen, Otto von. 1942. "Fredsförhandlingarna mellan Olov skötkonung och Olav Haraldsson." [Svensk] *Historisk tidskrift* 62:205–70.

Gade, Kari Ellen. 2000. Unpublished paper on *Morkinskinna* and *Orkneyinga saga.*

Gísli Sigurðsson. 1990. "On the Classification of Eddic Poetry in View of the Oral Theory." In *Poetry in the Scandinavian Middle Ages:* Atti del 12° Congresso internazionale di studi sull'alto medioevo, Spoleto 4–10 settembre 1988, 245–55. Spoleto: Presso la Sede del Centro Studi.

———. 1994a. "Another Audience—Another Saga: How Can We Best Explain Different Accounts in *Vatnsdœla saga* and *Finnboga saga ramma* of the Same Events?" In *Text und Zeittiefe*, ed. Hildegard L. C. Tristram, 359–75. ScriptOralia 58. Tübingen: Gunter Narr Verlag.

———. 1994b. "Aðrir áheyrandur—önnur saga? Um ólíkar frásagnir Vatnsdœlu og Finnboga sögu af sömu atburðum." *Skáldskaparmál* 3: 30–41.

———. 1997. "Methodology for the Study of the Oral in Medieval Iceland." In *Medieval Insular Literature between the Oral and the Written II: Continuity of Transmission,* ed. Hildegard L. C. Tristram, 177–92. Tübingen: Gunter Narr Verlag.

———. 1998. "Munnleg geymd og aldur Eddukvæða." In *Eddukvæði*, xv-xxiii. Reykjavík: Mál og menning.

———. 2002. *Túlkun Íslendingasagna í ljósi munnlegrar hefðar: Tilgáta um aðferð*. Reykjavík: Stofnun Árna Magnússonar á Íslandi; trans. Nicholas Jones as *The Medieval Icelandic Saga and Oral Tradition: A Discourse on Method.* Publications of the Milman Parry Collection of Oral Literature 2. Cambridge, MA: The Milman Parry Collection of Oral Literature, Harvard University, 2004.

Gimmler, Heinrich. 1976. "Die Thættir der Morkinskinna: Ein Beitrag zur Überlieferungsproblematik und zur Typologie der altnordischen Kurzerzählung." Ph.D. diss., Universität Frankfurt am Main.

Guðni Kolbeinsson and Jónas Kristjánsson. 1979. "Gerðir Gíslasögu." *Gripla* 3: 128–62.

Harris, Joseph. 1976. "Theme and Genre in Some *Íslendinga þættir.*" *SS* 44: 1–27; reprinted in his "*Speak Useful Words or Say Nothing*": *Old Norse Studies by Joseph Harris,* ed. Susan E. Deskis and Thomas D. Hill, 97–126. Islandica 53. Ithaca: Cornell University Library, 2008. http://cip.cornell.edu/DPubS/Repository/1.0/Disseminate?handle=cul.isl/1238784735&view=body&content-type=pdf_1

———. 1985. "Eddic Poetry." In *Old Norse-Icelandic Literature: A Critical Guide,* ed. Carol J. Clover and John Lindow, 68–156. Islandica 45. Ithaca: Cornell University Press; reprinted Toronto: Toronto University Press, 2005.

Helgi Þorláksson. 1979. "Hvernig var Snorri í sjón?" In *Snorri: Átta alda minning*, 161–81. Reykjavík: Sögufélag.

Heller, Rolf. 1977. "Zur Entstehung der Grönlandsszenen der Fóstbrœðra saga." In *Sjötíu ritgerðir,* ed. Einar G. Pétursson and Jónas Kristjánsson, 1: 326–34. 2 vols. Reykjavík: Stofnun Árna Magnússonar.

Heinemann, Fredrik J. 1974. "*Hrafnkels saga freysgoða* and Type-Scene Analysis." *SS* 46: 102–19.

Hermann Pálsson. 1999. *Oral Tradition and Saga Writing*. Studia Medievalia Septentrionalia 3. Vienna: Fassbaender.

Heusler, Andreas. 1913. "Die Anfänge der isländischen Saga." *Abhandlungen der Preussischen Akademie der Wissenschaften*, phil.-hist. Kl. 9: 1–87; reprinted in his *Kleine Schriften,* ed. Stefan Sonderegger, 2: 388–459. 2 vols. Berlin: de Gruyter, 1969.

———. 1941. *Die altgermanische Dichtung*. Potsdam: Athenaion. 2. Aufl. der neubearb. und verm. Ausg. Handbuch der Literaturwissenschaft; reprinted Darmstadt: Wissenschaftliche Buchgesellschaft, 1957.

Hofmann, Dietrich. 1972. "Reykdœla saga und mündliche Überlieferung." *Skandinavistik* 2: 1–26; reprinted in his *Studien zur nordischen und germanischen Philologie,* ed. Gert Kreutzer, Alastair Walker, and Ommo Wilts, 142–67. Gesammelte Schriften 1. Hamburg: Helmut Buske Verlag, 1988.

———. 1981. "Die Yngvars saga víðfǫrla und Oddr munkr inn fróði." In *Speculum norroenum: Norse Studies in Memory of Gabriel Turville-Petre,* ed. Ursula Dronke, Guðrún P. Helgadóttir, Gerd Wolfgang Weber, and Hans Bekker-Nielsen, 188–222. Odense: Odense University Press; reprinted in his *Studien zur nordischen und germanischen Philologie,* ed. Gert Kreutzer, Alastair Walker, and Ommo Wilts, 365–99. Gesammelte Schriften 1. Hamburg: Helmut Buske Verlag, 1988.

Holtsmark, Anne. 1951. "Studies in the Gísla saga." *Studia Norvegica Ethnologica et Folkloristica* 2, 6: 3–55.

Indrebø, Gustav. 1917. *Fagrskinna.* Kristiania: Grøndahl & Søn.

———. 1928. "Harald hardraade i Morkinskinna." In *Festskrift til Finnur Jónsson 29. maj 1928*, 173–80. Copenhagen: Levin & Munksgaard.

———. 1938–39. "Nokre merknader til den norröne kongesoga." *ANF* 54: 58–79.

Johnsen, Oscar Albert. 1916. "Friðgerðar-saga. En kildekritisk undersøkelse." [Norsk] *Historisk tidsskrift*, ser. 5, 3: 513–61.

Jón Jóhannesson. 1941. *Gerðir Landnámabókar.* Reykjavík: Félagsprentsmiðjan H. F.

———. 1974. *A History of the Old Icelandic Commonwealth.* Trans. Haraldur Bessason. University of Manitoba Icelandic Studies 2. Winnipeg: University of Manitoba Press.

Jón Jónsson. 1918. "Athugasemd um Þorgný lögmann." *ANF* 34: 148–53.

Jónas Kristjánsson. 1972. *Um Fóstbrœðrasögu.* Reykjavík: Stofnun Árna Magnússonar.

———. 1976. "The Legendary Saga." In *Minjar og menntir: Afmælisrit helgað Kristjáni Eldjárn 6. desember 1976*, ed. Guðni Kolbeinsson, Bjarni Vilhjálmsson, Jónas Kristjánsson, and Þór Magnússon, 281–93. Reykjavík: Bókaútgáfa Menningarsjóðs.

———. 1977. "Egils saga og konungasögur." In *Sjötíu ritgerðir*, ed. Einar G. Pétursson and Jónas Kristjánsson, 2: 449–72. 2 vols. Reykjavík: Stofnun Árna Magnússonar.

———. 1988a. "Íslendingasögur og Sturlunga: Samanburður nokkurra einkenna og efnisatriða." In *Sturlustefna: Ráðstefna haldin á sjö alda ártíð Sturlu Þórðarsonar sagnaritara 1984*, 94–111. Reykjavík: Stofnun Árna Magnússonar.

———. 1988b. *Eddas and Sagas: Iceland's Medieval Literature*. Trans. Peter Foote. Reykjavík: Hið íslenska bókmenntafélag.

———. 1990. "Var Snorri Sturluson upphafsmaður Íslendingasagna?" *Andvari* 32: 85–105.

Kalinke, Marianne E. 1984. "*Sigurðar saga Jórsalafara*: The Fictionalization of Fact in *Morkinskinna*." *SS* 56: 152–67.

Kellogg, Robert. 1958. "A Concordance of the Elder Edda." Ph.D. diss., Harvard University.

———. 1988. *A Concordance of Eddic Poetry*. East Lansing, MI: Colleagues Press.

———. 1990. "The Prehistory of Eddic Poetry." In *Poetry in the Scandinavian Middle Ages: Atti del 12° Congresso internazionale di studi sull'alto medioevo, Spoleto 4–10 settembre 1988*, 189–99. Spoleto: Presso la Sede del Centro Studi.

Kindlundh, Sten. 2009. "Om Reykdœla saga ok Víga-Skútu." *Gardar* 40: 26–48.

Koht, Halvdan. 1914. "Sagaenes opfattelse av vår gamle historie." [Norsk] *Historisk tidsskrift* 5, 2: 379–96; reprinted in *Rikssamling og kristendom*, ed. Andreas Holmsen and Jarle Simensen, 41–55. Norske historikere i utvalg 1. Oslo: Universitetsforlaget, 1967.

Kunin, Devra, trans. 2001. *A History of Norway and the Passion and Miracles of the Blessed Óláfr*. Ed. with an introduction and notes by Carl Phelpstead. London: University College London; Viking Society for Northern Research.

Kválen, Eivind. 1925. *Den eldste norske kongesoga: Morkinskinna og Hryggjarstykki*. Oslo: n.p.

Lämmert, Eberhard. 1955. *Bauformen des Erzählens*. Stuttgart: Metzler.

Lange, Gudrun. 1989. *Die Anfänge der isländisch-norwegischen Geschichtsschreibung*. Studia Islandica 47. Reykjavík: Bókaútgáfa Menningarsjóðs.

Lethbridge, Emily. "Dating the Sagas and *Gísla saga Súrssonar*" (forthcoming).

Lie, Hallvard. 1937. *Studier i Heimskringlas stil: Dialogene og talene*. NVAOS 2, hist.-filos. kl. 5. Oslo: Jacob Dybwad.

Liestøl, Knut. 1928. "Reykdœla saga: Tradisjon og forfattar." In *Festskrift til Finnur Jónsson 29. maj 1928*, 29–44. Copenhagen: Levin & Munksgaard.

———. 1930. *The Origin of the Icelandic Family Sagas*. Trans. A. G. Jayne. Cambridge, MA: Harvard University Press.

Lönnroth, Lars. 1963. "Studier i Olaf Tryggvasons saga." *Samlaren* 84: 54–94.

———. 1963–64. "Kroppen som själens spegel—ett motiv i de isländska sagorna." *Lychnos* 1963–64: 24–61.

———. 1964. "Tesen om de två kulturerna : Kritiska studier i den isländska sagaskrivningens sociala förutsättningar." *SI* 15: 1–97.

———. 1965a. "Det litterära porträttet i latinsk historiografi och isländsk sagaskrivning: En komparativ studie." *Acta Philologica Scandinavica* 27: 68–117.

———. 1965b. *European Sources of Icelandic Saga-Writing: An Essay Based on Previous Studies*. Stockholm: Thule.

———. 1971. "Hjálmar's Death-Song and the Delivery of Eddic Poetry." *Speculum* 46: 1–20; reprinted in his *The Academy of Odin* (2011) [see below], 191–218.

———. 1976a. *Njáls saga: A Critical Introduction*. Berkeley: University of California Press.

———. 1976b. "Ideology and Structure in *Heimskringla*." *Parergon* 15: 16–29; reprinted in his *The Academy of Odin* (2011) [see below], 141–62.

———. 1978. *Den dubbla scenen: Muntlig diktning från Eddan til Abba*. Stockholm: Prisma.

———. 1981. "Iǫrð fannz æva né upphiminn: A Formula Analysis." In *Speculum Norroenum: Norse Studies in Memory of Gabriel Turville-Petre*, ed. Ursula Dronke et al. , 310–27. Odense: Odense University Press; reprinted in his *The Academy of Odin* (2011) [see below], 219–41.

———. 2000. "The Baptist and the Saint: Odd Snorrason's View of the Two King Olavs." In *International Scandinavian and Medieval Studies in Memory of Gerd Wolfgang Weber*, ed. Michael Dallapiazza, Olaf Hansen, Preben Meulengracht Sørensen, and Yvonne S. Bonnetain, 257–64. Trieste: Edizioni Parnaso.

———. 2011. *The Academy of Odin: Selected Papers on Old Norse Literature*. [Odense]: University Press of Southern Denmark.

Lotspeich, Claude. 1903. *Zur Víga-Glúms- und Reykdæla saga*. Leipzig: Hesse.

———. 1909. "The Composition of the Icelandic Family Sagas." *JEGP* 8:217–24.

Louis-Jensen, Jonna. 1970. " 'Syvende og ottende brudstykke': Fragmentet AM 325 IVα 4to." In *Opuscula* 4. BA 30. Copenhagen: Munksgaard, 1–30.

———. 1977. *Kongesagastudier: Kompilationen Hulda-Hrokkinskinna*. BA 32. Copenhagen: Reitzel.

———. 1997. "Heimskringla—Et værk af Snorri Sturluson?" *Nordica Bergensia* 14:230–45; reprinted in her *Con Amore: En artikelsamling udgivet på 70-årsdagen den 21. oktober 2006*, ed. Michael Chesnutt and Florian Gammel, 217–32. Copenhagen: Reitzel, 2006.

———. "Dating the Archetype: *Eyrbyggja saga* and *Egils saga Skallagrímssonar*" (forthcoming).

Magnús Jónsson. 1940. *Guðmundar saga dýra: Nokkrar athuganir um uppruna hennar og samsetning*. Studia Islandica 8. Reykjavík: Ísafoldarprentsmiðja.

Magoun, Francis P., Jr. 1953. "The Oral-Formulaic Character of Anglo-Saxon Narrative Poetry." *Speculum* 28: 446–63.

———. 1955. "Bede's Story of Cædman: The Case History of an Anglo-Saxon Oral Singer." *Speculum* 30: 49–63.

Manhire, W. 1975–76. "The Narrative Functions of Source-References in the Sagas of Icelanders." *Saga-Book* 19: 170–90.

Maurer, Konrad. 1867. *Ueber die Ausdrücke: altnordische, altnorwegische & isländische Sprache*. Abhandlungen der Königlichen Bayerischen Akademie der Wissenschaften, 1. Cl., 11. Bd., 2. Abt. Munich: Verlag der Königlichen Akademie, 455–706.

Melsteð, Bogi Th. 1899. "Útanstefnur og erendisrekar útlendra þjóðhöfðingja á fyrri hluta Sturlungaaldar: 1200–1239." *Tímarit hins íslenzka bókmenntafélags* 20: 122–30.

Menéndez Pidal, Ramón. 1959. *La Chanson de Roland y el neotradicionalismo: Orígenes de la épica románica*. Madrid: Espasa-Calpe; trans. Irénée-Marcel Cluzel, *La Chanson de Roland et la traditon épique des Francs*. Paris: Picard, 1960.

Meulengracht Sørensen, Preben. 1993a. *Fortælling og ære: Studier i islændinge-sagaerne*. Aarhus: Aarhus University Press.

———. 1993b. "*Egils saga Skalla-Grímssonar.*" In his *Fortælling og ære*, 127–47.

Miller, William Ian. 2008. *Audun and the Polar Bear: Luck, Law, and Largesse in a Medieval Tale of Risky Business*. Leiden and Boston: Brill.

Moberg, Ove. 1941. *Olav Haraldsson, Knut den Store och Sverige: Studier i Olav den heliges förhållande till de nordiska grannländerna*. Lund: Gleerup.

Möbius, Theodor. 1852. *Über die ältere isländische Saga*. Leipzig: Giesecke & Devrient.

Müller, Peter Erasmus. 1817–20. *Sagabibliothek*. 3 vols. Copenhagen: I. F. Schultz.

Mundal, Else. 1977. *Sagadebatt*. Oslo: Universitetsforlaget.

———. 1990. "Den norrøne episke tradisjonen." In *Hellas og Norge: Kontakt, komparasjon, kontrast*, ed. Øivind Andersen and Tomas Hägg, 65–80. Bergen: Klassisk institutt i Bergen.

———. "The Dating of the Oldest Sagas of Early Icelanders" (forthcoming).

McDougall, David and Ian, trans. 1998. *Historia de Antiquitate Regum Norwagiensium: An Account of the Ancient History of Norwegian Kings*. With an introduction by Peter Foote. London: Viking Society for Northern Research.

McKinnell, John, trans. 1987. *Víga-Glúms Saga, with the Tales of Ögmund Bash and Thorvald Chatterbox*. Edinburgh: Canongate.

Nerman, Birger. 1916. "Torgny lagman." *ANF* 32: 302–15.

Netter, Irmgard. 1935. *Die indirekte Rede in den Isländersagas*. Leipzig: Hermann Eichblatt Verlag.

Niles, John D. 1983. *Beowulf: The Poem and Its Tradition*. Cambridge, MA: Harvard University Press.

Nordal, Guðrún. 1998. *Ethics and Action in Thirteenth-Century Iceland*. Odense: Odense University Press.

Nordal, Guðrún, Sverrir Tómasson, and Vésteinn Ólason. 1992. *Íslensk bókmenntasaga*, vol. 1. Reykjavík: Mál og menning.

Nordal, Sigurður. 1913. "Om Orkneyingasaga." *ÅNOH* 3, 3: 31–50.

———. 1914. *Om Olaf den helliges saga*. Copenhagen: Gad.

———. 1920. *Snorri Sturluson*. Reykjavík: Þór. B. Þorláksson; reprinted Reykjavík: Helgafell, 1973.

———. 1940. *Hrafnkatla*. Studia Islandica 7. Reykjavík: Ísafoldarprentsmiðja; trans. R. George Thomas as *Hrafnkels saga freysgoða: A Study by Sigurður Nordal*. Cardiff: University of Wales Press, 1958.

———. 1941. "Snorri Sturluson: Nokkurar hugleiðingar á 700 ártíð hans." *Skírnir* 115: 5–33.

Den norsk-islandske skjaldedigtning. Ed. Finnur Jónsson. Vols. IA-IIA (tekst efter håndskrifterne) and IB-IIB (rettet tekst). Copenhagen: Gyldendal, 1908–15; reprinted Copenhagen: Rosenkilde & Bagger, 1967 (A) and 1973 (B).

Ólafsson, Birgitte Spur. 1980. "Hver myrti Véstein?" *Mímir* 19: 60–67.

Ólafur Halldórsson. 1984. "Mostur og Sæla." *Gripla* 6: 101–12.

Ólsen, Björn Magnússon. 1904. "Landnáma og Egils saga." *ÅNOH* 2, 19: 167–247.

———. 1905a. "Landnáma og Hœnsa-Þóris saga." *ÅNOH* 2, 20: 63–80.

———. 1905b. "Landnáma og Eyrbyggja saga." *ÅNOH* 2, 20: 81–117.

———. 1908. "Landnáma og Laxdœla saga." *ÅNOH* 2, 23: 151–232.

———. 1910. "Landnáma og Gull-Þóris (Þorskfirðinga) saga." *ÅNOH* 2, 25: 35–61.

———. 1920. "Landnáma og Eiríks saga rauða." *ÅNOH* 3, 10: 301–7.

———. 1937–39. *Um Íslendingasögur*. Safn til sögu Íslands 6, 3–7. Reykjavík: Hið íslenzka bókmenntafélag.

Óskar Halldórsson. 1976. *Uppruni og þema Hrafnkels sögu*. Reykjavík: Hið íslenska bókmenntafélag.

———. 1989. "The Origin and Theme of *Hrafnkels saga*." In *Sagas of the Icelanders: A Book of Essays*, ed. John Tucker, 257–71. New York: Garland.

Paasche, Fredrik. 1922. "Tendens og syn i kongesagaen." *Edda* 1922: 1–17; reprinted in *Rikssamling og kristendom*, ed. Andreas Holmsen and Jarle Simensen, 56–75. Norske historikere i utvalg 1. Oslo: Universitetsforlaget, 1967.

Parry, Milman. 1971. *The Making of Homeric Verse: The Collected Papers of Milman Parry*. Ed. Adam Parry. Oxford: Clarendon Press; reprinted 1987.

Poole, Russell G. 1991. *Viking Poems on War and Peace: A Study of Skaldic Narrative*. Toronto: University of Toronto Press.

Sandvik, Gudmund. 1955. *Hovding og konge i Heimskringla*. Oslo: Akademisk forlag.

Sävborg, Daniel. 2007. *Erotik, känslor och berättarkonst i norrön litteratur*. Acta Universitatis Upsaliensis, Historia Litterarum 27. Uppsala: Uppsala Universitet.

Scholes, Robert, and Robert Kellogg. 1966. *The Nature of Narrative*. New York: Oxford University Press; reprinted 2006.

Schreiner, Johann. 1926. *Tradisjon og saga om Olav den hellige*. NVAOS 2, hist-filos. kl. 1. Oslo: Jacob Dybwad.

———. 1927. *Saga og oldfunn: Studier til Norges eldste historie*. NVAOS 2, hist.-filos. kl. 4. Oslo: Jacob Dybwad.

Scovazzi, Marco. 1960. *La saga di Hrafnkell e il problema delle saghe islandesi.* Arona: Paideia.

See, Klaus von. 1978. "Was ist Heldendichtung?" In *Europäische Heldendichtung*, ed. Klaus von See, 1–38. Wege der Forschung 500. Darmstadt: Wissenschaftliche Buchgesellschaft.

———. 1981. "Altnordische Literaturgeschichte als Textgeschichte." In his *Edda, Saga, Skaldendichtung: Aufsätze zur skandinavischen Literatur des Mittelalters*, 527–39. Heidelberg: Winter.

Sieg, Gerd. 1966. "Die Zweikämpfe der Isländersagas." *Zeitschrift für deutsches Altertum und deutsche Literatur* 95: 1–27.

Simpson, Jacqueline. 1957–61. "Advocacy and Art in *Guðmundar saga dýra.*" *Saga-Book* 15: 327–45.

Storm, Gustav. 1873. *Snorre Sturlassöns historieskrivning: En kritisk undersøgelse.* Copenhagen: Bianco Lunos bogtrykkeri.

———. 1893. *Otte brudstykker af den ældste saga om Olav den hellige.* Christiania: Grøndahl & Søns bogtrykkeri.

Stitt, Michael J. 1992. *Beowulf and the Bear's Son: Epic, Saga, and Fairytale in Northern Germanic Tradition.* New York: Garland.

Sveinbjörn Rafnsson. 1974. *Studier i Landnámabók: Kritiska bidrag till den isländska fristatstidens historia.* Lund: Gleerup.

Thomas Aquinas. 1947. *Summa Theologica.* Trans. Fathers of the English Dominican Province. 3 vols. New York: Benziger Brothers.

Tulinius, Torfi H. 2004. *Skáldið í skriftinni: Snorri Sturluson og Egils saga.* Reykjavík: Hið íslenska bókmenntafélag.

Turville-Petre, Gabriel. 1936. "The Traditions of Víga-Glúms Saga." *Transactions of The Philological Society* 1936: 54–75.

———. 1940. *Víga-Glúms saga.* Ed. G. Turville-Petre. Oxford and London: Oxford University Press and Humphrey Milford; 2nd ed., 1960; reprinted 1967.

———. 1953. *Origins of Icelandic Literature.* Oxford: Clarendon Press; reprinted 1967.

Ugulen, Jo Rune. 2002. "AM 39 fol., *Óláfs saga helga* og *Heimskringla*: Komparative analyser til utgreiing av overgangen mellom andre og tredje del av *Heimskringla*, og tilhøvet mellom nokre av handskriftene." Hovudfagsavhandling i norrøn filologi, Nordisk institutt, Universitetet i Bergen.

Úlfar Bragason. 2010. *Ætt og saga: Um frásagnarfræði Sturlungu eða Íslendinga sögu hinnar miklu.* Reykjavík: Háskólaútgáfan.

Vésteinn Ólason. 1998. *Dialogues with the Viking Age: Narration and Representation in the Sagas of Icelanders.* Reykjavík: Heimskringla.

———. 1999. "Gísli Súrsson—a Flawless or Flawed Hero?" In *Die Aktualität der Saga: Festschrift für Hans Schottmann,* ed. Stig Toftgaard Andersen, 163–75. Berlin and New York: Walter de Gruyter.

———. 2007. "The Icelandic Saga as a Kind of Literature with Special Reference to Its Representation of Reality." In *Learning and Understanding in the Old Norse World: Essays in Honour of Margaret Clunies Ross*, ed. Judy Quinn, Kate Heslop, and Tarrin Wills, 27–47. Turnhout: Brepols.

Viðar Hreinsson. 1994. "Frásagnaraðferð Sturlu sögu." In *Samtíðarsögur—*

The Contemporary Sagas: Níunda alþjóðlega fornsagnaþingið—The Ninth International Saga Conference, Akureyri 31 July—6 August 1994, 2: 803–17. 2 vols. Akureyri: n.p.

Vries, Jan de. 1964. *Altnordische Literaturgeschichte*. 2 vols. 2nd ed. Berlin: de Gruyter.

Weibull, Curt. 1921. *Sverige och dess nordiska grannmakter under den tidigare medeltiden*. Lund: Gleerup.

Wessén, Elias. 1928–29. "Om Snorres Prologus till Heimskringla och den särskilda Olavssagan." *Acta Philologica Scandinavica* 3: 52–62.

Whaley, Diana. 1991. *Heimskringla: An Introduction*. London: Viking Society for Northern Research.

www.ingramcontent.com/pod-product-compliance
Lightning Source LLC
Chambersburg PA
CBHW020934310726
48980CB00007B/766/J

* 9 7 8 0 9 3 5 9 9 5 1 4 5 *